Module Architecture View

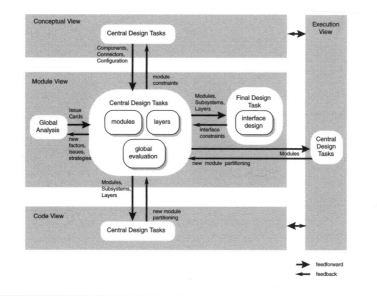

Design Activities

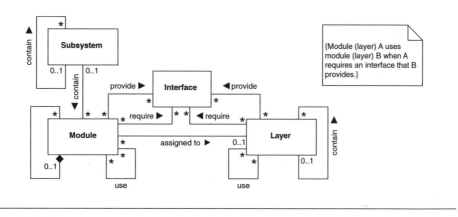

Meta-Model

The Addison-Wesley Object Technology Series

Grady Booch, Ivar Jacobson, and James Rumbaugh, Series Editors

For more information check out the series web site [http://www.awl.com/cseng/otseries/].

The Component Software Series

Clemens Szyperski, Series Editor

For more information check out the series web site [http://www.awl.com/cseng/csseries/].

Applied Software Architecture

Applied Software Architecture

Christine Hofmeister
Robert Nord
Dilip Soni

ADDISON–WESLEY

Boston • San Francisco • New York • Toronto • Montreal
London • Munich • Paris • Madrid
Capetown • Sydney • Tokyo • Singapore • Mexico City

Many of the designations used by manufacturers and sellers to distinguish their products are claimed as trademarks. Where those designations appear in this book, and we were aware of a trademark claim, the designations have been printed in initial capital letters or in all capitals.

The author and publisher have taken care in the preparation of this book, but make no expressed or implied warranty of any kind and assume no responsibility for errors or omissions. No liability is assumed for incidental or consequential damages in connection with or arising out of the use of the information or programs contained herein.

The publisher offers discounts on this book when ordered in quantity for special sales. For more information, please contact:

Pearson Education Corporate Sales Division
One Lake Street
Upper Saddle River, NJ 07458
(800) 382-3419
corpsales@pearsontechgroup.com

Visit AW on the Web: www.awl.com/cseng/

Library of Congress Cataloging-in-Publication Data
Hofmeister, Christine.
  Applied software architecture / Christine Hofmeister, Robert Nord,
Dilip Soni.
      p. cm. — (The Addison-Wesley object technology series)
  Includes bibliographical references (p.).
  ISBN 0-201-32571-3
  1. Application software—Development. 2. Computer architecture.
I. Nord, Robert.   II. Soni, Dilip.   III. Title.   IV. Series.
QA76.76.A65H654 1999
005.1—dc21   99–43579
                                                       CIP

ISBN 0-201-32571-3
Text printed on recycled paper
3 4 5 6 7 8—CRW—03 02 01
Third printing, April 2001

Contents

List of Figures

Chapter 5   Module Architecture View

Chapter 6   Execution Architecture View

Chapter 7   Code Architecture View

Part III   Software Architecture Best Practice

Chapter 8   Safety Vision

Chapter 11   Comm Vision

List of Tables

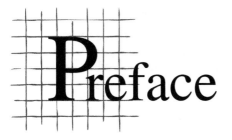

Preface

Software architecture is a recently emerged technical field, but it's not a new activity; there have always been good designers who create good software architectures. However, now the consensus is that what these designers do is qualitatively different from other software engineering activities, and we've begun figuring out how they do it and how we can teach others to do it.

Software architecture is not just a new label for an old activity; software architects today face new challenges. They are asked to produce increasingly complex software using the latest technologies, but these technologies are changing faster than ever. And they are asked to produce better quality software with a shorter time-to-market. Instead of seeing the architecture as necessarily complicated by these staggering requirements, we need to realize that the architecture is our most powerful tool in meeting them.

This book is a practical guide to designing, describing, and applying software architecture. The book began as a study of software architecture in industry, specifically at our company—Siemens. The study told us how practitioners define software architecture, what problems they are trying to solve with it, and how and why they choose particular architectural solutions.

We examined how architects design systems so that today's technology can be replaced with tomorrow's. We saw how the experts abstracted the essential aspects of their real-time, safety-critical, reliability, and performance requirements so that they could make good architectural decisions consistently. We also saw how good architecture descriptions improved the development process, making it easier to develop high-quality software in a shorter time. We saw how managers' understanding of the architecture was critical in organizing and scheduling the project. We saw how developers depended on the architecture to define interfaces and boundaries between their component and others, and to target maintenance activities.

This book also grew from our experience with software architecture as we applied the principles and techniques we saw the experts use. The description techniques helped uncover architectural problems in existing systems. The design principles guided us in defining architectures for new systems and for proposing solutions to problems in existing systems.

Road Map

Part I of this book provides important background information for understanding what we mean by software architecture, and how we structure the architecture design tasks. In Part II we define the architecture design tasks, and use a running example to show how they are applied to the design of a software architecture. The example system, IS2000, is an image acquisition and processing system. We don't provide its complete architecture design, but instead describe one of its subsystems in detail. The Additional Reading section at the end of each chapter in Parts I and II gives references to sources of more information on software architecture.

Part III contains detailed descriptions of four industrial systems. These systems come from our original industrial study and they represent the state-of-the-art in software architecture. Each chapter in Part III gives a broad overview of the software architecture of a case study; these studies don't have the same level of detail as IS2000. The four systems are

1. Safety Vision—A half-million lines of code (LOC) instrumentation and control system for nuclear power plants

2. Healthy Vision—A million LOC embedded patient monitoring system

3. Central Vision—A half-million LOC centralized patient monitoring system

4. Comm Vision—A multimillion LOC telecommunications system

The architects of these systems faced and solved some of the most difficult challenges confronting today's architects: designing large-scale, real-time, safety-critical, highly reliable systems.

In Part IV, we examine the software architect's role, describing what an architect must do beyond the software architecture design.

A Glossary and a Quick Reference to the architecture design tasks and artifacts are included at the end of the book. The four Quick Reference architecture views can also be found on the front and back endpapers.

We have selected the Unified Modeling Language (UML) to describe the software architecture, supplemented by tables or other notations when appropriate. We chose UML because it expresses well most of what we were trying to capture, and it is widely understood. Although the architecture notation is not the essential contribution of this book, we believe that a common notation and a common agreement about what is described will further the field of software architecture by improving our ability to communicate.

The main thing you'll learn from this book is a new way to tackle the problem of architecture design. You will learn what the issues are, when they should be addressed, and how they can be addressed. This book will increase your ability to recognize good solutions. Even if it does not change your eventual architectural solutions, it will help you arrive at those solutions more quickly.

Guide to the Reader

There are a couple of different ways you can read this book. To get a general overview, we recommend you read Parts I and IV. For managers or others who are interested in understanding what software architecture is and how it is used, this is sufficient.

Project managers, system architects, software developers, testers, and those who want a better understanding of the four software architecture views should read, in addition, at least some of Part II. You can get this overview by reading Part II; you may skip the sections that cover the example system. Thus, read the first few pages of Part II, then the first and last sections of chapters 3 through 7. Skip Chapter 2 and Sections 3.2 through 3.7, 4.2, 5.2, 6.2, and 7.2.

After this overview, you will be well prepared to read the case studies. This is an option for students of software architecture or others who want to see the architecture of a range of applications. As you would expect, the case studies are all independent, so you can pick any or all to read. Read the introductory pages of Part III to find out more about the characteristics of each case study.

The final option is to read the whole book. This is, of course, what we recommend for software architects and all others who want a thorough understanding of software architecture. However, we don't expect you to digest Part III all at once. The case studies can be read over time, as the need or interest arises.

Acknowledgments

This book would not have been possible without the contributions of Cornelis H. Hoogendoorn, Heinz Kossmann, Tony Lanza, Jeff Melanson, and Stephan Stöcker. They worked intimately with us to help us understand and describe the systems, which are included as case studies in Part III. We also thank the many Siemens architects and engineers who participated in our initial study of software architectures, those who participated in the Siemens Architecture Workshop, and those who worked with us while we were on assignment at various Siemens companies. We learned from their best practices and we appreciate their willingness to apply our ideas to their products.

We are indebted to Thomas Grandke, Thomas Murphy, and Dan Paulish, from Siemens Corporate Research. We also thank Detlef Fischer and Wolfram Büttner from Siemens, and Linda Northrop, from the Software Engineering Institute. Their support created an environment that made writing this book possible.

Len Bass, Frank Buschmann, Paul Clements, David Garlan, Hassan Gomaa, Steve Hanson, Dan Paulish, Gaynor Redvers-Mutton, Mary Shaw, Peter Sommerlad, John Vlissides, and Michal Young deserve special mention for their encouragement and advice.

Several dedicated colleagues at Siemens reviewed and/or used the material in its formative stages: Leonor Abraido-Fandino, Francois Bronsard, Ram Chintala, Paul Drongowski, Gilberto Matos, Dan Paulish, Michael Sassin, Bob Schwanke, Peter Spool, Veronika Strack, and Jim Wood. We also thank Mike Greenberg for contributing his expertise in software development to the Code Architecture View chapter.

We also owe a large debt to the many dedicated professionals, both known and unknown to us, who reviewed the book and/or contributed their expertise to specific chapters. Len Bass, Frank Buschmann, Martin Fowler, David Garlan, Cris Kobryn, Heinz Kossmann, Philippe Kruchten, Jeff Melanson, John Moody, Jim Ning, Jim Purtilo, Brett Schuchert, Bran Selic, and Stephan Stöcker all contributed insights that challenged us to improve the technical content and readability.

This book might not have been written if Mike Hendrickson had not approached us and encouraged us to write a book on software architecture. We owe a great deal to the staff of Addison-Wesley Professional, including associate editors Katie Duffy and Debbie Lafferty, who kept us grounded throughout the process.

Finally, we thank our families and friends for their encouragement and support.

# Foreword

Architecture is one of the oldest arts and one of the most ancient engineering disciplines. The history of building architecture can be traced back thousands of years to the pyramids in Egypt, the Great Wall in China, and the temples in Mexico. The history of software architecture is much shorter—the software industry began sometime after ENIAC started processing bits in the late 1940s. Although many architectural specializations (e.g., building architecture, naval architecture, aerospace architecture) are mature disciplines, software architecture is still in its nascency. It is noteworthy that software architecture is also much less mature than its sibling, computer hardware architecture, which boasts Moore's Law to predict regular improvements in performance.

The common excuses for software architecture's immaturity are its youth and uniqueness. Although these excuses may have played well a decade or two ago, they are less convincing today. The software industry is no longer callow, and the stakes are no longer trivial. The industry is a half-century old, and much of our new "information age" economy relies on its products.

Although a half-century may not seem like a long time compared with the thousands of years associated with building architecture, we need to keep in mind that software generations are much shorter than building generations. If we ignore legacy systems and use the heuristic that a software generation is approximately 3 years, we have had many opportunities to learn from more than 2^4 generations of software during the last half-century. (Of course, the number of generations is larger if you choose to apply "Internet years" to recent product lifecycles.) We should also realize that the software industry has been able to leverage the knowledge in other architectural disciplines, most notably its hardware counterpart. For example, the "software IC" concept was borrowed from the hardware industry over a decade ago, although component-based architectures have not yet realized their potential.

As for the uniqueness of software, there is no question that the base building material is more malleable and less visible than most other substances we use to construct work and play artifacts. The plasticity of software has allowed us to build and renovate software systems in months instead of years; it has also allowed us to patch together "ball-of-mud" architectures that more resemble slums than edifices. As a consequence, we can point to only a few reference architectures and only a small number of architectural patterns that are worth emulating. Currently software architectures are typically more implicit than explicit and are frequently more hacked than planned.

Unfortunately, the near invisibility of software has facilitated the perpetration of these irresponsible architectural practices. Surprisingly few software professionals, and almost no business users, can reliably assess the robustness and quality of software architectures. Because most software architectures are implicit (i.e., "see the source code for details"), and few are described by detailed blueprints (i.e., software models and related specifications), many persons evaluate software systems superficially on the basis of the only part that is readily seen, the user interface. Although users typically know something is wrong when they select a menu item and receive an error message or crash the system, they frequently cannot identify whether the problem is in the foundation (e.g., operating system), in the plumbing (e.g., network or middleware), or in an appliance (e.g., a word processing or custom business application).

What to do? From a business perspective, we need to show software stakeholders how software architectures can significantly improve product quality and (for those thinking further than the next economic quarter) profitability. From a technical perspective, we need to learn better from our mistakes and apply more rigorous architectural processes and techniques.

Applied Software Architecture provides an important step in improving the quality of software architecture practices. The authors have outlined a pragmatic approach to architecture that is grounded in their extensive experience at Siemens in architecting large software systems. One major strength of this work is its systematic analysis of a collection of case studies. The authors have successfully struck the difficult balance between theory and practice that many strive for but few achieve.

I applaud the authors' use of the Unified Modeling Language (UML) to illustrate their architectures. Using this de facto modeling standard saves us from learning yet another specification language and allows us to focus on the subject matter instead of splitting notational and semantic hairs about what boxes and lines mean. More important, the UML's graphic notation helps us to visualize the complex architectures presented, so that we can efficiently discuss the functional, behavioral, and aesthetic aspects of the systems. This approach is an important step toward achieving architectural blueprints for software.

I have enjoyed working with the authors to improve their innovative use of UML and their meta-modeling techniques. Their valuable feedback on the strengths and weaknesses of the language will help the UML Revision Task Force to better support architectural modeling in future revisions.

Much challenging work lies before us, but I am encouraged by books like this that substantially raise the quality bar for software architecture practices. I hope you will learn from it as I have, and that you will use your new insights to improve your own software architectures.

Cris Kobryn
Co-Chair, OMG UML
Revision Task Force

PART I

Software Architecture

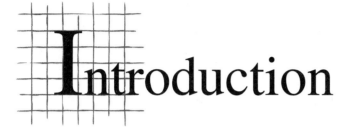# Chapter 1

Introduction

Because computer hardware has become more powerful and cost-effective, the need for new software applications has exploded. Suppliers of software applications have been addressing how they can specify the requirements for new products and then implement the software quickly and less expensively. The earliest software product to the market has an advantage over later products, but customers will abandon a product if the quality is not acceptable.

Having observed the fate of a large number of software product development efforts over the years, we believe a critical factor for a product's success is a good software architecture that is understood by the stakeholders (at the appropriate level of detail) and by the development team members. Although having a good software architecture does not guarantee that a product meets its requirements, having a poorly designed or ill-defined architecture makes it nearly impossible to meet the product requirements.

Unfortunately, software architecture is still very much an emerging discipline within software engineering. Architects have been limited by a lack of (1) standardized ways to represent architecture and (2) analysis methods to predict whether an architecture will result in an implementation that meets the requirements. Architects have had little guidance in how to go about designing the architecture: which decisions should be made first, how conflicting concerns should be satisfied, what level of detail the architecture should encompass, and what range of issues the architecture should cover.

The goal of this book is to provide you, the software architect, with practical guidelines and techniques so you can produce good architecture designs more quickly. Our philosophy is that you should not focus on designing the ideal architecture, but instead should focus on carefully evaluating trade-offs to arrive at a good solution when factoring in all the technical, marketing, personnel, and cost issues.

1.1 Putting Software Architecture in Context

The two main aspects of software architecture are that it provides a design plan—a blueprint—of a system, and that it is an abstraction to help manage the complexity of a system. In this section we discuss these two aspects, and some architecture terminology. This sets the stage for the rest of the chapter, which presents the four views of software architecture.

1.1.1 Software Architecture as a Design Plan

It has been said that all implemented software systems have a software architecture, regardless of whether they have explicit documentation describing it, or had a separately recognized task of designing the software architecture. Although we agree with this perspective as a philosophical statement about software architecture, we take a more pragmatic view here. In this book when we use the term *software architecture*, we are speaking of the purposeful design plan of a system.

The architect documents the architecture and makes sure it's understood by the stakeholders (at the appropriate level of detail) and by the developers.

This design plan isn't a project plan that describes activities and staffing for designing the architecture or developing the product. Instead, it is a structural plan that describes the elements of the system, how they fit together, and how they work together to fulfill the system's requirements. It is used as a blueprint during the development process, and it is also used to negotiate system requirements, and to set expectations with customers, and marketing and management personnel. The project manager uses the design plan as input to the project plan.

Having a distinct software architecture phase, with a documented architecture as the result, forces the architect or architecture team to consider the key design aspects early and across the whole system. Because the software architecture is the bridge between the system requirements and implementation, this design phase comes after the domain analysis, requirements analysis, and risk analysis, and before detailed design, coding, integration, and testing. We're not saying that the analysis tasks must end before the architecture design begins, or that later tasks have no impact on the architecture. This is just an approximate order of events, based on the primary dependencies between the tasks. There is some overlap and iteration between tasks.

The diagram in Figure 1.1 shows how the software architecture fits in with other product development tasks. In this book we don't advocate a particular software process. Instead we identify tasks based primarily on the results they produce, then describe the input needed for a task and how its results affect other tasks. We use this approach throughout the book, describing tasks and activities in terms of their dependencies.

The architect reviews requirements and negotiates them.

The analysis tasks produce the requirements for the system, and may produce things like a domain model, a requirements model, and an organizational model. Although none of these are part of the software architecture, the requirements are a key input to the software architecture design. As the archi-

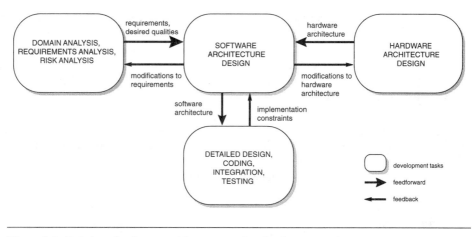

Figure 1.1. Relation of software architecture to other development tasks

The architect pro-
vides requirements
to the system archi-
tect, who configures
the hardware archi-
tecture.

tect or architecture team reviews the requirements and proceeds with the
architecture design, they may need to return to the stakeholders to negotiate
changes to the requirements.

The team also works closely with the system architect, who configures the
hardware architecture. The hardware architecture is another key input to the
software architecture design. The software architect or team in turn gives
requirements to the system architect, and may suggest modifications as the
software architecture design progresses.

The software architecture then guides the implementation tasks, including detailed design, coding, integration, and testing. Although some people
consider things like coding patterns and implementation templates to be part
of the architecture, we think of these code-level artifacts as implementation
mechanisms, not as the software architecture. Although ideally all of the
technical constraints that must be accommodated during implementation
would have been anticipated and addressed in the software architecture, this
isn't realistic. Inevitably there will be some unforeseen implementation constraints that cause changes to the architecture.

The architect
makes sure the
architecture is fol-
lowed.

1.1.2 Software Architecture as an Abstraction

The other main aspect of software architecture is that it is an abstraction that helps manage
complexity. The software architecture is not a comprehensive decomposition or refinement of the system: Many of the details needed to implement the system are abstracted
and encapsulated within an element of the architecture.

Without experience or guidance, an architect could easily pick the wrong details to expose in the architecture and could miss the important ones. The reason there's so much controversy over the definition of *software architecture* is that we can't yet succinctly describe which design details are important over all domains and system sizes.

The architect makes sure the architecture meets its requirements.

The software architecture should define and describe the elements of the system at a relatively coarse granularity. It should describe how the elements fulfill the system requirements, including which elements are responsible for which functionality, how they interact with each other, how they interact with the outside world, and their dependencies on the execution platform.

The architect keeps up with innovations and technologies.

Although many of the nonfunctional requirements or qualities are explicitly given as requirements, there may be additional qualities that the system should have. The architect should consider the kinds of changes to which the system will need to adapt; for example, the modifiability and portability of the system. Another quality to consider is the buildability and testability of the system.

Although the previously described elements are unquestionably architecture-level issues, there are things that are considered important architectural and implementation details, such as class structure or algorithms. These are important to the architecture when they are at the boundaries of architecture elements, describing how the elements interact with each other, the outside world, and with the execution platform. When

The architect develops a prototype, simulates, and gathers whatever information is necessary to identify, understand, and reduce risks.

these details are contained within the elements, they aren't important to the architecture. They can and should be fleshed out only during detailed design.

The purpose of the software architecture is not only to describe the important aspects for others, but to expose them so that the architect can reason about the design. This makes it easier to analyze trade-offs between conflicting requirements. For example, in a system that has custom hardware for gathering data, the architect knows that it must accommodate new kinds of hardware in the future. One solution is to encapsulate the hardware control in separate elements. However, there is a real-time requirement for this data gathering, which argues against inserting a layer between the hardware and the rest of the application. The architect must decide which requirement gets priority, and design a solution that adequately addresses both requirements.

The architect makes design trade-offs.

In the end these design trade-offs can only be resolved by sacrificing or compromising a requirement or other desired quality. The compromise could be in the form of

- Renegotiating a requirement
- Reducing the modifiability, portability, or other desired system quality
- Sacrificing simplicity by using a more complex design or implementation, or additional optimizations

We don't believe in striving for the ideal software architecture. Instead, the goal should be to design a good architecture—one in which, when the system is implemented according to the architecture, it meets its requirements and resource budgets. This means that it must be possible to implement the system according to the architecture. So an architecture that isn't explicit, comprehensive, consistent, and understandable is not good enough.

1.1.3 Software Architecture Terminology

When we talk about the software architecture of a system, we always mean the previously discussed set of issues. Sometimes people use the term in a narrow way. For example, sometimes the phrase "the software architecture of CORBA" refers to a description of how to build applications with it. We don't use the term in that way. For us, "the software architecture of CORBA" describes how CORBA itself is designed. That certainly includes information about how external applications use CORBA (as part of its interface to the outside world), but the software architecture also defines how it is structured internally and how it interacts with the execution platform.

Architectural style, architectural pattern

Table 1.1 shows a comparison of some of the terms used to describe software architectures. In the first row, the terms *architectural style* and *architectural pattern* are used in similar ways. They define element types and how they interact. We prefer to call this a *style*, to distinguish it more clearly from other kinds of patterns (for example, coding patterns, design patterns, analysis patterns, domain patterns, or organizational patterns).

An example of an architectural style is pipes and filters, which has two types of elements—a pipe and a filter. A pipe can be connected to a filter, but pipes cannot connect to pipes, nor filters to filters. This particular style also puts some constraints on how functionality is mapped to the architecture elements: Processing is mapped to the filters, and the pipes act as data conduits.

Reference architecture, domain-specific software architecture

The next two terms, *reference architecture* and *domain-specific software architecture*, are also used in similar ways. Like architectural styles, they define element types and allowed interactions, but in this case they apply to a particular domain. Thus they define how the domain functionality is mapped to the architecture elements.

An example of a reference architecture is a compiler. There is a general notion of the basic elements of a compiler (for example, front end, back end, symbol table), what they should do, and how they're interconnected. Someone designing a new compiler would not start from scratch, but would begin with this basic reference architecture in mind when defining the software architecture of the new compiler.

Product-line architecture

A *product-line architecture* generally applies to a set of products within an organization or company. This idea has grown from the realization that when a company has a family of similar products, they are more consistent and can be developed more cost-effectively if they share a common design and perhaps parts of the implementation.

A product-line architecture, like a reference architecture or domain-specific software architecture, defines element types, how they interact, and how the product functionality is

Term	Defines Element Types and How They Interact	Defines a Mapping of Functionality to Architecture Elements	Defines Instances of Architecture Elements
An **architectural style** or **architectural pattern** (usually not domain specific)	Yes	Sometimes	No
A **reference architecture** or **domain-specific software architecture** (applies to a particular domain)	Yes	Yes	No
A **product-line architecture** (applies to a set of products within an organization)	Yes	Yes	Sometimes
A **software architecture** (applies to a system or product)	Yes	Yes	Yes

Table 1.1. Comparison of Software Architecture Terms

mapped to them. It may also go further, by defining some of the instances of the architecture elements. For example, if all products in the family use the same error-reporting component, this component would be designed and implemented once, and used in all of the products. The product-line architecture would specify this particular component for error reporting.

The last row in Table 1.1 shows how a particular software architecture fits this comparison. It applies to one system and describes the element types, how they interact, how functionality is mapped to them, and the instances that exist in the system. This is the level of specificity you need to design a system.

These terms are not mutually exclusive. A reference architecture, a domain-specific software architecture, a product-line architecture, and a software architecture all make use of architectural styles in their design. Similarly, a product-line architecture or a software architecture can be based on a reference architecture or domain-specific software architecture. And lastly, a software architecture can be part of a product line, using the product-line architecture for its design.

Architecture description language

Particularly in the research community, people have been working on architecture description languages. In theory, an architect could use an architecture description language to describe any of the things listed in Table 1.1: an architectural style or pattern, a reference or domain-specific architecture, a product-line architecture, or a particular software architecture. In practice, not all languages support all of these equally well. Different architecture description languages have different strengths.

An architecture description language provides a way of specifying the elements used in the architecture, generally both as *types* and *instances*. It also provides support for interconnecting element instances to form a *configuration*. In order for the language to work well for describing a product line, an architecture description language must provide a way to specify how individual products can vary across the product line.

In addition to the language itself, many architecture description languages have accompanying tools that provide part of the implementation. In this case, the architect need only describe the architecture using the language and provide an implementation of the element instances. The tools provide the parts of the implementation needed to interconnect them.

Design pattern

There are two other terms that often come up in discussions of software architecture: *design patterns* and *frameworks*. Design patterns as a technology are sometimes relevant to architecture and sometimes only relevant to detailed design. When a design pattern describes the interactions between architecture elements, we consider it to be part of the software architecture. When it describes the structure and interactions within architecture elements, it is part of the detailed design.

Framework

Frameworks also specify structure, and the flow of control and/or data. Although this is architecture-level information, in a framework it is specified by giving a partial implementation—an implementation of the infrastructure. Like design patterns, frameworks are not domain specific, but they are specific to an execution platform. So frameworks are generally a hybrid of architecture-level information and implementation.

1.2   Where the Four Views Came From

This book grew out of a study we made of software architectures for large, complex industrial systems. The purpose of the study was first to understand the architectural issues facing designers, then to understand current practices, including best practices. We were looking for commonalities across domains and for underlying principles that led to a good and useful software architecture.

The systems we studied came from different domains: There were image and signal processing systems, a real-time operating system, communication systems, and instrumentation and control (I&C) systems. These systems ranged in size from fewer than 100,000 lines of code (LOC) to more than one million LOC. Table 1.2 summarizes their key characteristics. Three of the case studies described in Part III were part of the original study: Healthy Vision, Safety Vision, and Comm Vision.

For the original study we interviewed architects and designers, and examined design documents and code to look for important system structures and their uses. We started with a questionnaire about the software architecture, which we used to structure the initial

Application Domain	Size*	Important System Characteristics
User interface	Small	Window management
Signal processing	Medium	Monitoring, real time
Image and signal processing	Medium	High throughput
Computing environment	Medium	Management of distributed information
Signal processing (Healthy Vision)	Large	Monitoring, real time, safety critical
Instrumentation and control (Safety Vision)	Large	Fault tolerant, multiprocessing, safety critical
Instrumentation and control	Large	Multiprocessing
Operating system	Large	Real time
Image and signal processing	Very large	High throughput
Communication	Very large	Multiprocessing
Communication (Comm Vision)	Very large	Distributed, heterogeneous, multiprocessing

*Small = fewer than 100 KLOC; medium = 100–500 KLOC; large = 500 KLOC–1 MLOC; very large = more than 1 MLOC. KLOC = thousand lines of code; MLOC = million lines of code.

Table 1.2. Summary of the Case Study Systems

interviews. The follow-up interviews took place after we had a chance to examine the design documents and sometimes the code.

Our goal in our original study was to discover the principles that guided the software architecture in these systems. More specifically, for each system, we wanted to

- Understand the problem
- Understand the software architecture and how it addresses the particular problem
- Find out what approaches and methods the architects used in designing the software architecture
- Find out how they used the architecture during development, maintenance, and evolution, and how they used it for other products in the same family or successors of the product

This search for commonalities and principles led us to see that a software architecture has four distinct views: conceptual, module, execution, and code. The idea of separating software architecture into different views is not unique. Although there is not yet a general agreement about which views are the most useful, the reason behind multiple views is always the same: Separating different aspects into separate views helps people manage complexity.

Our four views are based on what we observed in practice. Each of them describes a different kind of structure. Between views the structures are loosely coupled and address different engineering concerns. We observed that architects have been making use of these different views, although without necessarily recognizing them as separate architectural views.

1.2.1 Loose Coupling Between Views

Over time, as the characteristics of software systems have changed, certain structures have come to be less tightly coupled with the rest of the architecture. The code view was the first of these.

Code View

Initially, the source code for a program resided in a single file. Today a system's source code is usually split into many files, and many kinds of files (for example, for the interface specification, for the body of a module, and so forth). Today's systems also have more sophisticated building approaches. Object code and binary code are artifacts in their own right, and these must be mapped to libraries and/or files. In addition, there are generally multiple versions of these artifacts, so configuration management is an important task.

The organization of the source code into object code, libraries, and binaries, then in turn into versions, files, and directories strongly affects the reusability of the code and the build time for the system. This is the *code view*.

Module View

As systems increased in size and in number of programmers, techniques arose for handling complexity due to size, and for partitioning work among programmers. Abstraction, encapsulation, and the notion of an interface became well-known concepts, and specific techniques for supporting them were designed, such as Ada packages and module interconnection languages.

Although the design of individual classes or procedures is usually too fine grained to be considered part of software architecture design, the decomposition of the system and the partitioning of modules into layers is the main purpose of the *module view*.

Execution View

Systems have always had a dynamic aspect. Even when programs were strictly sequential, languages such as IBM's Job Control Language arose to describe the sequencing of programs, and the files that were read and written. As systems became distributed, programmers had to decide how to allocate functional components to runtime entities; how to handle communication, coordination, and synchronization among them; and how to map them to the hardware. Software engineering researchers responded to these challenges by designing interconnection languages that address these dynamic structural issues.

Now these issues are generally recognized as being architecture-level issues. They are better handled by the architect early on in the project, rather than being handled by the programmer as development progresses. This is the work of the *execution view.*

Conceptual View

A more recent development in software architecture is the advent of what we call *the conceptual view.* It describes the system in terms of its major design elements and the relationships among them.

Some of today's advanced systems were designed with an explicit conceptual view. This view is usually tied closely to the application domain. Some models of conceptual views use communicating objects as the basic design element; others use assemblies of components and connectors.

In a few systems, the conceptual view plays a primary role. The module, execution, and code views are defined indirectly via rules or conventions, and the conceptual view is used to specify the software architecture of a system, perhaps with some attributes to guide the mappings of the other views. Then, with the help of tools, the implementation of the system is generated automatically.

Each of these four architecture views are present in every system. Sometimes two or more of the views mirror each other, meaning that the views have the same elements and the same relationships. An example is when there is a one-to-one correspondence between runtime entities in the execution view and files in the code view. Only in the most simple of systems is this the case. Today, creating executable files requires a complex sequence of preprocessing, compiling, and linking steps, with many dependencies among the source, intermediate, and executable components.

Thus, most systems today have a loose coupling between the execution and the code views. A runtime entity in the execution view has a corresponding file image in the code view, but the code view contains many additional source and intermediate components. In turn, the execution view may contain elements such as threads, which have no direct correspondence to elements in the code view.

1.2.2 Different Engineering Concerns Addressed by Different Views

Each of the four architecture views addresses different engineering concerns. In the previous section we introduced the views in the order in which they came to be decoupled, but this is roughly the reverse of the order in which they should be designed: conceptual, module, execution, and code. This order is driven by the engineering concerns of each view.

Conceptual View

The conceptual view is tied most closely to the application domain. In this view, the functionality of the system is mapped to architecture elements called *conceptual components*, with coordination and data exchange handled by elements called *connectors*. For the pipes and filters style, for example, the filters are components and the pipes are connectors.

In the conceptual view, problems and solutions are viewed primarily in domain terms. They should be relatively independent of particular software and hardware techniques. The engineering concerns addressed by the conceptual view include the following:

- How does the system fulfill the requirements?
- How are the commercial off-the-shelf (COTS) components to be integrated and how do they interact (at the functional level) with the rest of the system?
- How is domain-specific hardware and/or software incorporated into the system?
- How is functionality partitioned into product releases?
- How does the system incorporate portions of the prior generations of the product and how will it support future generations?
- How are product lines supported?
- How can the impact of changes in requirements or the domain be minimized?

Module View

In the module view, the components and connectors from the conceptual view are mapped to *subsystems* and *modules*. Here the architect addresses how the conceptual solution can be realized with today's software platforms and technologies. The primary engineering concerns are the following:

- How is the product mapped to the software platform?
- What system support/services does it use, and exactly where?
- How can testing be supported?
- How can dependencies between modules be minimized?
- How can reuse of modules and subsystems be maximized?
- What techniques can be used to insulate the product from changes in COTS software, in the software platform, or changes to standards?

Execution View

The execution view describes how modules are mapped to the elements provided by the runtime platform, and how these are mapped to the hardware architecture. The execution view defines the system's *runtime entities* and their attributes, such as memory usage and hardware assignment.

An important part of the execution view is the flow of control. The conceptual view describes the logical flow of control, but in the execution view interest lies in flow of control from the point of view of the runtime platform. Other engineering concerns for the execution view are the following:

- How does the system meet its performance, recovery, and reconfiguration requirements?
- How can one balance resource usage (for example, load balancing)?
- How can one achieve the necessary concurrency, replication, and distribution without adding too much complexity to the control algorithms?
- How can the impact of changes in the runtime platform be minimized?

Code View

For the code view, the architect determines how runtime entities from the execution view are mapped to *deployment components* (for example, executables), how modules from the module view are mapped to source components, and how the deployment components are produced from the *source components*. Important engineering concerns for this view are the following:

- How can the time and effort for product upgrades be reduced?
- How should product versions and releases be managed?
- How can build time be reduced?
- What tools are needed to support the development environment?
- How are integration and testing supported?

By segregating different engineering concerns in different views, the architect can address the higher priority decisions first, and can more easily analyze the design trade-offs.

1.3   Using the Four Views

By making the four views distinct, we are able to articulate differences between views that, in practice, are already loosely coupled. Also, by separating a conceptual view, we can articulate differences that some of the more advanced systems are making. In most systems today, the conceptual view is closely tied to the module view.

After seeing the motivation for and benefits of separating these four views, people often ask us how to design a software architecture to get the most benefit from the four views. Our approach is to prioritize the design decisions, then determine all the dependencies among them. The result is a set of design activities based on the artifacts the architect produces during design, and an order based on their dependencies. This is not a methodology or a software process; this approach fits within most of the processes in use today.

Because we're describing a design approach rather than a software process, in Part II we don't include details about who participates in the various design activities. There is a separate chapter in Part IV on the role of the architect. For the same reason, in Part II we don't describe how external evaluations are incorporated into the design process. We do discuss how the architect evaluates the design as it progresses, but a good software process should include architecture evaluation.

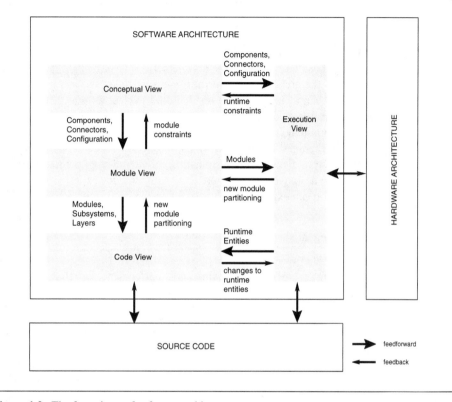

Figure 1.2. The four views of software architecture

The basis for our design approach is the four views, their design activities, and the dependencies among them. Figure 1.2 shows the views and their dependencies. Because these views are loosely coupled, not disjoint, there is some feedback and iteration among them. For each view, most of the design decisions are independent of the other views, but there are some decisions that are affected by the views that are designed later.

In addition, unless the new system poses no new challenges, the architect cannot finalize all decisions up front, before detailed design and implementation begins. If the system is very similar to a previous one, then it is theoretically possible to make the architecture decisions irrevocable. But in most cases, the architect must make the decisions that are the most reasonable, and then iterate back to the architecture and make changes when necessary. The goal is for those inevitable changes to have as little impact as possible, that is, to minimize their number, magnitude, and scope.

Earlier we mentioned that architecture description languages often have an accompanying infrastructure to bridge the gap between what the language can model and what the underlying platform can execute. We use the module, execution, and code views to bridge this gap. Components and connectors in our conceptual view can't be directly executed on any arbitrary runtime platform. The module and execution views explicitly define how components and connectors are mapped to the runtime platform.

Using these four views gives a systematic way of designing a software architecture, which helps the architect set priorities, analyze trade-offs, and make sure that nothing is missed. We can't guarantee the result is the perfect architecture, because such a thing doesn't exist. We also can't guarantee the result is the best architecture. There is rarely a single solution that is inarguably the best; there are usually multiple solutions that work, and each of them has different drawbacks. We can't even guarantee the result is an acceptable architecture. Even with a systematic approach to architecture design, and guidance on how to make design decisions, there is no substitute for experience.

What you can expect from this design approach is guidance in

- Tracing influencing factors and requirements through the architecture
- Sequencing the design activities
- Making design trade-offs
- Supporting system-specific qualities like performance or reliability
- Supporting general qualities like buildability, portability, testability, and reusability
- Ensuring that no aspects of the architecture are overlooked
- Producing useful documentation of the architecture

1.4   Notation

One word about our software architecture notation: Originally we used boxes-and-lines notation to describe software architectures. Then, late in 1998, we began to replace this with the Unified Modeling Language (UML). UML is a general-purpose modeling language with standardized graphical notation and associated semantics. We chose UML because it supports most of what we need to describe. One of our concerns was that UML emerged from object-oriented design, so it is most commonly used to describe things at the detailed-design level. This means that some of our architecture concepts are not directly supported by existing UML elements; however, our biggest concern was that we may cause more blurring between software architecture and detailed design. All in all, we think the benefits to be gained by using a standardized, well-understood notation outweigh the drawbacks.

Our use of the UML graphical notation is completely consistent with the current UML standard. But UML has a very particular meaning associated with each symbol. Rather than making up completely new elements and semantics, we use existing ones when the fit is close enough. For example, our "subsystem" in the module view means approximately the same thing as a UML subsystem, even though some of the details differ. The UML elements we use are listed in the summary tables of Chapters 4 through 7. We expect there will be a closer alignment between our semantics and those of UML in the future, because UML is being used more and more to describe software architecture.

Additional Reading

The IEEE Architecture Planning Group was chartered in 1995 by the IEEE Software Engineering Standards Committee to set the direction for architecture-related standards and practices for the IEEE. The IEEE Architecture Working Group was formed with the responsibility of implementing the planning group's recommendations and is chartered with developing IEEE P1471, *Recommended Practice for Architectural Description* (IEEE Architecture Working Group, 1999).

Shaw and Garlan (1996) describe software architecture and present the component-connector model and architecture styles. Bass, Clements, and Kazman (1998) introduce the need for multiple structures in software architecture and the role of reference architectures and product lines. The Software Engineering Institute (SEI) maintains a growing Web site containing information on software architecture, analysis, and product lines (Software Engineering Institute, 1999). Buschmann, Meunier, Rohnert, et al. (1996) describe a pattern-oriented approach to software architecture and the relationship of architectural patterns, frameworks, and design patterns. Buschmann (1999) describes how to use patterns for software architecture by considering both human and technical aspects of software development.

Soni, Nord, and Hofmeister (1995) present the results of our survey of software architectures for large, complex industrial systems that led us to see that a software architecture has four distinct views. Kruchten (1995) describes an alternate 4 + 1 view of software architecture. These views are carried over into the modeling of a system's architecture by Booch, Rumbaugh, and Jacobsen (1999). In their study, architecture is described in terms of five interlocking views: use-case view, design view, process view, implementation view, and deployment view. There is growing interest in describing software architecture with UML now that it is an Object Management Group (OMG) (1998, 1999) standard. Hofmeister, Nord, and Soni (1999), and Medvidovic and Rosenblum (1999) describe their experiences and reflect on areas in which UML worked well and areas in which it was deficient.

PART II

Designing, Describing, and Using Software Architecture

In this part of the book, we describe the architecture design tasks and use an example system, IS2000, to show how to design a software architecture.

Each of the four views has its own design tasks, but all are structured in a similar way (see Figure II.1). The first task for each view is global analysis. In the global analysis task, you first identify the external influencing factors and critical requirements that could affect the architecture. Then you analyze them to come up with strategies for designing the architecture. If the influencing factors and requirements can't all be satisfied, you must either decide which has priority, renegotiate a requirement, or change some external factor to come up with workable strategies for the architecture.

The second group of tasks is the central design tasks. You first define the elements of the architecture view and the relationships among them, and then (if it's appropriate for that view) define how these elements are configured. Different views have different types of elements. They could be conceptual components, modules, processes, files, or other kinds of elements. These design tasks are grouped together because they are more tightly coupled: There is more feedback among them than with other tasks.

Also in the central design tasks is a global evaluation task. This task doesn't produce a separate output; it is an ongoing task throughout the central design tasks. The central design tasks for most of the views have multiple sources of input, so one aspect of global evaluation is deciding which source of information to use at which time. The second aspect is checking whether decisions made as part of the central design have an impact on other, prior design tasks. If so, you follow the feedback arrows back to the earlier design task, and revise the design. The third aspect of global evaluation is evaluating the central design decisions for their impact on each other.

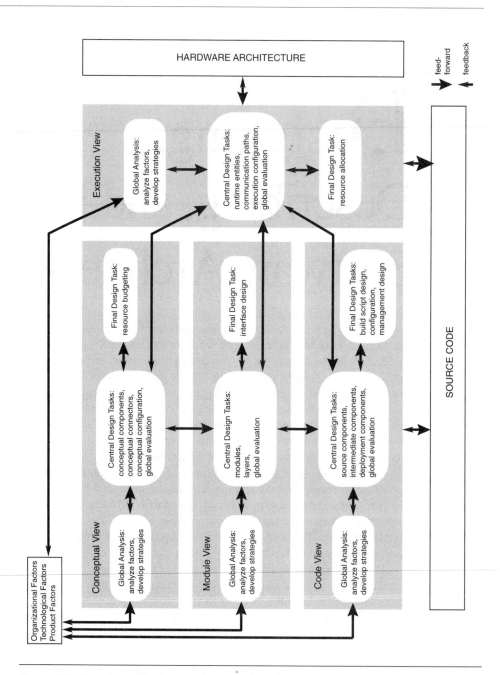

Figure II.1. Overview of the design tasks for the four views

The final design task for each of the four views is less tightly coupled. Examples of this final design task are resource budgeting and interface definition. There may be some feedback to the central design tasks, but most of the prior design decisions should not be affected by this final task.

For the most part, we have structured Part II so that it follows the approximate sequence of design activities. The exception is for global analysis: We added an extra chapter for this task, both because this task is similar for all views and because it needed a more detailed explanation.

The chapter on global analysis is followed by one chapter for each of the four views. Each of these contains

- An overview of the design tasks for the architecture view

- A detailed explanation of how to apply the design tasks using the IS2000 system

- A summary of the view, including how it is used

Chapter 2

IS2000: The Advanced Imaging Solution

In this chapter we introduce the image acquisition and processing system that illustrates the architecture concepts described in Part II. IS2000 is a fictional system, but it is inspired by actual systems we've studied. The resulting composite was simplified and generalized into a generic imaging system. Such an imaging system could be part of a product used for circuit board inspection, remote sensing, or multimedia applications.

2.1 System Overview

IS2000's hardware configuration is shown in Figure 2.1. The basic functionality of the product is to capture an image using the camera on the probe. The source of the image could be from visible light, which is one form of electromagnetic radiation, from another frequency in the electromagnetic spectrum, from heat, or from some other source of radiation. To supplement the images, sensor readings provide additional information, such as the distance of the camera to the object being imaged. To make the images, IS2000 has to acquire this raw data and convert it into sensor readings and images suitable for viewing.

The IS2000 user may wish to take a single image, a series of images at different time intervals, or to create a motion picture. The user may wish to keep the camera stationary or move it to take images from different angles. Each of these options is an example of an *acquisition procedure*. The system has a set of built-in acquisition procedures, which can be customized by setting parameters before or during the acquisition. The system also allows the user to define a new acquisition procedure.

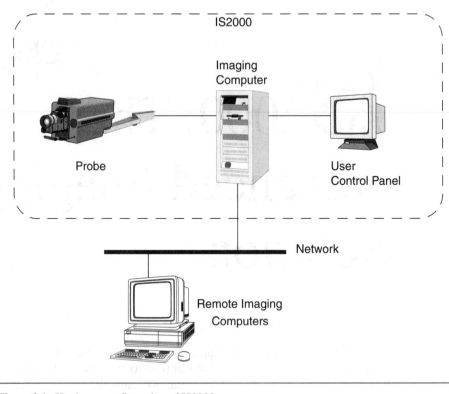

Figure 2.1. Hardware configuration of IS2000

When the acquisition procedure is underway, the user is able to monitor it by viewing the raw data as it is transformed into a raw image. After the raw images are acquired, the user can perform a number of processing operations to enhance the images for viewing. The user can elect to transfer them to a remote imaging system for remote viewing or processing.

2.2 Product Features

IS2000 provides a range of image acquisition and processing operations on two-dimensional and three-dimensional images, data storage for the images, and network access to the images. Its key marketing features are the following:

- IS2000 has a user-friendly operator environment.
- IS2000 has a comprehensive catalog of built-in acquisition procedures.
- The user can define custom acquisition procedures.

- The throughput of image acquisition is 50 percent higher than for previous products.
- Image display can be as fast as the maximum hardware speed.
- At runtime the user can make a trade-off between acquisition speed and image quality.
- IS2000 is designed for easy upgrade to new platforms.
- IS2000 has open platform connectivity to on-site or remote viewing and image postprocessing workstations.
- IS2000 can be connected to peripherals, including printers and digital imagers.

A single acquisition control panel is provided with each IS2000 unit. Additional independent viewing stations are also available.

2.3 System Interactions

IS2000 interacts with three things in its environment:

1. The user controlling the acquisition
2. The object being probed
3. The network connecting the system to other viewing stations

IS2000 has a corresponding piece of hardware for each of these interactions: the user control panel, the probe hardware, and the network connector. These in turn each have an interface to IS2000's software, which runs on the imaging computer:

- The user control panel interface is used for setting the parameters for an acquisition, monitoring the acquisition, and selecting images for export.
- The probe hardware interface is used for controlling and receiving data from the probe hardware.
- The network connector interface is used for exporting image data over the network.

2.4 The Future of IS2000

IS2000 must be designed to be extensible, maintainable, and portable. Its design must be flexible enough to accommodate certain expected changes. The product requirements may change somewhat during development and certainly will change over the lifetime of the product. The physical characteristics of the probe/camera may change as new models are introduced. The way users interact with the system is likely to change as they become more sophisticated in using the system and want more efficient ways of using it. As the processing power of the system increases, more and more work that was the responsibility of the users will shift to the system.

Other product features will also likely change. Over time, the built-in acquisition procedures will evolve. Image processing is constantly being improved, and new kinds of processing filters may be added. The product needs to remain compatible with new or evolving standards for file formats and communication of image information.

In addition, the technology affecting the software components is likely to change over the lifetime of the system. Even if the requirements for the functionality of an image processing filter don't change, its implementation might change, for example, to improve performance. IS2000 may have to be improved to handle upgrades to commercial components that are part of the product, and the target software environment is likely to change as upgrades are introduced.

In the next five chapters, we present how the design of IS2000's software architecture meets these challenges. Some of the design constraints are ones that every software designer faces and some of them are unique to the IS2000 functionality and marketplace.

Chapter 3
Global Analysis

The purpose of global analysis is to analyze the factors that influence the architecture and to develop strategies for accommodating these factors in the architecture design. Global analysis starts before the conceptual, module, execution, and code architecture views are defined, and it continues throughout the architecture design.

Global analysis begins with identifying factors that affect the architecture design. These influencing factors fall into three categories:

1. Organizational factors

2. Technological factors

3. Product factors

Organizational factors constrain the design choices. Some of them, such as development schedule and budget, apply only to the product you are currently designing. Other organizational factors, such as organizational attitudes and the software process, carry over to every product developed by an organization. If you ignore these factors, the architecture may not be able to be implemented.

The technological factors have a more obvious influence on the architecture. Your design choices are limited by the kinds of hardware and software, architecture technology, and standards that are currently available. But the state of technology changes over time, and products must adapt, so your architecture should be designed with flexibility in mind.

The product factors are the primary influence on the architecture. This category covers the functional features of your product, and qualities like performance, dependability, and cost. These factors may be different in future versions of the product, so your architecture should be designed to support the changes you can reasonably expect.

We call this activity *global* analysis for three reasons:

1. Many of the factors affect the entire system; they can't necessarily be localized in one component of the architecture. The strategies should address the global concerns, but provide guidance for implementing them locally.

2. Global analysis occurs throughout the architecture design rather than at one point in time. As you design each of the architecture views, you focus on developing strategies that help you design that view. New factors, issues, or strategies can arise at any time during the design, as the details of the architecture are pinned down.

3. During global analysis you consider the factors as a group instead of independently. These factors are not all independent; some of them may even contradict each other. You must sort out the conflicts and resolve them, either by prioritizing the factors or by negotiating changes to factors when you can.

Global analysis is meant to complement the risk analysis and/or requirements analysis that you perform—not replace it. It's possible that after completing the requirements and risk analyses you will already have a thorough analysis of the factors that affect the architecture. Then the focus of global analysis is to develop strategies for the architecture design.

The primary purpose of global analysis is to give you a systematic way of identifying, accommodating, and describing the factors that affect the architecture. The three types of factors are analyzed separately, with the results recorded in separate *factor tables*. You then develop strategies for accommodating the factors, and you describe them on *issue cards*.

In this chapter we describe this analysis and apply it to IS2000. We analyze the organizational factors first, then the technological and product factors. This is probably the reverse of the order you will address them, but we wanted to introduce the less obvious factors first, ending with the more familiar product factors.

3.1 Overview of Global Analysis Activities

The architecture design of a large software system is influenced by a variety of factors. Many of these have an impact over the entire system, and some directly contradict other factors. Some factors, such as requirements for fault tolerance, can affect the design in a fundamental manner. To avoid expensive rework, these factors must be addressed from the beginning of design. There is a tension between factors that constrain the design and factors that make it more flexible. These factors have to be balanced so that the system is able to be implemented and adapted to future needs.

During global analysis, you uncover the most influential of these factors, then develop strategies for designing the architecture so that it accommodates these factors and reflects global and future concerns. You should record the results of the analysis process as a part of the architecture so that individual developers can use these results while making decisions to address specific design problems. Without strategies that reflect global and future concerns, developers may choose a local solution that does not support anticipated changes. As the architecture design proceeds, the architect should monitor the efficacy and relevance of these strategies, and make changes when necessary.

To arrive at these strategies, there are two basic activities—analyze factors and develop strategies—each with three steps (Figure 3.1). Global analysis is the first task in each of the four architecture views, and its results are used in the central design tasks of that view. As you see in Figure 3.1, during the central design tasks, new issues or strategies may arise that cause you to return to the global analysis and to revise or expand your factor tables or issue cards.

3.1.1 Analyze Factors

The analyze factors activity takes as input the organizational, technological, and product factors. If these factors are not yet explicit, then part of the first step is to make them explicit.

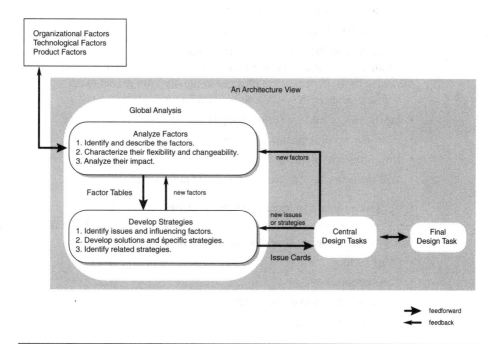

Figure 3.1. Global analysis activities

Step 1: Identify and Describe the Factors

At this early stage in the architecture design, the primary factors to consider are those that have a significant global influence, those that could change during development, those that are difficult to satisfy, and those with which you have little experience.

To determine whether a factor has significant global influence, you should ask

- Can the factor's influence be localized to one component in the design, or must it be distributed across several components?
- During which stages of development is the factor important?
- Does the factor require any new expertise or skills?

Step 2: Characterize the Flexibility or the Changeability of the Factors

The flexibility of a factor describes what is negotiable about the factor. The negotiating could be with any of the stakeholders: your managers, marketing personnel, the customers, the users, the system architect, or the developers. Use this information when factors conflict or for some other reason become impossible to fulfill.

To characterize the flexibility of a factor, you should ask

- Is it possible to influence or change the factor so that it makes your task of architecture development easier?
- In what way can you influence it?
- To what extent can you influence it?

The changeability of a factor describes what you expect could change about the factor, both in the near and more distant future. The changeability could be due to a change in the factor itself, or because of changes in the way you expect to use it in the future.

To characterize the changeability of a factor, you should ask

- In what way could the factor change?
- How likely will it change during or after development?
- How often will it change?
- Will the factor be affected by changes in other factors?

Step 3: Analyze the Impact of the Factors

Here you analyze the impact of the factors on the architecture. If the factor was to change, which of the following would be affected and how:

- Other factors
- Components
- Modes of operation of the system
- Other design decisions

You should record the impact of factors and their changeability in terms of impact on particular components, but this won't be possible if the components have not yet been defined or identified. Some experienced architects, even at this early stage, have a notion of the high-level components of the system. But even if you're making guesses during the early stages, it is important to capture your assumptions to get feedback as soon as possible.

As the design progresses, the impact of factors can be determined more precisely, and you should revise the documentation accordingly. We recommend that you use the format presented in Table 3.1, which we call a *factor table*, for recording the results of analyzing the factors. Keep three tables, one for each type of factor (organizational, technological, and product). We use a label for each factor that identifies its factor category (O1 or O2 in Table 3.1), and a unique sequencing number (O1.1, O1.2, and so on). The labels for organizational factors begin with the letter O, technological factors begin with T, and product factors begin with P.

Organizational Factor	Flexibility and Changeability	Impact
O1: <Factor category>		
O1.1: <Factor name>		
<Description of factor>	<What aspects of the factor are flexible or changeable?>	<Components affected by the factor or changes to it>
O1.2: <Factor name>		
<Description of factor>	<What aspects of the factor are flexible or changeable?>	<Components affected by the factor or changes to it>
O2: <Factor category>		
O2.1: <Factor name>		
<Description of factor>	<What aspects of the factor are flexible or changeable?>	<Components affected by the factor or changes to it>

Table 3.1. Sample Format of Organizational Factor Table

3.1.2   Develop Strategies

The second global analysis activity is to develop strategies for the architecture design or for implementation. This activity also has three steps.

Step 1: Identify Issues and Influencing Factors

Using the factor tables, you first identify a handful of important issues that are influenced by the factors and their changeability.

- An issue may arise from limitations or constraints imposed by factors. For example, an aggressive development schedule may make it impossible to satisfy all of the product requirements.

- An issue may result from the need to reduce the impact of changeability of factors. For example, it is often important to design the architecture to reduce the cost of porting the product to another operating system.

- An issue may develop because of the difficulty in satisfying product factors. For example, a high throughput requirement may overload the CPU.

- An issue may arise from the need to have a common solution to global requirements such as error handling and recovery.

Usually there are several factors that affect an issue, and when these factors conflict, or when fulfilling all of them is too expensive, then you must negotiate a change in the factors.

Step 2: Develop Solutions and Specific Strategies

For each issue, develop strategies that address the issue and ensure the implementation and changeability of the architecture design. Design each strategy to be consistent with the influencing factors, their desired/required changeability, and their interactions with other factors. Your strategies should address one or more of the following goals:

- Reduce or localize the factor's influence.
- Reduce the impact of the factor's changeability on the design and other factors.
- Reduce or localize required areas of expertise or skills.
- Reduce overall time and effort.

Step 3: Identify Related Strategies

When a strategy belongs with more than one issue, don't repeat the strategy: Describe it in just one place, and reference it as a related strategy in the other issues where it applies.

Use a standard format to describe each issue, its influencing factors and their impact, a general discussion of its solution, and the strategies that address it. Here is the format we recommend for describing an architecture design issue: We call this an *issue card*.

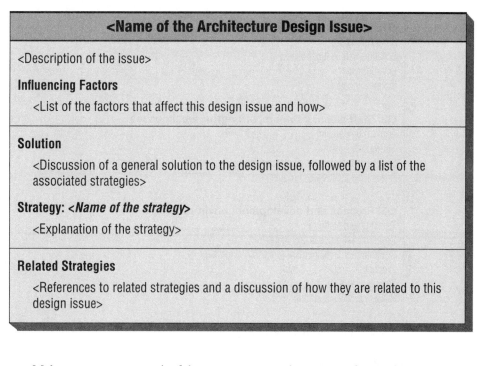

<Name of the Architecture Design Issue>

<Description of the issue>

Influencing Factors

<List of the factors that affect this design issue and how>

Solution

<Discussion of a general solution to the design issue, followed by a list of the associated strategies>

Strategy: *<Name of the strategy>*

<Explanation of the strategy>

Related Strategies

<References to related strategies and a discussion of how they are related to this design issue>

Make sure you use meaningful names to capture the essence of strategies and to make it easy to communicate. The importance of communication can't be overemphasized when it comes to strategies that will be applied by other developers.

You may want to summarize your strategies with a table that cross-indexes issues, influencing factors, and strategies (look ahead to Table 3.5 for an example). This overview acts as a guide for developers to find and to apply the appropriate strategy.

3.2 Analyze Organizational Factors

Next we present a detailed example of applying the global analysis to IS2000, starting with the analysis of the organizational factors. Certain factors that arise from the business organization itself affect the design of the architecture. We call these factors *organizational factors*. They include aspects of the project such as the schedule and budget, and the skills and interests of the people involved.

In Figure 3.2, we identified five categories of organizational factors: management, staff skills, process and development environment, development schedule, and development budget. Within these five categories we listed examples of typical organizational factors.

O1: Management
Build versus buy
Schedule versus functionality
Environment
Business goals

O2: Staff skills, interests, strengths, weaknesses
Application domain
Software design
Specialized implementation techniques
Specialized analysis techniques

O3: Process and development environment
Development platform
Development process and tools
Configuration management process and tools
Production process and tools
Testing process and tools
Release process and tools

O4: Development schedule
Time-to-market
Delivery of features
Release schedule

O5: Development budget
Head count
Cost of development tools

Figure 3.2. Typical organizational factors

The organizational factors don't describe the product; instead, they capture aspects of
the organization that could affect the architecture. Although the factors in Figure 3.2 are
the concerns of a project manager, they also concern an architect because of their potential
impact on the architecture. They constrain the design choices while the product is being
designed and built, and if they are ignored, the architecture may not be able to be implemented. For example, if the schedule is aggressive, there may not be enough time to train
developers in a new technology, which rules it out for the architecture design.

For most of these factors, your primary concern is to determine their flexibility, to
help you negotiate the constraints if necessary. If a factor is likely to change during devel-

opment, due to a change in management or market conditions for example, you should also analyze its changeability.

Step 1: Identify and Describe the Factors

The first step in analyzing organizational factors is to identify the factors that may affect the architecture. Table 3.2 describes some of the organizational factors for IS2000. The factors in the management section reflect the organization's historic preference for developing software in-house rather than acquiring it outside, and the high importance of meeting the schedule, even at the expense of not providing all the functionality. For other systems, organizational attitudes may not be relevant, or they may neutral enough to have no effect on the architecture.

For the staff skills section, we identified the skills and the experience developers should have for this project, and compared them with the actual skills. Early in the architecture design, you won't always know which specialized skills are needed. In this case you have to make a prediction, and revise these factors as the architecture design progresses.

For IS2000, the schedule factors have a significant impact. The product has a two-year time-to-market, and the features to be delivered are prioritized. It is clear to all the stakeholders that this is a very aggressive schedule, so they agreed early to a prioritization of features.

Step 2: Determine the Flexibility and the Changeability of the Factors

The next step in analyzing organizational factors is to characterize the flexibility and changeability of each factor, keeping in mind the priorities set by management and the organizational attitudes.

For IS2000, the results of this step are shown in the middle column of Table 3.2. The company considers time-to-market (factor O4.1) more important than development cost (factor O5.1) or delivering all planned features (factor O4.2). The organization's attitudes (factors O1.1 and O1.2) are relatively neutral, and do not preclude any architectural design choices.

Note that the in-house personnel assignments were made before the architecture design began. These are fixed, but there is some flexibility in either hiring a few permanent employees or hiring contractors for the duration of the project.

Step 3: Analyze the Impact of the Factors

The third step is to analyze the impact of the organizational factors and their flexibility or changeability. The flexibility of management preferences can be used, for example, to postpone implementation of product features to meet the schedule. The skill deficiency of the staff in use of multiple threads and processes can have a severe impact on the ability of the system to meet its performance requirements. The schedule and flexible delivery of features have a large and pervasive impact on almost all of the architecture design.

Organizational Factor	Flexibility and Changeability	Impact
O1: Management		
O1.1: Build versus buy		
There is a mild preference to build.	The organization will consider buying if it is justified.	There is a moderate impact on meeting the schedule.
O1.2: Schedule versus functionality		
There is a preference for meeting the schedule over some features.	This is negotiable for several features.	There is a moderate impact on meeting the schedule and the first product release.
O2: Staff skills		
O2.1: Experience in structured design		
All in-house developers have these skills.	Flexibility is not applicable.	There is a small impact.
O2.2: Experience in object-oriented analysis and design		
Half of the in-house developers have these skills.	It is feasible to hold training.	There is a moderate impact on achieving good design.
O2.3: Experience in multithreading		
One in-house developer has this skill.	The subject area is too complex to rely on training alone.	There is a moderate impact on meeting performance.
O2.4: Experience in building multiprocess systems		
Two in-house developers have this skill.	Training supplemented with software abstraction may alleviate lack of skills.	There is a large impact on meeting performance.

Table 3.2. Organizational Factors for IS2000

Organizational Factor	Flexibility and Changeability	Impact
O4: Development schedule		
O4.1: Time-to-market		
Time-to-market is two years.	There is no flexibility.	There is a large impact on design choices in all areas.
O4.2: Delivery of features		
The features are prioritized.	The features are negotiable.	There is a moderate impact on meeting the schedule.
O5: Development budget		
O5.1: Head count		
There are 12 developers.	The organization can hire one or two permanent developers or a large number of contractors.	There is a moderate impact on meeting the schedule.

Table 3.2. Organizational Factors for IS2000 *(continued)*

3.3 Begin Developing Strategies

After analyzing some of the factors you can begin identifying key issues in the architecture design and determine whether any solution strategies are emerging. Later in the global analysis, as you consider the technological factors and product requirements, you refine or revise these strategies. In practice, as you design each architectural view, you may need to identify additional strategies to handle design problems that become apparent only after some of the design has been completed.

Step 1: Identify Issues and Influencing Factors

After reviewing the analysis summarized in Table 3.2, we identified two issues: Aggressive Schedule and Skill Deficiencies. Obviously we can't know for certain the aggressiveness of the schedule or what skills are lacking without knowing certain key product factors, without having decided certain aspects of the architecture design, and without having at least a rough estimate of the resources needed to implement the product. At this point in the analysis we rely on past experience with similar products to identify the key issues for this product. It is possible that these issues will be addessed as we proceed further with the analysis and architecture design, but more likely we will refine the issue and modify the strategies for resolving it.

For the Aggressive Schedule issue, most of the influencing factors are organizational factors, but factor P7.2, COTS budget, is a product factor. This factor comes up later in our analysis, but we have included it here so we don't have to repeat the issue card again later.

Step 2: Develop Solutions and Specific Strategies

We propose three strategies to solve the Aggressive Schedule issue. The first two strategies mandate that we use existing software components whenever possible, either in-house or commercial software. The second strategy relies on the fact that features are prioritized and there is some flexibility in their delivery dates. If we design the architecture so that it is easy to add or to remove features, then we can adjust the feature set to meet the delivery dates.

For the Skill Deficiencies issue, past experience indicates that a system like this must be a multiprocess system. However, the development team overall is weak in the necessary skills. Thus the two strategies we propose are (1) to avoid using multiple threads and (2) to encapsulate multiprocess support. Later analysis may show these strategies to be infeasible or may support them.

Experienced architects begin to consider strategies such as these very early in the design process. They reconsider them as the architecture design progresses, so it is important to capture not only the initial strategies, but also the factors that prompt them. Having a record of the influencing factors gives you more information about the consequences of revising a strategy.

Step 3: Identify Related Strategies

At this point, for these two issues, there are no related strategies. Later we present other issues that are related to them.

Aggressive Schedule

The development schedule is aggressive. Given the estimated effort and available resources, it may not be possible to develop all the software in the required time.

Influencing Factors

O4.1: Time-to-market is short and is not negotiable. A rough estimate of effort required to redesign and reimplement all of the software suggests that it will take longer than two years.

O5.1: Head count cannot be increased substantially.

O1.1: Building is mildly preferred over buying.

O4.2: Delivery of features is negotiable. Low-priority features can be added to later releases.

P7.2: Budget for commercial off-the-shelf (COTS) components is flexible. Both the price and the licensing fees of COTS components must be considered.

Solution

Redesigning and reimplementing all of the software will take longer than two years. Three possible strategies are to reuse software, buy COTS, and to release low-priority features at a later stage.

Strategy: *Reuse existing in-house, domain-specific components.*

Several of the in-house domain-specific components are candidates for reuse. However, reuse of some existing components may need substantial redesign and reimplementation. Evaluate each of these components to determine whether it is advantageous to reuse it and whether it will save time and effort.

Strategy: *Buy rather than build.*

Buying COTS software has the potential of saving time and effort. However, the price and licensing fees for some COTS products may be too high. Learning to use new COTS software may increase time and effort. Purchase or license COTS software when it is advantageous and when it will reduce development time substantially.

Strategy: *Make it easy to add or remove features.*

One way to reduce the develop time is to reduce the functionality by delaying delivery of some of the features to a later release. If it is easy to add or to remove functional features without substantial reimplementation, then it is feasible to adjust the functionality to meet the delivery schedule.

> ## Skill Deficiencies
>
> We know from experience with the previous product that it will be a challenge to meet this product's performance requirements, which are considerably tighter than for the prior system. Common techniques to achieve higher performance are to use multiple threads and multiple processes. However, the development team is deficient in the necessary skills.
>
> ### Influencing Factors
>
> O2.3: There is only one developer who has experience with the use of multiple threads.
>
> O2.4: There are only two developers who have experience with the use of multiple processes.
>
> ### Solution
>
> Two possible strategies are to avoid the use of multithreading and to encapsulate multiprocess facilities.
>
> **Strategy: *Avoid the use of multiple threads.***
>
> Multithreading can be quite complex, difficult to use, and error prone. A training course alone would not be sufficient for a developer to achieve proficiency in multithreading. Rather than hiring someone with multithreading experience, avoid multithreading whenever possible and use it only when absolutely necessary.
>
> **Strategy: *Encapsulate multiprocess support facilities.***
>
> Because we have very few people with multiprocessing skills, our strategy is to maximize the available skills by encapsulating the multiprocess support facilities in a layer, and to provide a simpler interface that's tailored to the specific project needs.

3.4 Analyze Technological Factors

We now continue the global analysis with the technological factors. These factors arise from the external technology solutions that are embedded or embodied in the product. They are primarily hardware and software technologies and standards. Typical categories of technological factors are general-purpose and domain-specific hardware, software technologies such as the operating system and user interface, architecture technologies such as patterns and frameworks, and standards such as image data formats (Figure 3.3). For each of these categories, consider whether there are general-purpose and/or domain-specific solutions appropriate for your product. Also consider whether the available solutions are commercially available or belong to the company, whether for a product family or a specific product.

T1: General-purpose hardware
Processors
Network
Memory
Disk

T2: Domain-specific hardware
Probe hardware
Probe network

T3: Software technology
Operating system
User interface
Software components
Implementation language
Design patterns
Frameworks

T4: Architecture technology
Architecture styles
Architecture patterns and frameworks
Domain-specific or reference architectures
Architecture description languages
Product-line technologies

T5: Standards
Operating system interface
Database
Data formats
Communication
Algorithms and techniques
Coding conventions

Figure 3.3. Typical categories of technological factors

Although, like the organizational factors, these factors do not describe the product itself, its design and implementation directly depends on them. These factors are likely to change, which in turn forces the design and implementation of the software system to change accordingly. Your architecture should be designed to minimize the difficulty of adapting to expected changes in technological factors.

In analyzing the technological factors, you follow the same three steps as for the organizational factors, and produce a factor table that summarizes the technological factors. These steps should be clear by now, so for IS2000, let's go directly to the technological factor table (Table 3.3).

Technological Factor	Flexibility and Changeability	Impact
T1: General-purpose hardware		
T1.1: Processor type		
A standard processor has been selected.	Increases in processor speed are frequent. As technology improves, the processor type could change every four years.	The change in processor type is expected to be transparent, provided the operating system does not change.
T1.2: Number of processors		
Only one processor has been deemed to be sufficient initially.	If any additional functionality or performance is required, and available processor speeds do not increase, an additional processor may be required.	The change can be transparent if the operating system (OS) supports multiprocessing. If not, components at processor boundaries will be affected drastically.

Table 3.3. Technological Factors for IS2000

Technological Factor	Flexibility and Changeability	Impact
T1.3: Memory		
A total of 64MB of memory has been selected due to constraints in budget.	If memory prices drop, then this size could be increased. No significant decrease is expected during development.	More complex signal processing may become possible when memory size can be increased.
T2: Domain-specific hardware		
T2.1: Probe hardware		
This is the hardware to detect and process signals.	The probe hardware may be upgraded every three years as technology improves.	The impact will be large on components involved in acquisition and image processing.
T2.2: Probe network		
This is the network connecting components of the probe hardware and general-purpose hardware.	The probe network is expected to change every four years as technology improves.	The impact will be large on components involved in acquisition and image processing.
T3: Software technology		
T3.1: Operating system		
The OS on the general-purpose processor is a real-time OS. A nonreal-time OS will be used on additional CPUs if they are deployed.	OS features change every two years. The OS itself may change every four years.	Changes are transparent provided they conform to the current standard for OS interface. Otherwise, the impact will be large.

Table 3.3. Technological Factors for IS2000 *(continued)*

Technological Factor	Flexibility and Changeability	Impact
T3.2: OS processes		
Memory overhead and overhead for creation/destruction of a process are important considerations. Overhead for creation/destruction of processes is small on the real-time OS.	Overheads will be reduced with improvements in OS implementations. They may increase for a new OS, however.	The impact is large on allocation of modules to processes and threads in the execution view.
T5: Standards		
T5.1: Standard for OS interface		
POSIX has been selected as the OS interface standard.	This standard is stable.	There is large impact on all components.
T5.2: Standards for sensor data format		
The standards affect the format of the data available from the probe hardware.	There is no stable standard for this format.	There is a large impact on components involved in acquisition, image processing, and postprocessing.
T5.3: Standards for image data formats		
The format of image data is standardized in this domain.	The standard is somewhat stable, but is likely to change every three years.	There is a large impact on image-processing and postprocessing components.

Table 3.3. Technological Factors for IS2000 *(continued)*

Technological Factor	Flexibility and Changeability	Impact
T5.4: Domain-specific algorithms and techniques		
These are the algorithms for signal processing, image construction, and image processing.	The field is quite mature. Improvements will be minor and infrequent.	There is a minor impact on components involved in acquisition, image processing, and postprocessing.

Table 3.3. Technological Factors for IS2000 *(continued)*

For the general-purpose hardware category we have three factors: T1.1 and T1.2 record our initial choice of a single standard processor, which we expect to provide sufficient computing power, and T1.3 records our 64MB memory size. The general-purpose hardware platform is one of the major technological factors that is likely to change. As technology improves, the goal is to take advantage of faster processors or even move to a multiprocessor architecture. At this point a single CPU is planned, but we may add a second if one CPU cannot cope with the expected system load. To keep costs down, though, the memory limit is pretty firm.

Next let's consider the implications of a change in the processor type. Because the operating system provides a layer over the hardware, such a change will likely be transparent, provided the hardware change does not require a change to a different operating system. Adding one or more processors would mean adding functionality to support multiprocessing. This change would have a large impact on all components at the processor boundaries.

For domain-specific hardware, we have the probe hardware (factor T2.1) and probe network (factor T2.2). Here we need to build in flexibility to introduce new models of the probe and probe networks, and to specify different hardware configurations (for example, for low-end to high-end products). Achieving this kind of flexibility will be a challenge, because changes to either the probe hardware or the network will affect all components involved in the acquisition or image processing.

In the software technology category, there are factors for the operating system (factor T3.1) and operating system processes (factor T3.2). The operating system is likely to change, for example if the requirements are updated to include support for new hardware platforms. We expect this change to be transparent, provided the operating system still conforms to our selected interface standard.

For the operating system processes, we don't expect to run up against the limit for the number of operating system processes, but each operating system process uses resources that are limited. If, during development, the system meets these limits, we may have to set limits on the use of operating system processes.

The final category, standards, lists the standards related to the operating system interface (factor T5.1), sensor data format (factor T5.2), image formats (factor T5.3), and domain-specific algorithms (factor T5.4). The system is connected to a network that transports the domain-specific data. Here we want to take advantage of vendor solutions, using standards when available so that we can upgrade to new versions. We also need to use the interface standard available for the sensor data format, although it is much less stable.

A change to the standards for sensor and image data formats would affect both acquisition and image-processing components as well as the postprocessing components (factors T5.2 and T5.3). If, however, the standard for the operating system interface (factor T5.1) were to change, it would have a large impact on all components of the system.

We want to incorporate standard domain-specific techniques (for example, edge detection in image processing), and to be prepared to upgrade them as appropriate. Because the application domain of the product is mature, the algorithms and techniques for this product are the same ones that have been used in prior products. They are unlikely to undergo any major changes during the life of the product. This is fortunate because such a change could affect components involved in acquisition, image processing, and postprocessing, although the impact would be localized to the particular algorithm or technique (factor T5.4).

3.5 Continue Developing Strategies

The next step is to review the analysis thus far to identify key issues that arise from the technological factors and their changeability, and to develop strategies to address them. Some of the strategies can introduce new technological factors, which causes us to revisit some of the previous steps to assess the impact of these newly introduced factors. Later in this chapter, when we consider the product requirements, we may refine or revise these strategies.

In reviewing the analysis summarized in Table 3.3, we identify the following two issues:

1. **Changes in General-Purpose and Domain-Specific Hardware**—Changes in both the general-purpose and the domain-specific hardware are anticipated on a regular basis. The problem is to adapt to these changes quickly.

2. **Changes in Software Technology**—Changes in software technology will affect several important components. The problem is to reduce the effort in adapting the affected components.

Changes in General-Purpose and Domain-Specific Hardware

Changes in both the general-purpose and the domain-specific hardware are anticipated on a regular basis. The challenge is to reduce the effort and time involved in adapting the product to the new hardware.

Influencing Factors

T1.1: The processor speed is likely to change very frequently, even during development. As technology improves, the goal is to take advantage of faster processors or even move to a multiprocessor architecture.

T2.1: The probe hardware is expected to change every three years. Changes in the probe hardware can change performance requirements as well as sensor data formats. This, in turn, affects the components involved in acquisition and image processing.

T2.2: The probe network is expected to change every four years. This may change the throughput of signal data, and therefore the acquisition components. The higher data rate may also affect the memory requirements of image-processing components.

Solution

Separate the software that directly interacts with the hardware.

The following strategies should be applied first in the conceptual view to introduce components that encapsulate the hardware and to separate them from the application components. They should then be applied in the module view to encapsulate the software related to conceptual components in corresponding modules. The strategies are also useful in separating software related to hardware components from software related to application components.

Strategy: *Encapsulate domain-specific hardware.*

The system interacts with the domain-specific hardware of the probe. The system should be flexible in allowing for new models of the probe to be introduced and new hardware configurations to be specified. Use an abstraction for the probe to minimize the effects of any changes to the probe hardware.

Strategy: *Encapsulate general-purpose hardware.*

Encapsulate the system hardware to allow changes to be made to the hardware with little or no impact on the applications. Conversely, this strategy will support the introduction of new application features without requiring modifications to the software that manages the hardware.

Changes in Software Technology

Off-the-shelf components such as the operating system have a large impact on a significant number of system components. The challenge is to reduce the effort and time necessary to adapt the system when these changes arise.

Influencing Factors

T3.1: Operating system features change every two years. The operating system itself may change every four years. The impact of these changes is large unless they conform to the selected operating system interface standard.

T3.2: Changes in operating system process models have a large impact on the allocation of modules to processes and threads in the execution view.

T5: Standards exist for many of the external components. In some cases such standards are unstable, whereas in others they do not exist at all.

Solution

Use standards when possible and develop internal, product-specific interfaces to commercial off-the-shelf components.

Strategy: *Use standards.*

Use standards when possible to reduce the impact of changes on software technology. Use a standard operating system interface such as POSIX to facilitate porting to another operating system in the future.

Strategy: *Develop product-specific interfaces to external components.*

When standards are unstable or absent, create internal standards. Develop product-specific interfaces to reduce dependencies on external components and unstable standards. A good candidate for the application of this strategy is sensor communication.

Related Strategies

Related and synergistic strategies are *Buy rather than build* and *Reuse existing in-house, domain-specific components* (issue, Aggressive Schedule).

3.6 Analyze Product Factors

The remaining type of factors to be analyzed are the product factors. They describe the product's requirements for functionality, the features seen by the user, and qualities such as performance. Figure 3.4 shows typical categories of requirements: functional features; user interface; performance; dependability; failure detection, reporting, recovery; service; and product cost.

P1: Functional features
Functional features

P2: User interface
User interaction model
User interface features

P3: Performance
Acquisition performance
Sensor data rate
Start-up and shutdown times
Recovery time

P4: Dependability
Availability
Reliability
Safety

P5: Failure detection, reporting, recovery
Error classification
Error logging
Diagnostics
Recovery

P6: Service
Service features
Software installation and upgrade
Maintenance of domain-specific hardware
Software testing
Maintenance of software

P7: Product Cost
Hardware budget
Software licensing budget

Figure 3.4. Typical categories of product factors

The product factors have a larger impact on the architecture than either the organizational factors or the technological factors. As the market changes, the product factors may also change, sometimes drastically. The product factors can also change during development. The architecture should be designed so that it can satisfy the requirements and easily accommodate anticipated changes.

Although we emphasized flexibility with the organizational factors and changeability with the technological factors, here we need to characterize both the flexibility and the changeability of the product factors. Examine the flexibility of product factors to ensure the implementation of your design, and examine the changeability of requirements to ensure system evolution.

In analyzing the product factors, we again follow the process outlined in Section 3.1. The results of applying this to IS2000 are shown in Table 3.4.

This system converts raw data into images and provides a range of image-processing operations on two- and three-dimensional images. The user sets up parameters for an acquisition procedure, then the system runs the acquisition interactively. The system normally acquires data without interruption, but the user can interrupt and exert some control over the acquisition. The user can also select from acquisition and image-processing algorithms to balance the acquisition speed and the image quality.

Product Factor	Flexibility and Changeability	Impact
P1: Functional features		
P1.1: Acquisition procedures		
Acquire raw signal data and convert it into two- and three-dimensional images. The system has a number of standard acquisition procedures.	New acquisition procedures may be added every three years.	This feature affects acquisition performance, image processing, and the user interface.
P1.2: Image processing		
A range of two- and three-dimensional image-processing algorithms are supported.	New image-processing algorithms can be added on a regular basis.	This feature affects the user interface and acquisition performance.

Table 3.4. Product Factors for IS2000

Product Factor	Flexibility and Changeability	Impact
P1.3: Image types		
A range of image types are supported.	New image types can be added with new processing algorithms.	This feature affects persistence of storage, acquisition and image-processing components, and communication over a network.
P2: User interface		
P2.1: User interaction model		
The user can control image acquisition interactively.	This feature must adapt to new paradigms and to new domain standards every three years.	This feature affects the user interface component, and may affect the acquisition and storage components.
P2.2: User-level acquisition control		
The user can set up parameters for an acquisition procedure, select acquisition algorithms, and start, pause, and stop the acquisition.	Requirements for user-level acquisition control are stable.	This feature affects the acquisition and storage components.
P3: Performance		
P3.1: Maximum signal data rate		
This is the rate at which the probe can acquire data.	The maximum data rate changes with changes in the probe hardware.	This factor affects acquisition performance.

Table 3.4. Product Factors for IS2000 *(continued)*

Product Factor	Flexibility and Changeability	Impact
P3.2: Acquisition performance		
Acquisition performance is measured by the size and number of images, and acquisition response time is measured in terms of end-to-end deadlines.	The acquisition performance requirements are slightly flexible. Their effect on performance requirements of individual components is likely to change during development when the system is tuned or whenever the product is modified.	A large impact on all components involved in acquisition and image processing, storage, and display can be expected.
P7: Product cost		
P7.1: General-purpose hardware budget		
The budget for the general-purpose hardware is limited and the part allocated to memory restricts the maximum memory size to 64MB.	There is no flexibility in the budget.	The budget has a moderate impact on the components for acquisition and image processing.
P7.2: Commercial off-the-shelf (COTS) budget		
The maximum limit for licensing COTS software is $2,000.	There is some flexibility if time-to-market can be reduced.	There is a moderate impact on meeting the schedule.

Table 3.4. Product Factors for IS2000 *(continued)*

Advances in hardware, software, and the application domain will likely drive changes in requirements as technology enables the user to do new things. We expect to add or to enhance acquisition procedures and algorithms every few years. New image-processing algorithms are expected to be added on a regular basis. Adding these new features may affect the system's performance.

The user interaction model is likely to change as users want to perform more sophisticated tasks and, at the same time, have the system take on more of the administrative functions, thereby making the system easier to use. Changes to the user interaction model will affect the system interface.

For IS2000, the performance factors describe the maximum rate at which the signal data can be acquired by the probe hardware, and they describe acquisition performance. The maximum signal data rate is expected to change every few years as faster versions of the probe hardware become available.

There are several different measures of the acquisition performance of a system. The system must keep up with the raw events coming into the system, process them, and then make them available for viewing in a timely manner. Responsibility for meeting this requirement is completely distributed (there are no central aspects), although the requirement doesn't necessarily affect the entire system. To meet this requirement, we need to acquire people who have expertise in data acquisition and image processing, communications, control/coordination, and knowledge of the performance properties of the hardware and software platforms.

The requirements for acquisition performance will change when the maximum data rate changes or when new acquisition procedures and image-processing algorithms are offered. Responsibility for acquisition is shared among a wide cross-section of components, each of which is assigned a performance budget. The overall acquisition performance is dependent on such performance budgets, the performance of the software platform (for example, performance of communication mechanisms), and decisions related to process and processor boundaries. These parameters are likely to change as the system is tuned during development and when performance bottlenecks occur, when the system can be run at full capacity, and after initial performance experiments. The acquisition performance requirements are slightly flexible and can be negotiated if changes are small.

The impact of the performance requirements is expected to be large. We need to reduce the scope of this impact to the minimal number of components, because satisfying real-time requirements requires more overhead (for example, special hardware, a real-time software platform, stringent guidelines/constraints on components, and rigorous analysis) and introduces more complexity and higher risk to the project.

3.7 Continue Developing Strategies

Again let's try to identify new issues using the additional information about the product factors and the strategies we've developed so far. Some of the strategies could introduce or modify product factors. In this case, we need to revisit some of the previous steps to assess the impact of the new factor.

Because of the changeability of the functional features and the user interaction model, we identified the issue of Easy Addition and Removal of Features. This also arises from the strategy *Make it easy to add and remove features* (from the Aggressive Schedule issue), which is a very general strategy. By raising it to the level of an issue, we now add more specific strategies for achieving it.

Easy Addition and Removal of Features

Making it easy to add or remove features will help meet the aggressive schedule by trading off function with time. However, designing a system for easy addition and removal of features is a nontrivial problem.

Influencing Factors

O4.1: Time-to-market is short.

O4.2: Delivery of features is negotiable.

P1: New varieties of features may be added every three years.

P2.1: The user interaction model must be adapted to new paradigms and standards.

Solution

Use the principle of separation of concerns to develop specific strategies to address particular problems with features and the user interface.

Strategy: *Separate components and modules along dimensions of concern.*

Follow the principle of separation of concerns to incorporate flexibility to accommodate change in the module view. Separate or decompose modules along important dimensions of concern, including processing, communication, control, data, and user interface aspects of the software design. For example, when designing an acquisition procedure, you want to separate the processing aspects from the control aspects. This provides the possibility of using the processing modules in other acquisition procedures or in contexts that cannot be foreseen at this time. Application of this strategy will also allow you to allocate and trace the requirements to the design elements. When the requirements change, it will be easier to reuse the existing framework and to plug in new components to get a new solution more quickly.

Strategy: *Encapsulate features into separate components.*

To isolate the effects of change to product features, organize related product features into separate components (for example, movement of the probe, image processing, connectivity to the network).

Strategy: *Decouple the user interaction model.*

To isolate the effects of change in the way the user interacts with the system, decouple the user interaction model from the rest of the applications.

Related Strategies

See also *Encapsulate general-purpose hardware* (issue, General-Purpose and Domain-Specific Hardware).

Table 3.5 summarizes the strategies we have developed so far. We will continue to analyze factors and to develop strategies in the next four chapters, which describe the design of the four architecture views. Table 3.5 also summarizes the factors and strategies not yet presented; they are included in the shaded rows.

Issue	Influencing Factors	Applicable Strategy
Aggressive Schedule	O4.1, O5.1, O1.1, O4.2, P7.2	*Reuse existing in-house, domain-specific components.*
		Buy rather than build.
		Make it easy to add or remove features.
Skill Deficiencies	O2.3, O2.4	*Avoid the use of multiple threads.*
		Encapsulate multiprocess support facilities.
Changes in General-Purpose and Domain-Specific Hardware	T1.1, T2.1, T2.2	*Encapsulate domain-specific hardware.*
		Encapsulate general-purpose hardware.
Changes in Software Technology	T3, T5	*Use standards.*
		Develop product-specific interfaces to external components.
Resource Limitations	T1.3, T3.2, T3.4	*Limit the number of active processes.*
		Use dynamic interprocess communication connections.
Easy Addition and Removal of Features	O4.1, O4.2, P1, P2.1	*Separate components and modules along dimensions of concern.*
		Encapsulate features into separate components.
		Decouple the user interaction model.

Table 3.5. Summary of Strategies

Issue	Influencing Factors	Applicable Strategy
Easy Addition and Removal of Acquisition Procedures and Processing Algorithms	O4.1, O4.2, P1.1, P1.2, P1.3	*Use a flexible pipeline model for image processing.*
		Introduce components for acquisition and image processing.
		Encapsulate domain-specific image data.
High Throughput	P7.1, T1.2, T3.2, T3.3, O2.3, O2.4	*Map independent threads of control to processes.*
		Use an additional CPU.
Real-Time Acquisition Performance	T1, T3.1, T3.2, T3.3, T3.4, T2.1, P3.1, P3.2	*Separate time-critical from nontime-critical components.*
		Develop guidelines for module behavior.
		Use flexible allocation of modules to processes.
		Use rate monotonic analysis to predict performance.
		Use shared memory to communicate between pipeline stages.
Implementation of Recovery	P5.4	*Introduce a recovery mode of operation.*
		Make all data at the point of recovery persistent and accessible.
Implementation of Diagnostics	P5.1, P5.2, P5.3	*Define an error-handling policy.*
		Reduce the effort for error handling.
		Encapsulate diagnostic components.
		Use standard logging services.

Table 3.5. Summary of Strategies *(continued)*

Issue	Influencing Factors	Applicable Strategy
Architectural Integrity	O3.2, T3.5, T5.6	*Preserve module view hierarchies.*
		Separate organization of public interface components.
Concurrent Development Tasks	O4.2, O3.4	*Separate organization of deployment components from source components.*
		Preserve execution view.
		Use phased development.
		Release layers through static libraries.
Limited Availability of Probe Prototypes	O3.2, O3.3, O3.4, O4.3	*Develop an off-line probe simulator with an appropriate abstraction.*
		Use a flexible build procedure.
Multiple Development and Target Platforms	T1.1, T1.2, O3.1, O3.2	*Separate and encapsulate code dependent on the target platform.*

Table 3.5. Summary of Strategies *(continued)*

3.8 Global Analysis Summary

The purpose of the global analysis is to identify the important factors that affect the architecture, analyze their changeability and impact, and develop strategies to guide the architecture design. Three kinds of influencing factors are considered during global analysis:

1. Organizational factors that constrain the design choices
2. Technological factors that are embedded or embodied in the product
3. Product factors that include functional features and qualities of the product

Typical categories of these three kinds of factors are summarized in Table 3.6.

Global analysis is an activity that should be performed as part of the design of each of the four architecture views. The issue cards produced during global analysis are used in the central design tasks of each view. Decisions made when performing the central design tasks could also cause a return to the global analysis to add or to modify factors, issues, or strategies.

Organizational Factors	Technological Factors	Product Factors
O1: Management	T1: General-purpose hardware	P1: Functional features
O2: Staff skills, interests, strengths, weaknesses	T2: Domain-specific hardware	P2: User interface
O3: Process and development environment	T3: Software technology	P3: Performance
O4: Development schedule	T4: Architecture technology	P4: Dependability
O5: Development budget	T5: Standards	P5: Failure detection, reporting, recovery
		P6: Service
		P7: Product cost

Table 3.6. Typical Categories of Influencing Factors

Global analysis has two activities, each with three steps. During the first activity, analyze factors, you must do the following:

1. Identify and describe the factors.
2. Characterize their flexibility and changeability.
3. Analyze their impact.

The result of this activity is a factor table for each of the three types of factors.

During the second activity, develop strategies, you must do the following:

1. Identify issues and influencing factors.
2. For each issue, develop a solution and specific strategies.
3. For each issue, identify related strategies.

The result of this activity is an issue card for each issue you identify. It is also useful to summarize the strategies in a table that cross-indexes issues, influencing factors, and strategies.

When global analysis is complete (at the end of architecture design), you will have characterized the important influencing factors and developed strategies for ensuring buildability, implementation, and changeability of the product and its architecture.

Additional Reading

Meszaros and Doble (1997) capture some of the best practices of pattern writing to make them more understandable and usable. This chapter follows some of the recommendations made in this paper. Coplein (1995) has more information on organization or process patterns.

Rechtin and Maier (1997) describe many important strategies for designing a system architecture that are applicable to software architecture. Davis (1995) describes 201 general strategies for software development. These strategies are useful as a starting point for selecting your own, either using them directly or adapting them for the needs of your system.

Dorofee et al. (1996) describe a method for continuous risk management for the entire development spectrum and a taxonomy of factors. Risk is defined as "the possibility of suffering loss." If the event is a certainty, it is not a risk but a problem. Managing risk is one aspect of global analysis. Other aspects of global analysis include identifying factors that impact the software architecture, the resulting problems and issues, and their associated strategies that guide design decisions.

Requirements engineering (Davis, 1993) addresses similar concerns as analyzing product factors that influence the architecture. Requirements engineering analysis tasks include grouping and organization, dependency and conflict analysis, and requirements quantification. Global analysis broadens this specialty to include organizational and technology factors to ensure the system is buildable and uses the results of the analysis to develop strategies that guide design.

Chapter 4

Conceptual Architecture View

The conceptual architecture view is closest to the application domain because it is the least constrained by the software and the hardware platforms. In the conceptual view, you model your product as a collection of decomposable, interconnected conceptual components and connectors.

In this component-connector model, the components are independently executing peers. The notion of building a system by interconnecting components is appealing because of the potential for reuse and for incorporating off-the-shelf components, but that isn't possible without unbundling much of the communication and control aspects and putting them in connectors. So a critical goal of this model is to keep the control aspects of the components simple, and to isolate control in the connectors.

Because today's software technology doesn't directly implement this computational model, you need the other architecture views to show how the component-connector model is mapped to today's programming languages, operating systems, communication mechanisms, and so forth.

When designing the conceptual view, in addition to mapping your product's functionality to components and connectors, you must also treat global properties such as performance and dependability. Not all properties should be considered in the conceptual view. For example, portability is primarily a concern of the module architecture view, because there you must consider the factors relating to the software and the hardware platform.

For the global properties that you do address in the conceptual view, you will have begun to design an architecture that fulfills them, but you still have to consider them in other views. For example, the design of your conceptual view should address the performance requirements. But in the execution view, when you map modules to hardware, you must revisit the performance requirements to make sure they are fulfilled.

If you are using a domain-specific or reference architecture, this could be the starting point for your conceptual view. Whether it can be the starting point depends on whether the architecture uses a computational model consistent with the conceptual view. Sometimes a domain-specific or reference architecture is defined in terms of the module or execution view, or it is a mix of several of the views.

When the conceptual architecture view for your system is complete, you will be able to reason about the ability of the system to fulfill functional requirements and global properties. If you are using use-cases and/or scenarios to capture the system's desired behavior, your conceptual view should be able to handle satisfactorily all the use-cases and scenarios that describe interactions with outside actors (the user, other systems, and so on).

This chapter has three main sections. The first section describes the design activities for the conceptual view. Section 4.2 presents a detailed example of how to design this view using the IS2000 system. The third section, Section 4.3, summarizes the results of designing this view, describing its elements, relations, artifacts, and uses.

4.1 Design Activities for the Conceptual Architecture View

There are three phases to the conceptual view design: global analysis, central design tasks, and the final design task. Figure 4.1 shows these design tasks and their relations to other tasks.

The central design tasks consist of four tightly coupled tasks. During this phase you identify the components and connectors for building your system and use them to construct it. Throughout this process, you use the issue cards developed during global analysis, and evaluate your design decisions with respect to the criteria established in the global analysis task.

The results of the central design tasks—the components, connectors, and configuration—are fed to the final design task, which is resource budgeting. Here you assign resources to the components and connectors in your configuration. These budgets are refined later during the execution view, but the initial budgets help you identify potential resource problems. These additional constraints are fed back to the central design tasks, where you can adjust the design to accommodate them or, if that's not possible, return to the global analysis to develop new strategies. In the most extreme case, you would revisit the system requirements and negotiate changes with the system stakeholders.

The conceptual architecture view provides input to the design tasks of both the module and the execution views, but can be influenced by them as well. It is the first part of the architecture that you will design.

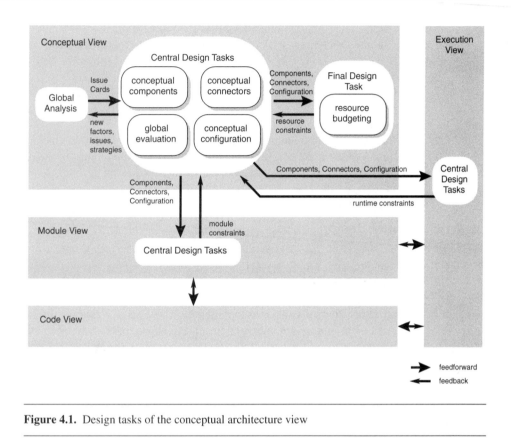

Figure 4.1. Design tasks of the conceptual architecture view

4.1.1 Global Analysis

The first step in conceptual view design is the global analysis task. This task is described fully in the previous chapter, so here we only mention aspects most important for the conceptual view.

Before beginning the global analysis for the conceptual view, you should have reviewed the product requirements, use-cases, and the system requirements and interactions. Make sure you understand the interface to the environment, the users, and other systems that interact with this system. Identify the modes of operation for the system. Look at the functional requirements, and pay particular attention to system qualities and global properties.

Next you analyze the product, technological, and organizational factors, producing factor tables for the three categories. Then you identify issues and develop strategies to solve them. Because the factors drive the issues and strategies, you should now focus on the factors most relevant to the conceptual view.

For this view, you should look at all the product factors. For the technological factors, those in the categories of domain-specific hardware and architecture technology are important. In the standards category, you should consider primarily the domain-specific standards.

Of the organizational factors, those from the categories of management, development schedule, and perhaps development budget are most likely to have an impact on the conceptual view.

It is not realistic to think that you'll be able to identify all of the factors at the beginning of the architecture design, but you should have captured most of them, and the most important ones. New factors may come up during the central design tasks, and during the design of the other views.

4.1.2 Central Design Tasks

To complete the central design tasks, you use the strategies developed during global analysis to guide design decisions and to improve the ability of the system to respond to change. You define the components and the connectors of the system, and define how the system is built using them. From the requirements and the application domain come the majority of components. Others may arise to support global properties. Using the results of the global analysis task as inputs, you may need to adjust component boundaries, or add new components or connectors. You do the following four activities during central design:

1. Define component and connector types.

2. Define how component and connector types interconnect.

3. Map the system functionality to components and connectors, concentrating functional behavior in the components and control aspects in the connectors.

4. Define the instances of the component and connector types that exist in the product, and how they are interconnected.

The order in which you do these things is not fixed. For example, you may start with the third activity in the list, in conjunction with the fourth, then do the first and second activity. You will also likely repeat many of these activities as you refine the design.

If you're starting with a domain-specific or reference architecture, you can expect it to provide the component and connector types, and some constraints on how they interact. It should also give you information regarding how to map the system functionality to components and connectors, at least for portions of your system.

A product-line architecture provides a similar starting point, and it may define some of the instances of the components and connectors. In this case, you would also expect it to provide the implementation of these components and connectors because they are used for all products in the family.

When performing the central design tasks you have to decide whether it's appropriate to use an available architectural style, and for which parts of the system. An architectural style defines component and connector types, and constrains how they interconnect. You need to execute the third and fourth activities before you know whether the style works for your system.

The strategies from global analysis constrain or guide many of your decisions. You must continually evaluate the results, particularly for the third and fourth activities, to make sure you're following the strategies. You should also review the factor tables to make sure you account for the relevant factors, and to see if any are missing.

Conceptual Components

For the conceptual components task, you define the components that exist in your system by defining both component types and instances. It is not absolutely necessary to define component types first, then instances of those types, but we recommend it. If you don't define types, you'll have to describe all the properties of a component for every instance.

A component contains ports, which are the interaction points for the component. A port is not the same as the common notion of an interface for several reasons. First, an interface defines services or operations that the component provides, but not what it uses. With this kind of asymmetry between "provides" and "uses," components would not be true peers. Ports in our model do not have this bias: They define both incoming and outgoing messages (operations), so the components can truly be peers. Second, interfaces are commonly defined as having no associated implementation; they are just a list of the operations provided. In our case, ports can have an implementation, so they can incorporate functionality to adapt, combine, or otherwise process incoming and outgoing operations. Lastly, each port has an associated protocol that mandates how the incoming and outgoing operations can be ordered.

A component can be decomposed into components and connectors. Figure 4.2 contains a UML diagram that summarizes the aspects of components we've just described. The boxes are the UML class notation, so we have elements for a component, a port, a protocol, and a connector.

The lines in the diagram are relations. The lines with the solid diamond are a standard UML relation that means composition: The class at the diamond end of a relation is decomposed into or contains the class at the other end. The multiplicity of the relation is shown by a number (or an asterisk, for zero or more) near the end of the relation. So a component contains zero or more ports, and a port is contained by at most one component. A port obeys exactly one protocol, but a protocol can be obeyed by zero or more ports.

Figure 4.2 is part of the meta-model of the conceptual view that we show at the end of the chapter. We call it a *meta-model* because it describes how the elements of this view are related to each other. This is in contrast to a normal UML model, which we reserve for describing the component and connector types, instances, and relations for a particular system. A meta-model diagram doesn't necessarily look any different from a model diagram, but the term *meta-model* tells you that you've stepped up a level of abstraction.

We use meta-models to describe the elements of each architecture view and how they are related to each other.[1] A meta-model is a compact, precise description, but it takes

---

1. Our meta-models are not intended to be part of the UML meta-model, which serves to define UML. We use the term *meta-model* in a more general way—to mean, simply, a model of a model.

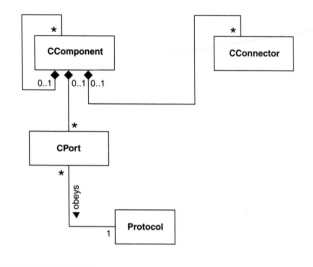

Figure 4.2. Definition of a conceptual component

some practice to understand it easily. Feel free to just skim over the meta-models and focus instead on the examples for IS2000 and the case studies.

In addition to describing the structure of a component, you should also describe its behavior. You may want to describe aspects of its behavior, such as control aspects, formally with a UML Statechart Diagram. This description would likely be associated with a component type rather than the instances, because it shouldn't vary across instances. To describe functional behavior, either of a component type or an instance, you can use a natural language description or a UML Statechart Diagram.

Conceptual Connectors

For the conceptual connectors task, you, in a similar way, define connector types and instances. Again, it is not essential that you define types, but we recommend it.

Whereas components had ports, connectors have roles as the point of interaction with other architecture elements. The roles, like ports, obey an associated protocol. Connectors can also be decomposed into components and connectors. These aspects of a connector are summarized in Figure 4.3. The formal names of these elements start with C for conceptual (for example, CComponent) to avoid confusion with existing UML terms.

You should also describe the connector behavior. Because the functional behavior of the system is concentrated in the components, and control is concentrated in the connectors, to describe connector behavior you must focus on the control aspects.

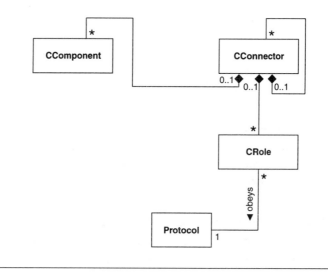

Figure 4.3. Definition of a conceptual connector

Conceptual Configuration

During the conceptual configuration task you define the relations among your components and connectors. A conceptual configuration that contains component and connector types constrains how instances of these types can be interconnected. A conceptual configuration that contains instances defines which instances exist in the product and how they interconnect.

Components and connectors are interconnected through their ports and roles. Figure 4.4 shows the rules for these relations: A port can be connected to zero or more roles, and vice versa. We used a UML Note to describe additional constraints on the "cconnection"

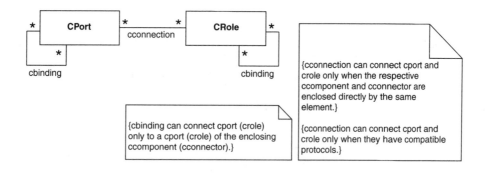

Figure 4.4. Definition of the relations between ports and roles

relation—constraints that would be hard to capture with the graphical notation alone. Connections are possible only when the associated protocols are compatible and only when the elements are nested within the same component or connector.

The binding relation is used when a component or connector is decomposed to bind an inner port to a port of the enclosing component, or to bind an inner role with a role of the enclosing connector.

Global Evaluation

We described earlier how you must continually evaluate your design decisions to see that you are following the results of the global analysis. During the central design tasks you must also periodically evaluate the interactions among your decisions.

4.1.3   Final Design Task: Resource Budgeting

The remaining task is to budget resources for the component and connectors instances identified during the central design tasks. This is done after the other tasks have been accomplished. Typically, resources get allocated rather late in the design process. Establishing budgets at the time the conceptual view is designed gives you the opportunity to evaluate properties of the architecture earlier in the design process.

With these budgets, you are able to use the conceptual structure as an application-level model for performing early analysis. The model may show you that the system meets certain properties, but it could make assumptions that are overly optimistic if it does not factor in overhead associated with the execution environment. If the application-level model does not meet the requirements, then you know that a major redesign of the system is needed.

During this resource budgeting phase you identify critical application-level resources that are limited or are to be shared, and assign budgets. For example, you might assign memory budgets to the components involved in data-intensive activities or communication bandwidth. You might also assign computation time budgets to the components responsible for time-critical activities. The architecture-level decisions were made during the central design tasks, so the decisions at this stage are more localized.

4.2   Design of Conceptual Architecture View for IS2000

Let's now go through these design activities in detail using IS2000 as an example. We won't do the complete design of the conceptual view, but for one section of the system—the ImagePipeline—let's go down to a final level of detail.

4.2.1 Global Analysis

In the previous chapter we began the global analysis for IS2000. Let's now continue it, looking specifically for strategies that are useful in designing the conceptual view. Of the strategies developed so far, the following should be useful here:

Issue: Aggressive Schedule
  Strategy: *Make it easy to add or remove features.*

Issue: Changes in General-Purpose and Domain-Specific Hardware
  Strategy: *Encapsulate domain-specific hardware.*

Issue: Easy Addition and Removal of Features
  Strategy: *Separate components and modules along dimensions of concern.*
  Strategy: *Encapsulate features into separate components.*
  Strategy: *Decouple the user interaction model.*

We explained earlier that the third issue is an expansion of the strategy *Make it easy to add or remove features.* Now we specialize this issue further by creating a new issue, Easy Addition and Removal of Acquisition Procedures and Processing Algorithms, and provide strategies for solving it.

Also in the previous chapter we identified product factors related to the system's performance, but provided no specific strategies for addressing it. So we also add the issue Real-Time Acquisition Performance. The strategy listed for this issue applies to the conceptual view. Later, as we design the other views, we expect to add more strategies.

Easy Addition and Removal of Acquisition Procedures and Processing Algorithms

There are many acquisition procedures and processing algorithms. Implementation of each of these features is quite complex and time-consuming. There is a need to reduce complexity and effort in implementing such features.

Influencing Factors

  O4.1: Time-to-market is short.

  O4.2: Delivery of features is negotiable.

  P1.1: New acquisition procedures can be added every three years.

  P1.2: New image-processing algorithms can be added on a regular basis.

Continued

Easy Addition and Removal of Acquisition Procedures and Processing Algorithms *(continued)*

P1.3: New types of image and signal data may be required on a regular basis as the probe hardware changes.

Solution

Define domain-specific abstractions to facilitate the task of implementing acquisition and processing applications.

Strategy: *Use a flexible pipeline model for image processing.*

Develop a flexible pipeline model for implementing image processing. Use processing components as stages in the pipeline. This allows the ability to introduce new acquisition procedures quickly by constructing pipelines using both old and new components.

Strategy: *Introduce components for acquisition and image processing.*

Develop components for domain-specific acquisition and image processing to minimize the effects of any changes to the application domain. Developing a component model for domain-specific processing makes it easier to add or to upgrade components that are more efficient, and to offer new features.

Strategy: *Encapsulate domain-specific image data.*

To add or to upgrade to improved image-processing techniques, introduce components for domain-specific processing. Thus we can take advantage of industry standards and vendor solutions for transporting data over the network.

Related Strategies

See also *Encapsulate domain-specific hardware* (issue, Changes in General-Purpose and Domain-Specific Hardware).

4.2.2 Central Design Tasks: Components, Connectors, and Configuration

Next we turn to the central design tasks of the conceptual view: defining components and connectors, how they are configured, and global evaluation. These tasks cannot be done in a strictly sequential order. As you will see with IS2000, the design activities are interleaved.

Real-Time Acquisition Performance

Meeting real-time performance requirements is critical to the success of the product. There is no separate source code for meeting the real-time performance requirements directly. The source code that implements functional processing must also meet the performance constraints.

Influencing Factors

T1, T3: A single standard processor running a real-time operating system is expected to provide sufficient computing resources.

P3.1, T2.1: The maximum signal data rate changes with changes in the probe hardware.

P3.2: Acquisition performance requirements are slightly flexible.

Solution

Partition the system into separate components for algorithms, communication, and control to provide the flexibility to implement several different strategies.

Strategy: *Separate time-critical components from nontime-critical components.*

To isolate the effects of change in the performance requirements, partition the system into components (and modules) that participate in time-critical processing and those that do not. This requires careful consideration at the interface between the real-time and nonreal-time sides of the system.

Related Strategies

See also *Separate components and modules along dimensions of concern* (issue, Easy Addition and Removal of Features).

The Conceptual Configuration

Let's start by representing the IS2000 system as a component with ports for its interactions with the outside world: the user, the probe hardware, and the network. The three kinds of interactions with the user are for controlling an acquisition procedure, displaying images on the monitor during the acquisition, and exporting the acquired images. Let's model these as three separate ports. The interactions with the probe hardware are to send

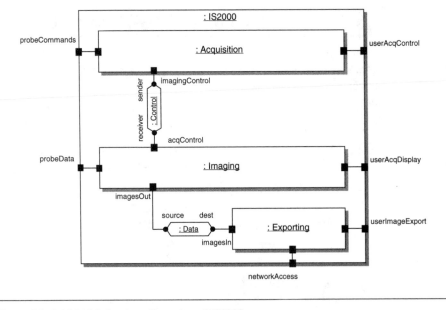

Figure 4.5. Initial high-level configuration of IS2000

commands and to receive data, so let's also make these separate ports. There is also a port for network access.

Next let's start decomposing the system. Here the new strategy *Introduce components for acquisition and image processing* is applicable, so IS2000 is decomposed into an Acquisition component, an Imaging component, and a third component for the rest of the system's functionality, which is to export the images. This initial high-level configuration is shown in Figure 4.5. We haven't yet precisely defined the connectors, but we know that the connector between the Acquisition and Imaging components functions as a control exchange, and the connector between the Imaging and Exporting components primarily passes data.

Although Figure 4.5 doesn't look like typical UML, it is actually a UML Class Diagram. Components, ports, connectors, and roles are modeled as stereotyped classes. For each of these we use a special graphical symbol to make the diagrams more clear. The symbol for a component is a shadowed rectangle, and its ports are shown as small black squares at the edge of the component, with the port name near the port symbol. The symbol for a connector is an elongated hexagon, and its roles are small black circles at the edge of the connector, with the role name nearby.

There are three kinds of relations in Figure 4.5: composition, binding, and connection. To show the decomposition of a component (IS2000) into a set of interconnected components and connectors, we use the UML convention of nesting the decomposition inside the containing class. A binding between ports is shown with a UML association (a line), as is a connection between a port and a role.

To continue refining the conceptual configuration, let's apply the strategy *Encapsulate domain-specific hardware*. Because both the Acquisition and the Imaging components interact with the probe hardware, within each of these we must create a component that is responsible for communicating with the probe. This helps insulate the rest of the system when the hardware changes. It also gives us more reuse opportunities, for example, COTS components for motion control and in-house components for camera and sensor control, which we identified during global analysis.

In the Acquisition component, ProbeControl sets up the probe and controls it during the acquisition. In the Imaging component, DataCollection accepts the image data from the probe, and receives formatting information from ProbeControl that is interjected into the image data (Figure 4.6). Later, in the module architecture view, we will likely put the

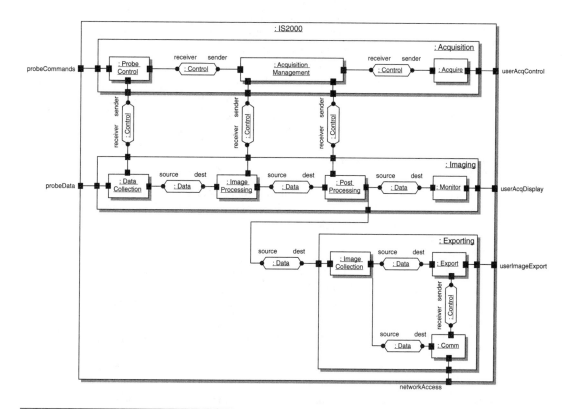

Figure 4.6. Refined high-level configuration of IS2000

modules for ProbeControl and DataCollection into the same layer, but in this view they are in separate components.

Similarly, applying the strategy *Decouple the user interaction model*, we introduce separate components within Acquisition, Imaging, and Exporting to handle the interaction with the user. In Figure 4.6 these are Acquire, Monitor, and Export.

To finish decomposing the Acquisition component, let's create the component AcquisitionManagement, which sets the policies for processing and organizing images. These are different for each acquisition. This is the result of applying the general strategy *Separate components and modules along dimensions of concern*. The Imaging component must abide by these policies, so there is a control connector from AcquisitionManagement to Imaging.

In Figure 4.6 there are actually two control connectors from AcquisitionManagement to Imaging, because we split the processing of images into two components: ImageProcessing and PostProcessing. Functionally these components are responsible for framing the raw data and processing it into images. But the strategy *Separate time-critical from nontime-critical components* indicates that one of the components (ImageProcessing) should contain only the time-critical initial processing of the raw data, and the rest of the processing should be put into the PostProcessing component.

The processed images are retained for as long as 24 hours, and the ImageCollection component is responsible for storing this information. This information also needs to be available to other systems over the network. The Export component is responsible for moving data to other systems, and Comm is responsible for the domain-specific communication of the image data. Here we applied the strategy *Encapsulate domain-specific image data* to guide the decomposition of the Exporting component into the Image Collection, Export, and Comm components.

All of these decisions are reflected in Figure 4.6, but this is not the final configuration: Not all the ports have been named, and the connectors are only roughly defined. As we continue with the design of each of the inner components, the missing details of the ports and connectors will be pinned down.

The ImageProcessing Component

Next let's look at the design of the ImageProcessing component in more detail. Image processing is responsible for framing raw data (arriving at the rawDataInput port) into images (sent out via the framedOutput port). The DataCollection component will do some buffering, but ImageProcessing must keep up with the buffered data to meet its real-time requirements. Image processing is controlled according to the acquisition procedure through the acqControl port.

ImageProcessing is decomposed into a Packetizer and possibly multiple ImagePipelines. Here we can apply the strategy *Use a flexible pipeline model for image processing*. The Packetizer bundles the incoming data into packets suitable for additional processing, which takes place in the ImagePipelines. This decomposition is shown in Figure 4.7.

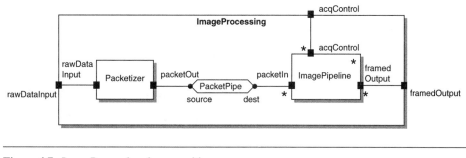

Figure 4.7. ImageProcessing decomposition

The fact that there can be zero or more ImagePipelines is shown with the UML notation for multiplicity. We use the convention that when the multiplicity of a class or association is not given, it is 1. So in Figure 4.7, there is exactly one Packetizer and one
PacketPipe in ImageProcessing. The asterisk in UML means a multiplicity of 0 or more,
so there can be zero or more ImagePipelines in ImageProcessing. The multiplicity on the
binding between acqControl ports shows that the acqControl of ImageProcessing is bound
to each of the ImagePipelines (a one-to-many binding). Similarly, the dest role of Packet-
Pipe is connected to each of the ImagePipelines. All pipelines receive the same data from
the Packetizer and filter out what they don't need.

You may have noticed that the names of components and connectors in Figure 4.6 are
underlined and preceded by colons, but in Figure 4.7 they're not. In UML this signifies the
distinction between an object (an instance) and a class. Here, in the conceptual configuration diagrams, we use this notation to distinguish between a component or connector
instance (underlined and preceded by a colon) and a component or connector type. So
Figure 4.6 shows exactly one configuration, and Figure 4.7 shows a set of configurations.

Whenever an aspect of the structure is reused, either in a different place of the configuration or in a different product, it is easier to describe it as a component, port, connector,
or role type, with properties that apply to all instances of that type. In Figure 4.7, the properties that apply to instances of the components, ports, connectors, and roles are the association constraints—specifically, the decomposition, bindings, and connections.

Other properties of components, ports, connectors, and roles that we haven't yet discussed are their functional behavior and protocols. In the next section, we show how you
can model these aspects using UML. If you'd prefer not to get into this topic yet, you can
skip ahead to the next section, and read about describing behavior and protocols at a later
time.

Defining Protocols and Behavior

The upper part of Figure 4.8 repeats some of the information that was in Figure 4.7. For
example, the Packetizer component contains the rawDataInput port and the packetOut
port, which is connected to the source role of the PacketPipe connector. The lower part of

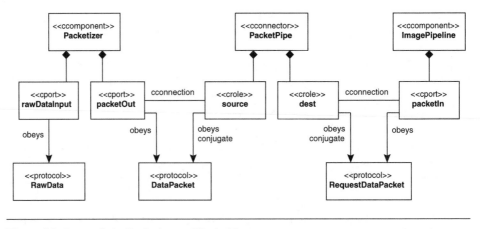

Figure 4.8. Protocols for Packetizer and PacketPipe

this figure shows the protocols obeyed by each of the ports or roles. In this section we use UML to describe these three protocols and the behavior of the Packetizer component and the PacketPipe connector.

A protocol is defined as a set of incoming message types, outgoing message types, and the valid message exchange sequences. The rawDataInput port of the Packetizer component obeys the RawData protocol specified in Figure 4.9. The declaration on the left side of the figure shows that the Packetizer receives two incoming messages and sends one outgoing message. The rawData message contains the raw data, rd. The sequence diagram on the right side of the figure shows the interleaving of the messages. The Packetizer receives a notice that the data is ready. It makes a request for the data and then receives it.

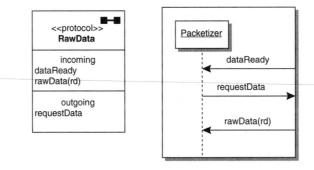

Figure 4.9. RawData protocol

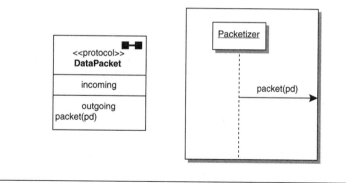

Figure 4.10. DataPacket protocol

The reason for the three-phase protocol is to give the Packetizer the opportunity to finish what it is doing and put itself into a state in which it is prepared to receive the data.[2]

The packetOut port adheres to the DataPacket protocol shown in Figure 4.10. The port sends the packets as they are available.

Since the beginning of the conceptual view design, we have kept decomposing components into sets of interconnected components and connectors. The Packetizer is not decomposed further, so it is time to define its behavior. Figure 4.11 uses a UML Statechart Diagram to define the behavior of the Packetizer in terms of the messages it sends and receives over its ports.

Transitions between the states have three parts, of the form Event [Guard] /Action, all of which are optional. Event represents an incoming message received by the component, and it triggers a state change. Action here is the component sending an outgoing message through one of its ports. Guard is a logical condition. A guarded transition occurs only if the guard resolves to true.

In the UML Statechart Diagram, the Packetizer initializes an empty packet, then waits. When data becomes available it adds this to the packet. When there is enough data to complete the packet, it sends out a message containing the packet and returns to the initial state.

The packetIn port of the ImagePipeline component adheres to the RequestDataPacket protocol shown in Figure 4.12. First it issues a subscription request. When it is ready for work it requests a packet and waits to receive one. Because ImagePipeline only requests a packet when it is ready to process one, no buffering is necessary. When it is notified to shut

---

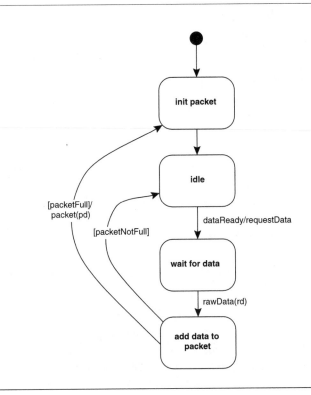

Figure 4.11. Packetizer behavior

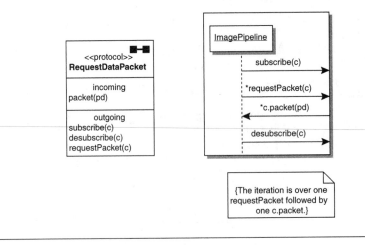

Figure 4.12. RequestDataPacket protocol

down, ImagePipeline cancels its subscription. Because of the indeterminate number of requests that can be generated and packets that can be received, let's add an asterisk and a constraint to express the message interleaving.

PacketPipe connects the Packetizer to one or more ImagePipelines. Its interfaces are called roles and, like ports, they adhere to protocols. In Figure 4.7, PacketPipe has two roles, source and dest. The source role obeys the conjugate of the DataPacket protocol. Being a conjugate means that the ordering of the messages is reversed so that incoming messages are now outgoing and vice versa. The source role of PacketPipe is connected to the packetOut port of Packetizer. Only ports and roles with compatible protocols can be connected to each other, and a common way of ensuring compatibility is to use a protocol and its conjugate. Protocol compatibility can be defined more broadly, and this is an area of active research.

The dest role obeys the conjugate of the RequestDataPacket protocol, so it is compatible with the packetIn port of ImagePipeline.

The behavior of the PacketPipe connector defines how its two roles interact; that is, how the outgoing messages are dependent on and interleaved with the incoming messages. The state machine in Figure 4.13 shows the behavior of the PacketPipe connector. Each of the image pipelines first subscribes for data. Each of them requests packets when it is ready for work, but no pipeline can process the next packet until all the other pipelines are also ready to receive it. In this way the pipelines stay synchronized. The PacketPipe connector must handle this synchronization among pipelines and provide some buffering to support it.

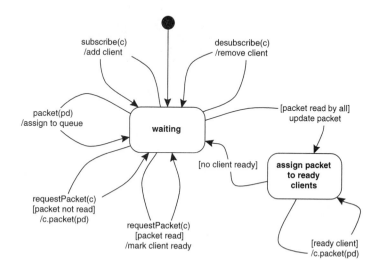

Figure 4.13. PacketPipe connector behavior

The ImagePipeline Component

With the definition of the Packetizer component and the PacketPipe connector complete, let's turn to the definition of ImagePipeline to complete the definition of image processing. The image pipeline has packets of raw data coming in (packetIn port) and framed images going out (framedOutput port). Its acqControl port responds to control messages from AcquisitionManagement.

Again, using the strategy *Use a flexible pipeline model for image processing*, let's decompose ImagePipeline into a number of stages and a pipeline manager (Figure 4.14). This makes it easier to reuse a stage across multiple pipelines, add new stages to a pipeline, or create new pipelines for new kinds of acquisition procedures. There is one PipelineMgr and one Framer per ImagePipeline, and one or more Imager components.

The Framer is always the first stage of the pipeline. It is connected to ImagePipe, which is connected to the imageIn port of an Imager. The imageOut port of an Imager is either connected to another ImagePipe or, when it is the last stage in the pipeline, is bound to framedOutput. The number of stages depends on the acquisition procedure selected by the user.

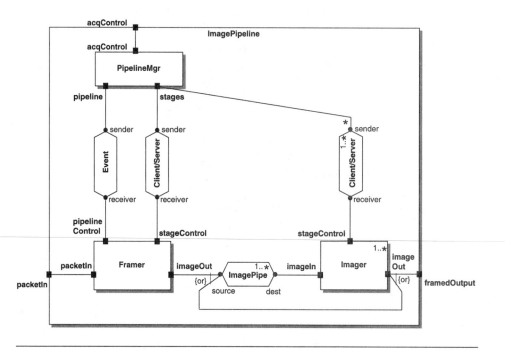

Figure 4.14. ImagePipeline decomposition

Although the specific processing is different, the stages share common features. They act as filters in the sense that they process a continuous stream of data, and pass it on to the next stage. They also all respond to control messages to start or stop processing. Almost all have ports for stageControl, imageIn, and imageOut. The first stage in the pipeline is the exception. It accepts packets of raw data rather than images and responds to messages for controlling the pipeline in addition to those for controlling the stage.

The connectors between stages are ImagePipes that transmit a stream of data from one stage to another. They have a source role for accepting input and a dest role for providing output. The imageOut ports and dest roles obey the same protocol, and the source roles and imageIn ports obey its conjugate. An ImagePipe has the property that it preserves the order of the data: The first item in is the first item out (FIFO queue).

PipelineMgr handles initialization and control messages from outside the system. Note that this high-level management or "control" is different from the control of the data flowing between the pipeline stages. The first provides the kind of acquisition control seen by the user, and it should be considered in the conceptual view. The second is part of the behavior of the connectors between the pipeline stages, and the details of its implementation are handled in the module view. Although these two kinds of control could end up in the same module in the module view, having an explicit conceptual view gives us the advantage of separating these two concepts in the design.

Control of the pipeline is through the pipeline and stages ports. There are commands to set up and to shut down the stages for an acquisition procedure, and to adjust the processing of the individual stages. The connector between the PipelineMgr and each of the stages is called Client/Server. On the sender side, control requests are accepted, and on the receiver side the control request is sent and a corresponding reply is received. On the pipeline port, the PipelineMgr sends commands to signal the start, stop, pause, and end of images, and no reply is expected.

After initialization, the Framer checks for any messages from the PipelineMgr. When a message is received to start framing images, the Framer requests packets from the Packetizer and processes them repeatedly until notified of the end of the image. It then passes the framed image on to the next stage in the pipeline before checking for new messages and repeating the cycle.

The Imager component's functionality is a subset of that of the Framer. It does not have a pipelineControl port. It receives images rather than packets, and thus it does not have the added complexity of constructing the framed image.

We've summarized the behavior of the ImageProcessing component in Figure 4.15. This is a UML Sequence Diagram, so it can only show a particular sequence of interactions among instances. Here, to emphasize the relationships among the components, we show only component instances, not ports, connectors, or roles.

The acquisition manager (not shown) starts an acquisition by sending a message to PipelineMgr. PipelineMgr is created for this particular acquisition. It in turn creates the stages to do the necessary processing, here shown as instances of Framer and Imager. The Packetizer has already been initialized at system start-up. When there is enough raw data to make up a packet, it gets sent to the first stage in the image pipeline—the Framer. The Framer does its processing and then passes the image along to the next stage and so on

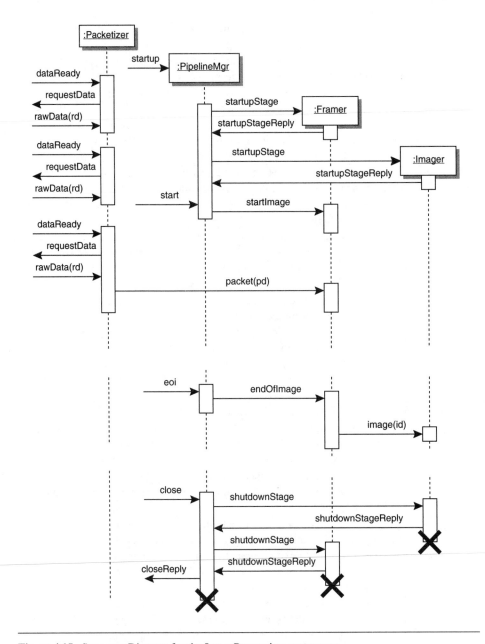

Figure 4.15. Sequence Diagram for the ImageProcessing component

Pipeline	Stages
pipeline1: ImagePipeline	stage1: Framer, stage2: Imager, stage3: Imager, stage4: Imager

Table 4.1. Sample Pipeline Instances

down the line (if there are any additional stages). The acquisition manager controls the acquisition and sends messages to signal the start and end of images and to signal when it is time to shut down the acquisition.

Notice that ImagePipeline decomposition depicted in Figure 4.14 contains only classes (component and connector types), not instances. The final step would be to define exactly which component instances are used for each acquisition protocol. Because each acquisition procedure has its own image pipeline, we could draw a diagram similar to Figure 4.14 for each acquisition procedure, containing all the instances it uses. But here, because the structure of an image pipeline is relatively simple, we prefer to use a table that lists the instances in each pipeline. Table 4.1 shows an entry for the instances in a pipeline. It records the configuration information that can vary among pipelines, that is, the number and order of stages in each pipeline. Information about the pipeline manager and the connectors is not included because this information is derived from Figure 4.14.

Recovery and Diagnostics

Up to this point, our focus has been on introducing components to support the functional features. One exception was the global property for real-time processing, which influenced how we divided the system into components.

Now let's consider additional global properties, from the category of failure detection, reporting, recovery. Because we have not yet considered product factors in this category, let's return to the global analysis to add product factors, then develop additional strategies for handling them.

One product factor is that the image data must be recoverable in the event of a failure. Raw data that has been captured should be recovered and processed when the system is back on-line. Acquisitions may take a long time. If an acquisition consists of 100 images and the system fails during acquisition of the ninety-ninth image, the first 98 images should be recoverable. Recovery affects a number of components: During normal processing, components must gather the data needed to recover. After a failure, the system needs to process the recovered data, which includes recovering a possibly incomplete acquisition.

Depending on the available resources, recovery may have a major impact on the architecture design. If the data to be recovered is already in a persistent store (for example, a file or database) or if there are enough resources to take "snapshots" of the internal state and input/output, then the job is practically done. If not, we need to design the architecture so that the data is accessible when it needs to be recovered. Once the architecture approach is determined, the impact of future changes can be localized to one or more of the recovery components. Table 4.2 shows the analysis of product factor P5.4, recovery.

Product Factor	Flexibility and Changeability	Impact
P5: Failure detection, reporting, recovery		
P5.1: Error classification		
System errors are classified according to their type and severity.	Error classification is likely to change during development. It is affected by functional features, the user interaction model, and the probe model.	There is a moderate impact on all components. Error logging is affected.
P5.2: Error logging		
Error logging is used to capture diagnostic, clinical, and software trace events.	Error logging is affected by error classification, error-handling policy, and the hardware platform. It is likely to change during development.	There is a moderate impact on all components. Acquisition performance may be affected.
P5.3: Support for use of error logs		
Error logs can be retrieved and viewed for the purpose of error tracking and diagnosis.	Requirements for the use of an error log are expected to be quite stable.	There is a minimal impact on components.
P5.4: Recovery		
Acquired imaged data must be recoverable in the event of a system failure.	Recovery requirements are stable. They are flexible to adapt to changes in acquisition size, data rate, format, and recovery support by the data storage system.	There is a moderate to large impact on all components involved in recovery.

Table 4.2. Factors Added During Design of Conceptual View

The other new product factors in this table are related to diagnostics: error classification, error logging, and support for using error logs in diagnosis. Error classification and logging affect all parts of the system and all its modes (for example, acquisition, recovery, diagnostics) of operation. Because performance is critical, any strategy for error logging must minimize its impact on performance. To reduce its scope, we can encapsulate it, but it cannot be localized. The distributed part of logging that interacts with the rest of the system should be easy to use and easy to incorporate.

From these product factors, we identify two new issues: Implementation of Recovery and Implementation of Diagnostics. The strategies for these issues need to show how we handle two requirements that have a global impact.

Implementation of Recovery

Recovery is the responsibility of many components. We need to ensure that support for recovery is uniformly implemented by all relevant components.

Influencing Factors

P5.4: Acquired imaged data must be recoverable in the event of a system failure. Recovery requirements are stable and can be flexible to reduce effort of implementation.

Solution

Apply the principle of separation of concerns to introduce a separate recovery mode of operation for each component. Ensure that the data to be recovered is accessible to all components.

Strategy: *Introduce a recovery mode of operation.*

Introduce a recovery mode to localize change. This means introducing components for cleanup, shutdown, and crash recovery. The scope of impact can be reduced cost-effectively by introducing a recovery mode for processing the recovered data. Using a separate recovery model means that we don't have to worry about affecting the system's performance during an acquisition. However, users may wish to execute recovery in parallel with other activities in the future. Existing components involved in processing will now have an additional responsibility to provide an interface to run in recovery mode. We also want to encapsulate file system and database recovery support.

Strategy: *Make all data at the point of recovery persistent and accessible.*

Make data at the point of recovery persistent and accessible through an interface at the architecture level for easier implementation of a recovery mechanism. If it is not accessible, then recovery may require snapshots of the internal state.

Implementation of Diagnostics

Error logging will be used to support diagnostics. Responsibility for diagnostics is shared by all components. We need to ensure that support for diagnostics is uniformly implemented by all components.

Influencing Factors

P5.1: System errors are classified according to their type and severity. Error classification is likely to change.

P5.2: Error logging is affected by error classification, error-handling policy, and the hardware platform. It is likely to change.

P5.3: Requirements for the use of error logs are expected to be stable.

Solution

Support for diagnostics is needed during development, for tracing, and at runtime. The design of the diagnostics has many elements. It includes the log itself (which is a repository of the error information), the types of errors being reported, and the kinds of information captured (for example, component, error, location). Components need to log information, and the user needs to be able to read the logs.

Strategy: *Define an error-handling policy.*

Define a policy to avoid, detect, and handle different classes of errors. This includes how to define and use exceptions, and how to select an exception mechanism. Provide guidelines on how to avoid errors, as well as how to detect and report them.

Strategy: *Reduce effort for error handling.*

Error handling is tedious, and many developers dislike it. Make their task easier by using tools to support the error-handling policy. For example, there are tools that take an error classification scheme as input and generate code templates for error reporting.

Strategy: *Encapsulate diagnostics components.*

Localize the impact of error logging by encapsulating one component for error logging and another for the use of logs. Define product-specific interfaces so that their implementation can be easily replaced.

Strategy: *Use standard logging services.*

To meet the schedule and to take advantage of industry standards, use standard services such as message catalogs and the file system to read and review log files.

With these strategies in place, let's turn first to designing the architecture to support recovery. The strategy *Make all data at the point of recovery persistent and accessible* influences where we draw the boundaries among the components involved in processing the image data.

Revisiting Figure 4.6 to examine the components involved in an acquisition, we see that data is available in three places: at the point where data is coming into Image-Processing, between ImageProcessing and PostProcessing, and where data is leaving Post-Processing. If recovering data at one of these points is feasible and meets the requirements, then no structural changes to the architecture need to be made. If not, then we may need to divide one of the components to get access to the data at the appropriate point, or shift the boundary of responsibility between two components. Any potential changes must also be evaluated with respect to the strategies *Separate time-critical from nontime-critical components* and *Use a flexible pipeline model for image processing*, because these were the source of our earlier design decisions for this part of the system.

Now let's consider the implications of recovering the data at each of the three points. Recovering data at the point before ImageProcessing is not feasible because of the amount of raw data that needs to be stored. The point after ImageProcessing cuts down the volume to a manageable size, and ImageProcessing is so fast that we would only lose an image or two if we recovered data here. The point after PostProcessing doesn't reduce the volume of data much further. PostProcessing, however, takes much more time than ImageProcessing. If we recover at this point we would lose much of the image data in the beginning of the pipeline and not meet our recovery requirements. Thus we need to make image information recoverable at the point between ImageProcessing and PostProcessing.

Because the data must be available even if the system goes down, the connector between ImageProcessing and PostProcessing must have the property that the data it transfers is persistent. This is a new connector type, called PersistentDataPipe.

We also apply the strategy *Introduce a recovery mode of operation*. This causes us to add components that encapsulate the functionality for the recovery mode, and to add a new recovery port to existing components, such as PostProcessing, for when they run in recovery mode.

Next let's look at what is needed to support diagnostics. For error logging, let's introduce two new components: Logger and LogReader. The Logger is responsible for receiving and storing event messages in a log. To log an event with the Logger, existing components need a new logging port. The LogReader allows a user to review the logs.

4.2.3 Final Design Task: Resource Budgeting

The remaining task in the conceptual view is to budget resources for component and connector instances identified during the central design tasks. The resources we consider are those that are limited or are to be shared. If we can't come up with a balanced budget, meaning that we can't assign reasonable budgets to components and connectors without overrunning our available resources, then we must return to the central design tasks with additional information about resource constraints.

For example, we establish memory budgets for the components involved in data-intensive activities based on data flow rate. The FIFO queues for the pipes between the pipeline stages are given a budget based on predicted image size. The budget for PersistentDataPipe, the connector between ImageProcessing and PostProcessing, is based on the number of images that we predict will accumulate between the two, which is in turn based on their relative speed of processing an image.

We need computation time budgets for the components responsible for time-critical activities. These budgets are dictated by the end-to-end deadlines given in the requirements. For example, the time between detection of a real-time event (for example, stop) and its effect on event data must be less than 1 msec. This affects the budgets for DataCollection, ImageProcessing, and PostProcessing. This is an iterative process. Budgets are assigned to these top-level components. Budgets are then assigned to subcomponents and so on. A preliminary analysis can then be performed to ensure the latency requirement is met.

The system must be able to support a sustained data rate of 2MB per second generated by the probe hardware. This affects both the time budget and the buffer size for the Data-Collector component.

4.2.4   Design Summary for IS2000 Conceptual View

To design the conceptual view, we identified components based on our global analysis and captured their responsibilities and dependencies. We refined the dependencies by introducing connectors, with details about their communication protocols. We used these building blocks to configure our particular system. Global properties such as error logging, recovery, and real-time processing caused us to introduce additional components or to make adjustments in the interfaces or boundaries of existing components. Table 4.3 summarizes the main design decisions we made in this chapter, and the rationale for them.

Design Decision	Rationale
Global analysis	
Add new issue: Easy Addition and Removal of Acquisition Procedures and Processing Algorithms.	Strategy: *Make it easier to add or remove features.* Strategy: *Encapsulate features into separate components.*
Add new issue: Real-Time Acquisition Performance.	Product factors for performance

Table 4.3. Sequence of Design Decisions for IS2000 Conceptual View

Design Decision	Rationale
The conceptual configuration	
Decompose IS2000 into three main components: Acquisition, Imaging, and Exporting.	Strategy: *Introduce components for acquisition and image processing.*
Introduce components that are an abstraction of the probe hardware (ProbeControl, DataCollection).	Strategy: *Encapsulate domain-specific hardware.*
Introduce components for the user's interactions with the system (Acquire, Monitor, Export).	Strategy: *Decouple the user interaction model.*
Create AcquisitionManagement component.	Strategy: *Separate components and modules along dimensions of concern.*
Split processing of images into two components: ImageProcessing and PostProcessing.	Strategy: *Separate time-critical components from nontime-critical components.*
Introduce ImageCollection and Comm components	Strategy: *Encapsulate domain-specific image data.*
The ImageProcessing component	
Decompose ImageProcessing into Packetizer and multiple ImagePipe-lines, connected by a PacketPipe.	Strategy: *Use a flexible pipeline model for acquisition and image processing.*
Defining protocols and behavior	
Add RawData, DataPacket, and RequestDataPacket protocols. Describe behavior of Packetizer and PacketPipe.	Describe behavior of ports and roles using protocols. When components and connectors are not decomposed further, describe their behavior using UML Statechart Diagrams.

Table 4.3. Sequence of Design Decisions for IS2000 Conceptual View *(continued)*

Design Decision	Rationale
The ImagePipeline component	
Decompose ImagePipeline into a Framer and multiple Imager stages, connected by ImagePipes.	Strategy: *Use a flexible pipeline model for acquisition and image processing.*
Put one PipelineMgr in each ImagePipeline.	Provide support for user-level acquisition control.
Recovery and diagnostics	
Add new factors to the product factor table: P5.1: Error classification, P5.2: Error logging, P5.3: Support for use of error logs, and P5.4: Recovery.	Identify new factors during the analysis of global properties related to failure detection, reporting, and recovery.
Add new issue: Implementation of Recovery.	Identify new issues during the analysis of product factors for recovery.
Add new issue: Implementation of Diagnostics.	Identify new issues during the analysis of product factors for error classification, logging, and use of logs.
Introduce a recovery mode and recover data at the connector between ImageProcessing and PostProcessing.	Strategy: *Introduce a recovery mode of operation.* Strategy: *Make all data at the point of recovery persistent and accessible.*
Introduce Logger and LogReader components.	Strategy: *Define an error-handling policy.* Strategy: *Encapsulate diagnostic components.*
Resource budgeting	
Assign data budgets to connectors.	Budgets depend on image size, number of images, and relative processing speed of ImageProcessing and PostProcessing.
Assign time budgets to the time-critical components.	Budgets depend on end-to-end deadlines given in requirements.

Table 4.3. Sequence of Design Decisions for IS2000 Conceptual View *(continued)*

For IS2000, we began with the conceptual configuration of the system, mapping functionality to components and determining the rough behavior of the connectors.

If you start with a domain-specific or reference architecture, it will most likely provide you with similar information. It will probably give you a more precise indication of the component and connector types, but not all the details of the configuration, such as exactly which instances of components and connectors exist.

If you use instead an architectural style for some part of the architecture, you will not have specific configuration information, but you will have precise information about component and connector types, and which interconnections are allowed. It is up to you to decide how to map the functionality of the system to the components and connectors in the style.

4.3 Summary of Conceptual Architecture View

Table 4.4 shows the elements, relations, and artifacts of the conceptual architecture view. The elements and relations are the building blocks, and the artifacts are the architecture descriptions or documentation. For the elements and relations, we show which UML meta-model class (the kind of UML element) is used to represent them, and the notation we use in the diagrams that describe the conceptual view.

Element	UML Element	New Stereotype	Notation	Attributes	Associated Behavior
CComponent	Active class	<<ccomponent>>		Resource budget	Component behavior
CPort	Class	<<cport>>	■	—	—
CConnector	Active class	<<cconnector>>		Resource budget	Connector behavior
CRole	Class	<<crole>>	●	—	—
Protocol	Class	<<protocol>>		—	Legal sequence of interactions

Table 4.4. Summary of Conceptual Architecture View

Relation	UML Element	Notation	Description
composition	Composition	Nesting (or ↑)	A component or connector can be decomposed into a configuration of interconnected components and connectors.
cbinding	Association	——————	A port can be bound to a port of the enclosing component. A role can be bound to a role of the enclosing connector.
cconnection	Association	——————	A component's port can be connected to a connector's role when both are directly enclosed by the same element.
obeys	Association	—— obeys ——	A port or role obeys a protocol.
obeys conjugate	Association	obeys conjugate	A port or role obeys the conjugate of a protocol.

Artifact	Representation
Conceptual configuration	UML Class Diagram
Port or role protocol	ROOM protocol declaration (uses UML Sequence or Statechart Diagram)
Component or connector behavior	Natural language description or UML Statechart Diagram
Interactions among components	UML Sequence Diagram
ROOM = real-time object-oriented modeling; UML = Unified Modeling Language.	

Table 4.4. Summary of Conceptual Architecture View *(continued)*

Components and connectors can have a resource budget recorded as an attribute, and can have an associated description of their behavior. The description of this behavior is one kind of artifact: It can be represented by a natural language description or a UML Statechart Diagram.

For a protocol, the associated behavior describes the legal sequence of incoming and outgoing messages. A protocol description is another kind of artifact, represented by a real-time object-oriented modeling (ROOM) protocol declaration.

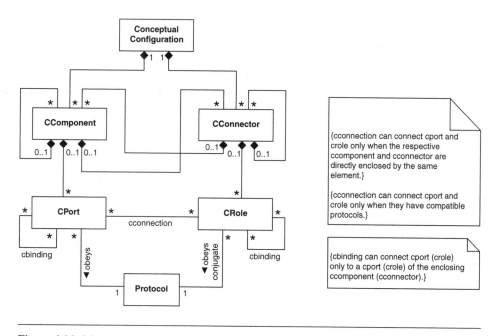

Figure 4.16. Meta-model of the conceptual architecture view

The main type of artifact is a conceptual configuration, which is represented by a UML Class Diagram that contains the elements and relations of the conceptual view. We define more precisely how the relations can be applied to the elements using the meta-model in Figure 4.16. Starting at the top, a conceptual configuration contains zero or more components and zero or more connectors.

Conceptual components contain ports that define how the component can interact with other elements of the configuration. Components can be decomposed further into a collection of components and connectors. When a component is decomposed, its ports can be bound to ports of the components it (directly) contains.

Conceptual connectors are analogous to conceptual components, except that their interaction points are called *roles* rather than *ports*. Connectors can also be decomposed into a set of components and connectors, and roles can be bound only to the role of an enclosing connector.

The connection relation is used to connect a component's port to a connector's role, but it is only allowed when the component and connector are directly enclosed by the same element. In addition, both ports and roles obey a protocol (or obey its conjugate), and a connection is allowed only when the associated protocols are compatible.

4.3.1 Traceability

Describing the relationships of the conceptual architecture view to requirements, external factors, and other architecture views provides traceability. During global analysis you create factor tables for characterizing the influencing factors, and you create issue cards for capturing strategies that accommodate the factors. A table such as Table 4.3 shows which strategies are used in each of the design decisions of the conceptual view. When one of the factors changes, its influence can be traced to the affected components. The following two items should be traceable in the architecture view:

1. *Critical requirements.* Product features and requirements can be traced to the conceptual elements. This helps you figure out the impact that existing or new requirements will have on the software architecture. Conversely, you can trace the design decisions to requirements, and determine how well they are met.

2. *Organizational and technological factors.* As mentioned at the beginning of the chapter, external factors and the strategies to deal with them have a direct impact on the conceptual view. Making them part of your recorded architecture description makes it easier to understand the implications of change during the design process and in the future.

As you continue the architecture design and introduce the module and execution architecture views, you will support traceability by recording how elements in the conceptual architecture view are mapped to modules or processes.

4.3.2 Uses for the Conceptual Architecture View

When the conceptual view is explicit, it can be used to reason about and/or predict important system properties. You may use the conceptual view for

- Use-cases and scenarios
- Performance estimation
- Safety and reliability analysis
- Target independent testing
- Understanding the static and dynamic configurability of the system
- Effort estimation (preliminary; not including the infrastructure)

Additional Reading

Shaw and Garlan (1996) provide a definition of software architecture in terms of components and connectors that is close to our conceptual view. They also provide additional information about work that addresses the conceptual view concerns of constructing systems as assemblies of components and first-class connectors, and information about protocol compatibility and interface checking.

Selic, Gullekson, and Ward (1994) describe a methodology for ROOM and strategies for dealing with complexity. ROOM is an example of an architecture description language that gives software engineers the ability to model aspects of the conceptual view, such as composing software systems using communicating objects. Our description for protocols is influenced by ROOM. Selic and Rumbaugh (1998) describe how certain ROOM constructs can be modeled in UML. Their notion of capsules, ports, and protocols is similar to our conceptual components, ports, and protocols.

Diagrams are useful for improving the understanding of normal operation or functionality of the system. Tables are useful for checking for completeness—to determine whether something is missing. To supplement the diagrams, tables of components, their responsibilities, and collaborations give additional details. CRC cards (Beck, 1991), documenting the component, its responsibility, and collaborations, are useful for capturing this information.

Drongowski (1993) describes the software architecture of a real-time system. Nord and Cheng (1994) perform an evaluation of this system to assess the performance properties based on the conceptual architecture and to demonstrate how this provides feedback to the architecture design decisions.

Chapter 5

Module Architecture View

The main purpose of the module architecture view is to bring you closer to the system's implementation in software. The reason for keeping the module view distinct from the conceptual view is that they each make explicit different things.

In the conceptual view, the functional relationships must be explicit, but in the module view that is secondary to making explicit how the functionality is mapped to the implementation. In the module view, the relationships among the implementing elements must be made explicit, including how the system uses the underlying software platform (for example, operating system services, other system services).

For example, in the image-processing pipeline of IS2000, the images are passed from one pipeline stage to the next. This is explicit in the conceptual view. In the module view, each stage requests a pointer to its image data from the pipeline manager, then reads and writes the image using this pointer. The pipeline manager ensures that the pointers are given successively to each of the stages, but this control information is now embedded inside the implementation of the pipeline manager, instead of being visible at the architectural level.

It is certainly not impossible to keep all the important control information visible in the module view, but this is one of the design trade-offs you must make. Often (as in this case) performance requirements force you to choose a more efficient implementation—one that sacrifices logical clarity for performance.

As another example, suppose in the conceptual view two components communicate over a connector with call/return semantics. If the two components are assigned to the same CPU, they are implemented as a local procedure call, and if they are on different CPUs, they are implemented as a remote procedure call (RPC). In the conceptual view you are interested in describing the behavior of these connectors: The functional behavior is the same, but the connectors could have different failure modes or timing differences.

However, because the implementation of the two variations is very different, in the module view they have different modules associated with them. In addition, for the RPC variant, the supporting services need to be included. These are not important in the conceptual view.

The module view is not simply a refinement of the conceptual view. Mapping conceptual elements to modules is a repartitioning. In IS2000 you'll see an example in which a component, three connectors, their roles, and two ports are grouped together, then split into two modules—one containing the processing and the other containing the data. Although the modules must fulfill the behavior specified for the conceptual elements, they must also take into account the implementation constraints.

The conceptual and module views are based on two fundamentally different models. In the conceptual view, components are where the main application functionality resides. They interact using connectors, which can have sophisticated control functionality, and use ports and roles to adapt or to mediate the interaction.

In the module view, all the application functionality, control functionality, adaptation, and mediation must be mapped to modules. Modules require and provide interfaces, but these have no associated implementation; they can't adapt or mediate the interactions between modules. Modules interact by invoking services declared in their required interfaces. They are passive with respect to their provided interfaces, waiting to be invoked by another module.

Unlike the conceptual and execution views, for the module view you do not define a configuration. You define the modules and their inherent relationships to each other, but not how they are combined into a particular product. That information is in the execution view, where you define how modules are mapped to runtime elements, including when and how they are created and destroyed.

Modules are organized into two orthogonal structures: decomposition and layers. The decomposition of a system captures the way the system is logically decomposed into subsystems and modules. A module is also assigned to a layer, which then constrains its dependencies on other modules.

This chapter, like the previous one, has three sections. Section 5.1 describes the design activities, Section 5.2 shows how they are applied to IS2000, and the final section summarizes the elements and relations of the module view, and how you should describe and use them.

5.1 Design Activities for the Module Architecture View

Figure 5.1 shows the design tasks for the module architecture view, and how they interact with other design tasks. Like the conceptual view, the module view has three basic phases:

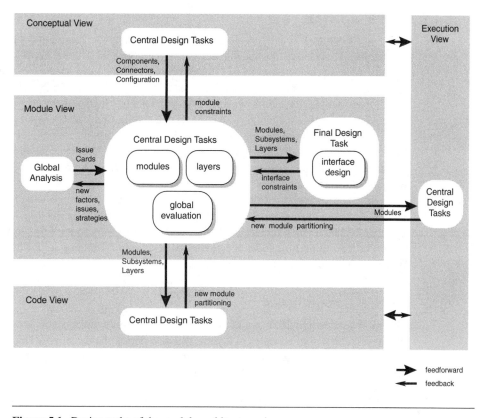

Figure 5.1. Design tasks of the module architecture view

global analysis, central design tasks, and interface design. The middle phase consists of three tightly coupled design tasks: modules, layers, and global evaluation.

This central phase uses the issue cards from global analysis, and the components, connectors, and configuration from the conceptual view as input. The results of this phase—the modules, subsystems, and layers—are used during interface design, and by the central design tasks of the execution and code architecture views.

During the central design phase you may identify new factors, issues, or strategies, causing you to revisit the global analysis task. You may also discover constraints about the modules or layers that cause you to make changes to the conceptual view.

After the central design phase, you may also get feedback from the interface design task, or from the execution or code architecture views, causing you to adjust the modules or layers.

5.1.1 Global Analysis

The first design task for the module view is global analysis. You have done much of the global analysis already, during the design of the conceptual view. When designing the module view, you may identify new factors or may create new issues and strategies, and the analysis of these follows the same approach described in Chapter 3, Global Analysis.

Before starting the central design tasks you should identify the strategies you expect to be relevant for the module view. Although you should check all the factors, certain categories are more likely to be relevant to this view. For the organizational factors, make sure you check the staff skills, process and development environment, and development budget categories. For the technological factors, the general-purpose hardware, software technology, and standards categories probably contain factors that affect this view.

Once you've identified the relevant factors, you then determine which strategies are influenced by them. Look for strategies related to modifiability, portability, and reuse. Use these strategies to guide the decisions for the module view. Also look for strategies related to properties like performance, dependability, and failure detection, reporting, recovery to make sure your module view design supports them.

5.1.2 Central Design Tasks

For the central design tasks you map conceptual elements to subsystems and modules, create layers, and assign modules to layers. You also determine the interfaces of the modules and layers. Guiding these decisions are the strategies from global analysis, experience with prior products, and general software engineering knowledge.

Modules

To design the modules you map the elements from the conceptual view to subsystems and modules. A subsystem usually corresponds to a higher level conceptual component (one that is decomposed into other components and connectors). It can contain other subsystems or modules.

A module can correspond to a single conceptual element (component, port, connector, or role) or to a set of them. Modules can also be decomposed into other modules, but in this case the parent module is really a container; only the leaf modules, in the end, correspond to implemented code. So a subsystem must eventually contain modules, if it is to have any implementation.

Figure 5.2 is a meta-model that describes these relations among subsystems and modules, and the relations between modules and interfaces. A module encapsulates data and operations to provide a service. The services provided by a module are defined by the interfaces it provides. A module may also need the services of another module to perform its function. These required services are defined by the interfaces it requires.

Modules can only interact with each other through these interfaces. Let's define the "use" relation (also called use-dependency) between modules as a relation derived from the "require" and "provide" relations. One module uses another when it requires the interface provided by the other.

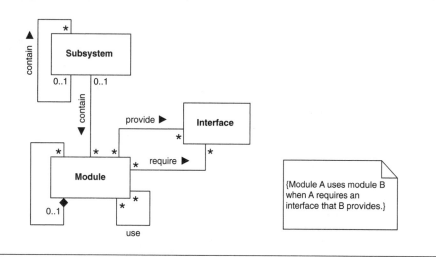

Figure 5.2. Meta-model for subsystems and modules

The conceptual elements get mapped to these modules. In the process of this mapping you assign the modules a responsibility, and determine their decomposition and use relationships. After the initial mapping you may decide to refine and split modules so they can be developed independently. Or, using strategies from the global analysis, you may decide to combine modules for efficiency.

You may also need to add supporting modules that don't have counterparts in the conceptual view. Look for factors that you can't pin down to a particular component, such as failure detection or recovery. Also look for services that are needed by existing modules and aren't provided by the software platform. These can lead to new modules.

Modules should be decomposed to the point when the responsibilities of each module are well understood, along with any implementation or integration risks. Modules grouped into a containing module are more tightly coupled than the modules contained in a subsystem, so they should be assigned as a group to a particular person or team.

Although the leaf modules are eventually implemented as source code, they are abstract modules. A module could, in the end, be implemented as an Ada package, a Modula module, a set of C++ classes, a set of C functions, or other programming language-specific elements.

Layers

Layers organize the modules into a partially ordered hierarchy. When a module is assigned to a layer, it can use any of the other modules in that layer. But whenever a module usage crosses a layer boundary, the interface required and provided by the modules must also be required and provided by the layers. Thus layers are used to constrain the module "use" relations.

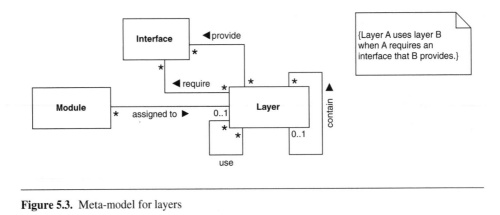

Figure 5.3. Meta-model for layers

The relations for layers are described in the meta-model in Figure 5.3. Layers can also contain sublayers to provide additional structuring within a layer.

Layers are a time-tested way of reducing complexity—for example, by encapsulating external components (such as COTS software or hardware) or by separating systems services from user interface software. They can be used to support reuse by assigning common services to an application services layer. Layers are also useful in providing independence between parts of the system so that, for example, a change in the operating system does not affect the entire system.

Although we present the design of modules and layers as two separate tasks, in practice you start identifying the layers as the modules are identified. You can do this in a bottom-up fashion, in which layers and the dependencies among them grow from the module responsibilities and their dependencies. The layers emerge as the modules are defined.

Another way is to begin with a set of layers based on your experience from similar applications in the domain. As they are identified, modules are assigned to the preexisting layers. In this top-down approach, the layers serve as a guide for defining modules.

The most common approach is to proceed with a combination of the two. Often, architects have in mind a coarse division of layers; for example, applications, user interface, and system services. As modules are defined they usually refine the layer model by adding additional layers for domain-specific functionality or by creating sublayers when a layer gets too complex.

Global Evaluation

To define the modules and layers, you get guidance from multiple sources: your conceptual view design, the strategies from global analysis, your experience with software architectures, and your general knowledge of architecture and software engineering. An important part of global evaluation is deciding which source of information to use at which time.

Global evaluation also means being on the lookout for feedback to the tasks and decisions you made earlier in the design. You should look for additional factors, issues, and strategies that feed back to the global analysis task. You need to evaluate whether any of your decisions about modules and layers warrant a change to the design of the conceptual view.

The third aspect of global evaluation is evaluating your module view decisions with respect to each other. You should expect to adjust the modules and subsystems based on your decisions about the layers, and vice versa. You will have to define new interfaces or revise them to satisfy the "require" and "provide" relations of both modules and layers.

5.1.3 Final Design Task: Interface Design

The final phase of module view design is to describe the interfaces for each of the modules and layers identified during the central design phase. This is done after the other tasks are complete. Here you do the detailed design of interfaces required or provided by modules or layers based on their use-dependencies. For this task you may decide to create new interfaces or to split or combine some. These decisions feed back to the central design tasks, and you may need to revise your modules or layers as a result.

5.2 Design of Module Architecture View for IS2000

Now that we have introduced the tasks for the module view design, let's look at how these are applied to the example system.

5.2.1 Global Analysis

Before starting the central design tasks for the module architecture view, let's revisit the global analysis. We need to look for applicable strategies, paying particular attention to those that have influencing factors related to staff skills, the process and development environment, general-purpose hardware, and software technology. We expect the following strategies to be applicable to the module view:

Issue: Aggressive Schedule
   Strategy: *Reuse existing components.*

Issue: Skill Deficiencies
   Strategy: *Encapsulate multiprocess support facilities.*

Issue: Changes in General-Purpose and Domain-Specific Hardware
   Strategy: *Encapsulate domain-specific hardware.*
   Strategy: *Encapsulate general-purpose hardware.*

Issue: Changes in Software Technology
   Strategy: *Use standards.*
   Strategy: *Develop product-specific interfaces to external components.*

Issue: Real-Time Acquisition Performance
Strategy: *Separate time-critical from nontime-critical components.*

Issue: Implementation of Diagnostics
Strategy: *Reduce the effort for error handling.*
Strategy: *Encapsulate diagnostic components.*

5.2.2   Central Design Tasks: Modularization and Layering

Next let's turn to the central design tasks of the module view: defining modules and organizing them into layers. As with the central design tasks of the conceptual view, these tasks are tightly coupled, so we need to switch back and forth between the tasks.

In this section let's start by using the conceptual components to come up with some initial layers, then map all the conceptual elements to subsystems and modules. Let's define the use-dependencies between the modules, then revisit the layers to refine them and add new supporting layers.

Initial Definition of Layers

One way to get started with the module view is to associate the main conceptual components with layers. When you start with the layer structure in this way, the layers you create come from your experience. We show such an initial layer definition in Figure 5.4. This is only a working diagram, because in the end we want the layer diagram to show modules assigned to layers, not to components. In all of our diagrams we use the UML package notation for a layer: It is drawn as a box with a tab attached to the upper left edge of the box.

Of the conceptual components in Figure 4.6, there are three components for the user interface: Acquire, Monitor, and Export. The graphical user interface (GUI) aspects of these components should be mapped to modules and put in a separate GUI layer. The Acquire component is mainly a user interface functionality, so it goes in the GUI layer.

The Monitor component contains GUI plus other functionality. The GUI functionality goes in the GUI layer, but the other functionality should be placed in a layer with similar components—in this case, a lower layer that we'll call Applications. The Export component contains GUI, image-processing, zoom, and image export functionality. The GUI part goes in the GUI layer, and the other modules also go in the Applications layer.

The GUI layer implements the graphical user interface for applications. Architecturally, a separate GUI layer is desirable for four reasons:

1. Design of GUI components is distinctly different from design of components with a programmatic application programming interface (API).

2. A separate GUI layer helps to promote a single, unified user interface design and reusable widgets for implementation.

3. Procedural and GUI components are enabled to be reused in other contexts.

4. Separation and decoupling of procedural and data components from GUI components reduces reworking resulting from changes to GUIs.

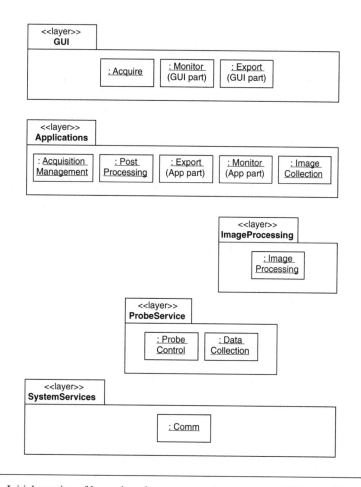

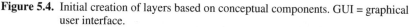

Figure 5.4. Initial creation of layers based on conceptual components. GUI = graphical
user interface.

We make the distinction that the GUI is responsible for defining and managing the
window display and handling user events, whereas the policy that defines what is done
when an event occurs is handled by the applications. For example, the acquisition applications interact with the acquisition GUIs to set up the acquisition parameters, display the
acquired data, display warning and error messages, and report the status of the acquisition.
The GUI handles all the user requests by presenting the user with interface screens that
can accept input from the keyboard, the mouse, and the menus on the screens. The GUI
isolates the applications from the low-level interface toolset (for example, X/Motif).

The AcquisitionManagement, PostProcessing, and ImageCollection components get
put in the Applications layer. You may recall that we used the strategy *Separate time-
critical from nontime-critical components* to split the processing of images into Image-

Processing and PostProcessing. For assignment to layers, we should follow the same strategy, and create a new ImageProcessing layer for time-critical processing.

Next let's look at the ProbeControl and DataCollection components, which encapsulate the probe hardware. We originally used the strategy *Encapsulate domain-specific hardware* to split these two components from the rest of the acquisition and imaging components. As before, the layering structure should support this strategy, so we create a new lower layer—ProbeService—for these two components.

The last of the components is Comm, which provides the network communication and domain-specific communication protocols. This goes in the SystemServices layer. This layer lets us hide the details of the communication-specific code from the modules implementing the high-level connector protocols. When we apply the strategy *Encapsulate multiprocess support facilities*, the modules that provide these services are also assigned to this layer.

Defining Modules for Image Processing

Now let's look at defining the modules for the image-processing components from the conceptual view. The image-processing subsystem produces framed images from the raw camera data. As defined in the conceptual view, image processing consists of a packetizer for collecting the raw data and one or more image pipelines that process the packets into images. An image pipeline is composed of a sequence of stages: The "packetized" data is input to the first stage, and each stage's output is input to the next stage. The output of the final stage is framed images. There are several types of possible image pipelines, each of which performs functions for a specific acquisition procedure. The conceptual configuration for ImageProcessing is shown in Figure 5.5.

For defining modules, let's start by assigning each component to a single module. In general we want to separate as much of the communication infrastructure as feasible into connector- and port-specific modules. Then the modules implementing a conceptual component are insulated from changes to the software platform.

First we need to map the ImageProcessing and ImagePipeline components to subsystems, and the Packetizer component to a module. Next we need to consider whether the PacketPipe connector should be mapped to a separate module. Here, experience suggests that because of the volume of data, we should use a central data buffer for the packetized data rather than give each pipeline its own copy. Therefore the Packetizer and the PacketPipe are implemented as the single central buffer manager MPacketizer.

The decisions about mapping components and connectors to modules generally come first, before you decide how to map the ports and roles to modules. Although in the conceptual view a port is contained in a component, we often want to introduce separate modules for ports. Ports play an important role in insulating a component from connector details, so the advantage of mapping ports to separate modules is to encapsulate connector-specific knowledge and code.

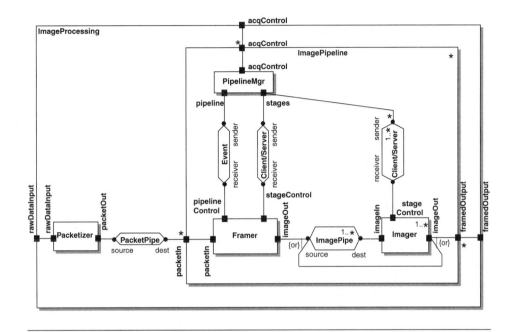

Figure 5.5. Conceptual configuration for ImageProcessing (from the conceptual view)

You get a similar benefit by mapping roles to separate modules. In the case of the PacketPipe, we've already made the decision to combine it with the Packetizer, so we have nothing to gain by putting their ports and roles in separate modules.

However, we do map the packetIn port on the ImagePipeline to a separate module— MPacketMgr. The pipeline uses module MPacketMgr to access the incoming data; it cannot access any other modules of the packetizer.

Similarly, the acqControl port on the ImageProcessing component is the interface used by the acquisition manager for controlling the ImagePipelines. We want to make sure the acquisition manager only has access to the MAcqControl module, not to the modules making up the pipeline directly, so this port also gets mapped to its own module. The decisions we've made so far are summarized in Table 5.1.

The PipelineMgr, its connections to the stages, and the connectors between the image pipeline stages themselves are mapped to the single central image pipeline manager MPipelineMgr in the module view. This manager controls and coordinates the stages of the pipeline. Because of the volume of data passed between the stages of the pipeline, again it will be more efficient to keep the data in a central buffer with each stage updating it in place, rather than passing the data between stages.

Conceptual Element		Module Element	
Name	Kind	Name	Kind
ImageProcessing	Component	SImaging	Subsystem
ImagePipeline	Component	SPipeline	Subsystem
Packetizer packetOut PacketPipe, source, dest	Component Port Connector and roles	MPacketizer	Module
packetIn	Port	MPacketMgr	Module
acqControl	Port	MAcqControl	Module

Table 5.1. Mapping Conceptual Elements to Module Elements: ImageProcessing

Next let's look at the relationship between the pipeline manager and its internal clients—the pipeline stages. We need to consider the ports on the pipeline manager, the connectors, and the ports on the clients.

Ideally we should encapsulate the high-level protocol specified by the client/server and event connectors as a single module. However, in practice, implementations for connectors are not always available and we are constrained by the available mechanisms in the software platform. When this is the case, the modules for the adjacent ports often have to implement what is missing.

Thus we combine the ports and connectors mediating the interactions between the stages (the clients) and the pipeline manager service with the MPipelineMgr module. The decision to use a single module comes down to a trade-off of providing an efficient implementation of our particular system versus building in flexibility for future uses. If we plan to reuse these components and ports in other systems that make up a product line for example, then we would be justified in devoting the necessary resources to implement a more general solution and add to our collection of implementations for domain-specific ports and connectors.

Now the pipelineControl, stageControl, imageIn, and imageOut ports on the stages are at the boundary of the new MPipelineMgr module. We group these ports into the MImageMgr module. The stages access this module only and do not have access to MPipelineMgr directly.

Conceptual Element		Module Element	
Name	Kind	Name	Kind
PipelineMgr	Component	MPipelineMgr	Module
pipeline, stages	Ports		
ImagePipe, source, dest	Connector and roles		
Client/Server, sender, receiver	Connector and roles		
Event, sender, receiver	Connector and roles		
pipelineControl, stageControl, imageIn, imageOut	Ports	MImageMgr	Module
Framer	Component	MFramer	Module
Imager	Component	MImager	Module

Table 5.2. Mapping Conceptual Elements to Module Elements: ImagePipeline

The stages in the pipeline such as Framer and Imager get mapped to their own modules. The mapping between conceptual elements and modules for ImagePipeline is summarized in Table 5.2.

Next let's begin to identify the decomposition dependencies among the modules and subsystems using the following rule:

> *Identifying decomposition dependencies.* If a conceptual component is decomposed into lower level components, there is a dependency from the corresponding parent module or subsystem to the child module or subsystem.

In the example, the dependencies among the conceptual elements give rise to the containment relationships shown in Figure 5.6. The notation we use for a module is a UML stereotyped class. Although people sometimes use the UML "component" notation for a module, it doesn't fit with our notion of an abstract module. A UML component is associated with a physical module of source code, so this notation is more appropriate for our code architecture view.

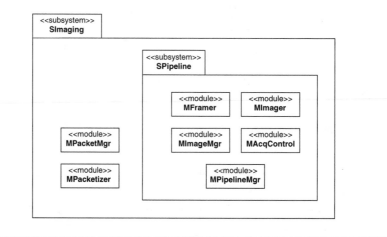

Figure 5.6. Initial containment relationships in imaging subsystem

The notation for a subsystem is a stereotyped UML package. Decomposition dependencies are shown by nesting the modules inside the containing module or subsystem. A subsystem can be decomposed into subsystems and modules (as in Figure 5.6), and a module can be decomposed into modules.

There are also use-dependencies among the modules based on the relationships among their corresponding conceptual elements.

> *Identifying use-dependencies.* If a conceptual component provides a service to another component, there is a dependency from the user to the provider of the service.

These dependencies are a little more difficult to determine because we must first identify the provider of the service and the client. It is helpful to look for patterns in control flow (for example, master/slave, service/client) or data flow direction. Note that there may be dependencies in both directions.

For each interaction between modules (derived from a relationship between their corresponding conceptual elements), we must define an interface through which the interaction occurs. One of the modules provides the interface, and the other requires it. The module that requires the interface "uses" the module that provides it.

For example, MAcqControl interacts with MPipelineMgr, so we need to define an interface—IPipelineControl—for this interaction. As we said earlier, the acqControl port is used by the acquisition manager to control the ImagePipelines. So in this case, the pipeline manager is the passive module, and it must provide the IPipelineControl interface.

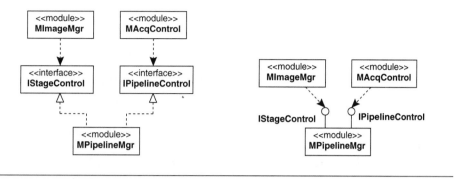

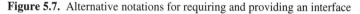

Figure 5.7. Alternative notations for requiring and providing an interface

The MImageMgr module also interacts with MPipelineMgr, but for a different purpose. The pipeline stages use MImageMgr to obtain their image data and to check for special processing requests from acquisition management. So MPipelineMgr provides a second interface—IStageControl—that is required by MImageMgr.

Figure 5.7 shows two different ways to describe these relationships in UML. On the left, the interfaces are shown as stereotyped classes, and the "provide" relation is shown as a dotted line with a triangle. The right side uses the "lollipop" notation for the interfaces, with the "provide" relation indicated by a solid line. In both notations the "require" relation is shown as a dotted line with an arrow pointing to the required interface.

Figure 5.8 shows the use-dependencies among the modules of the imaging subsystem. Let's add two new modules to this figure, enclosing some of the earlier modules. Because MAcqControl and MImageMgr act as proxies to request services of MPipelineMgr, these three modules are tightly coupled and should be implemented together. Thus let's group them in a containing module—MPipeline.

Let's do a similar thing with MPacketizer and MPacketMgr, and group them within MPacket. After adding these two higher level modules, the SPipeline subsystem isn't needed to organize the modules, so we can remove it.

In general, after you know which modules are in a subsystem, you should consider whether any of them should be grouped into a new containing module. Group modules that have many logical dependencies on each other, making them hard to develop independently. Then get rid of any subsystems or containing modules that are no longer needed.

We have often found it useful to produce separate diagrams for the decomposition and use-dependencies, although we combined them in one diagram here. Diagrams can then be organized according to different subsystems, providing more detailed views for each.

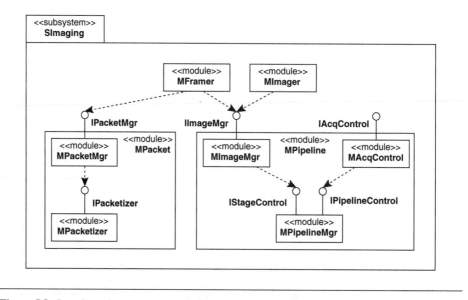

Figure 5.8. Imaging subsystem use-dependencies

Reviewing the ImageProcessing Layer

As planned during our initial layering task, we need to assign the image-processing modules to the ImageProcessing layer. Next let's take the modules corresponding to acquisition management and put them in the Applications layer. The acquisition manager client (MClient) accesses the MPipeline module through the IAcqControl interface. Therefore we can use it as an interface to the ImageProcessing layer as well.

For the probe services, let's apply the strategy *Reuse existing components*, and incorporate the existing modules MProbeControl and MDataCollect into our design. In both cases we must provide a separate module for adapting the old module. The new modules—MDataAcq and MDataMgr—provide the probe service's interface to the rest of the system. These four modules abstract and encapsulate the data aspects of the probe hardware, so let's assign them to the ProbeService layer.

The ProbeService layer provides a complete abstraction of the probe such that the layers above it need not use the hardware services directly. This makes it possible to switch the hardware without affecting higher layers.

Our assignment of modules to layers is summarized in Figure 5.9. We show the use-dependencies between modules, which are derived from the interfaces they require and provide.

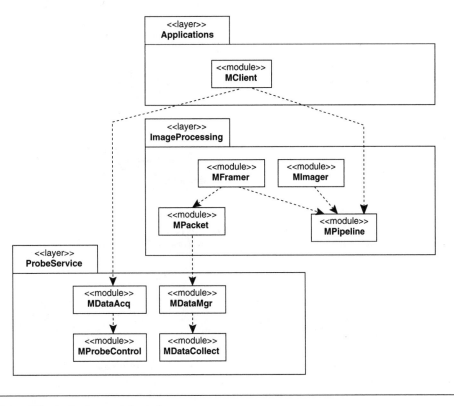

Figure 5.9. Assigning modules to layers

As the details of the module view are being worked out, it is useful to keep a current version of the layer diagram that fits on one page. Thus you can see at a glance the major partitioning of the system and get additional details by following the decomposition diagrams or looking up module assignments to layers in tables.

Now let's derive the dependencies between these three layers based on the dependencies among the modules belonging to them. For example, the data collector is used by the packetizer; thus the ImageProcessing layer depends on the ProbeService layer. The layers shown in Figure 5.10 follow the convention that arrows generally flow downward, meaning that layers positioned above are dependent on layers below them.

Within a layer, the layering does not impose any restrictions on module dependencies: Theoretically, any module can use any other within a layer. But the interfaces of a layer restrict what modules in other layers can use. Layers, like modules, can both provide and require interfaces. So two modules in separate layers can have a use-dependency only if one provides an interface that is also provided by its layer, and the other layer and module both require this interface.

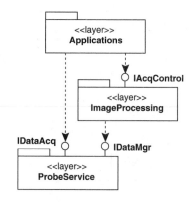

Figure 5.10. Use-dependencies between layers

For example, if we add another module to the Applications layer, it can use the services of modules in this layer as well as those provided by the ProbeService layer. (Although, if the Applications layer didn't previously require those services, we have to add the newly required interface.)

The layering scheme also facilitates buildability. Layers reduce and isolate external (for example, hardware and operating system) and internal dependencies, and facilitate bottom-up building and testing of various subsystems. Lower layer functionality can be implemented and tested before higher layers.

Adding Supporting Layers

In addition to mapping conceptual components, connectors, and ports to modules and organizing them into layers, an architect often needs to provide supporting layers. What is needed depends on the services the software platform provides.

For IS2000, because of the strategies *Encapsulate general-purpose hardware* and *Develop product-specific interfaces to external components*, we need to encapsulate the operating system, and use an operating system that is POSIX compliant. Thus let's introduce an OperatingSystem layer that supports a standard interface to operating systems.

Next let's look at the domain-specific support services for storage and communication. The ImageCollection component stores images for as long as 24 hours, but we haven't yet decided *how* these images will be stored. Let's use a commercial database to store these images, largely because a database has worked well for this purpose in past products. In addition, we can use the database to support recovery: It will implement the Persistent-DataPipe connector between the ImageProcessing and PostProcessing components.

This decision means we need to revisit the technological factors, adding new factors, analyzing them, and checking whether we have any new strategies. The particular database we use could change over the product's lifetime; for example, to maintain compatibility with other products. Other reasons for a database change are if a vendor goes out of business, if the product becomes obsolete, if a better platform becomes available, or if customers request features not available with the current database.

Recalling our strategy *Use standards,* and with a change in database likely, we decide to use an existing interface standard for the database, Open Database Connectivity (ODBC). This makes a change in database systems transparent, provided the new or upgraded system conforms to the interface standard. Changes to the standard itself would have a significant impact on many of our modules, but the standard is fairly stable.

The two new factors are listed in Table 5.3. After reviewing our existing issue cards, we update the issue Changes in Software Technology to add these influencing factors and to note that both existing strategies also apply to the database.

Technological Factor	Flexibility and Changeability	Impact
T3: Software technology		
T3.3: Database management system (DBMS)		
Use a commercial DBMS.	The DBMS may be upgraded every five years as technology improves.	The impact is transparent, provided it conforms to our DBMS interface standard. Change from a relational to an object-oriented DBMS may have a large impact on all components.
T5: Standards		
T5.5: Standard for DBMS interface		
Open Database Connectivity has been selected as the database access standard.	The standard is stable.	There is a large impact on components interfacing with the DBMS.

Table 5.3. Factors Added During Module View Design

Now, following the strategy *Develop product-specific interfaces to external components*, let's encapsulate the database, introducing a DatabaseService layer. The modules for image collection, which we had earlier placed in the Applications layer, are now moved to the DatabaseService layer.

A database service is a vendor-independent interface to a database management system (DBMS), and it provides support for data administration and management. We partition the DatabaseService layer into three sublayers. The DBMS is the lowest layer, and it supplies the mechanism for storing data. It is supplied by a vendor. The database interface at the next level is the vendor-independent interface to the DBMS. The top level is database administration, which is responsible for administration activities such as installation, configuration, maintenance, and database utilities.

To implement the requirements for error handling and logging, let's introduce modules for a logger and its interface. The interface is used by any other module that needs to communicate with the logger (strategy, *Encapsulate diagnostic components*). The logger is responsible for receiving and storing event messages in corresponding log files. Standard services such as message catalogs and the file system are used to review log files (strategy, *Reduce effort for error handling*). Let's collect these modules and put them into an ErrorHandling layer.

We may combine this ErrorHandling layer with the SystemServices layer later on. These kinds of services are often applicable to more than one product. If so, it makes sense to maintain them separately as part of a product-line architecture for a family of related systems. The final version of our layers is shown in Figure 5.11.

5.2.3   Final Design Task: Interface Design

For the final task in designing the module view we must describe the details of the interfaces, respecting the dependencies defined by the decomposition and layer structures. The protocol definitions from the conceptual view help us with this task. There isn't necessarily a one-to-one correspondence between a protocol definition and an interface definition because the ports or connectors that adhere to a protocol may be mapped to modules that are split or combined. However, using the protocol definitions is a good way to get started with supplying information about the details of the interface. Details of the interface include the names and characteristics of the operations of the modules. For operations, we must define the signature, including arguments and type information.

We also need to document the module with enough semantic information to describe what someone would need to know to use it (for example, preconditions, postconditions, exceptions). This is usually written in text. One way to integrate this documentation with the code is to establish coding conventions in which the detailed design is embedded in the comments in the header files. Instead of text, this semantic information could be written in a more formal assertion language.

We don't expect the architect to complete the entire interface design. Once the services provided and used are documented, these can be handed off to individual developers or teams to document the details. Details of the IAcqControl interface definition are shown in Figure 5.12.

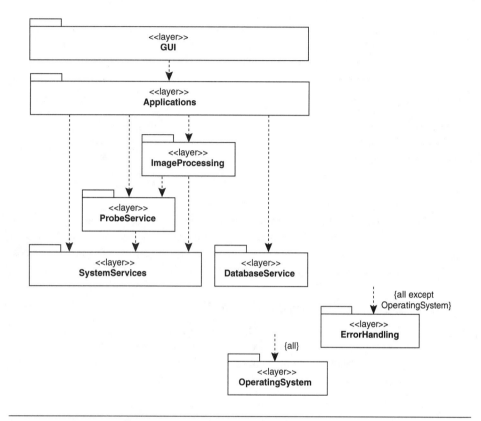

Figure 5.11. Final version of layers and their use-dependencies

```
Initialize()
   Client initializes interface with ImageProcessing.

Create(IP_id, Pipeline_config)
   Create an image pipeline with the given configuration.

Delete(IP_id)
   Stop execution of the pipeline and tear down the stages.

Terminate()
   Client terminates interface with ImageProcessing.

AdjustImage(IP_id, Stage_id, Message)
   Client adjusts the processing of the image
   (e.g., growth rate, persistence).
```

Figure 5.12. Interface definition for IAcqControl

Module Name	Description	Subsystem Name	Layer	Interfaces Provided
MPipelineMgr	Image pipeline manager	SImaging	ImageProcessing	IPipelineControl IStageControl
...				

Table 5.4. Sample Module Summary Table

Besides diagrams, tables are another useful description. Table 5.4 shows an entry from a summary of the modules of a system, with the layers and decomposition relationships. As the size of the system increases, tables for modules and interfaces become more important for managing and understanding the architecture.

5.2.4 Design Summary for IS2000 Module View

To design the module architecture view we identified modules that implement the conceptual elements, and we captured decomposition and use-dependencies among the modules. We also organized modules into layers. Table 5.5 summarizes the design decisions we discussed in this chapter.

Design Decision	Rationale
Initial definition of layers	
Create GUI layer.	Decouple GUI implementation from the rest of the application.
Create ImageProcessing layer.	Strategy: *Separate time-critical from nontime-critical components.*
Create ProbeService layer.	Strategy: *Encapsulate domain-specific hardware.*
Create SystemServices layer.	Strategy: *Encapsulate multiprocess support facilities.*

Table 5.5. Sequence of Design Decisions for IS2000 Module View

Design Decision	Rationale
Defining modules for ImageProcessing	
Implement Packetizer and PacketPipe as a centrally managed buffer (MPacketizer).	Recognize the high volume of data and real-time performance requirements.
Create separate modules for packetIn and acqControl ports.	Insulate the components from connector details.
Implement PipelineMgr, ImagePipe, Client/Server, and Event as a centrally managed buffer (MPipelineMgr).	Recognize the high volume of data and real-time performance requirements.
Create one module for pipelineControl, stageControl, imageIn, and imageOut.	Insulate Framer and Imager from details of MPipelineMgr.
Group MAcqControl, MImageMgr, and MPipelineMgr into a containing module.	Tightly coupled modules should be implemented together.
Group MPacketizer and MPacketMgr into a containing module.	Tightly coupled modules should be implemented together.
Remove subsystem SPipeline.	SPipeline not needed after adding containing modules.
Reviewing the ImageProcessing layer	
IAcqControl is provided by the ImageProcessing layer.	Provide module interfaces that are used by other layers.
Use existing modules MProbeControl and MDataCollect.	Strategy: *Reuse existing components.*
Adding supporting layers	
Create OperatingSystem layer.	Strategy: *Encapsulate general-purpose hardware.* Strategy: *Develop product-specific interfaces to external components.*

Table 5.5. Sequence of Design Decisions for IS2000 Module View *(continued)*

Design Decision	Rationale
Use a database for storing images (ImageCollection component) and for recovery (PersistentDataPipe connector).	Successful approach in past products.
Add new factors to the technological factor table: T3.3: Database management system, T5.5: Standard for DBMS interface.	The product uses a commercial database. Strategy: *Use standards.*
Create DatabaseService layer.	Strategy: *Develop product-specific interfaces to external components.*
Create ErrorHandling layer.	Strategy: *Encapsulate diagnostic components.*
Use standard services: message catalogs and file system.	Strategy: *Reduce effort for error handling.*
GUI = graphical user interface; DBMS = database management system.	

Table 5.5. Sequence of Design Decisions for IS2000 Module View *(continued)*

For IS2000, we started with an approximation of the layers, relying on experience and on strategies identified during global analysis. We then began to map conceptual elements to modules. We started by mapping a component to a module or subsystem. Next we looked at each connector, deciding whether to put it into an existing module or to create a new module for it. We did the same for ports and roles, sometimes creating a new module and sometimes putting them in an existing module.

Next we determined the decomposition and use-dependencies among modules and subsystems, and added interfaces for the modules. During this process we sometimes created new containing modules, and deleted containing subsystems.

We refined the layers, and defined interfaces for the layers. We also added supporting layers, relying on our global analysis strategies and the use-dependencies of the modules to determine the layers' relations. At the end, after the subsystems, modules, interfaces, and layers were stable, we performed detailed interface design.

5.3 **Summary of Module Architecture View**

Table 5.6 summarizes the elements, relations, and artifacts of the module architecture view. As in the conceptual view, the elements and relations are the building blocks for the architecture view, and the artifacts are the descriptions or documentation of the architecture. Note that the decomposition dependency is a form of the composition relation from the point of view of how a module is decomposed.

For the module view, one of the most important artifacts is the conceptual-module correspondence. Although this could be represented in a UML diagram, it's generally much more compact to put the mapping in a table. The Safety Vision case study (Chapter 8) contains an example of putting conceptual-module correspondence information in a UML diagram (see Figure 8.6).

The three kinds of UML Class Diagrams describing decomposition, module dependencies, and layer dependencies are essential artifacts for all systems. As we said earlier, particularly for large systems it is better not to put too many kinds of relations in a diagram. For example, the subsystem and module decomposition diagrams shouldn't have use-dependencies, and the use-dependency diagram shouldn't have decomposition dependencies or containment relations.

As you've seen in this chapter, we sometimes use diagrams that do combine these relations in a single diagram. Our module use-dependency diagram also showed containment and decomposition. A project should have conventions for the kinds of diagrams produced, so that the architecture description is consistent. You also have to decide which diagrams show interfaces explicitly, and which variant of the interface notation they use.

Element	UML Element	New Stereotype	Notation
Module	Class	<<module>>	<<module>>
Interface	Interface	—	O or <<interface>>
Subsystem	Subsystem	—	<<subsystem>>
Layer	Package	<<layer>>	<<layer>>

Table 5.6. Summary of Module Architecture View

Relation	UML Element	Notation	Description
contain	Association	Nesting	A subsystem can contain a subsystem or a module. A layer can contain a layer.
composition	Composition	Nesting (or ◆—)	A module can be decomposed into one or more modules.
use (also called use-dependency)	Usage	- - - - ->	Module (layer) A uses module (layer) B when A requires an interface that B provides.
require	Usage	- - - - ->	A module or layer can require an interface.
provide	Realization	—— (with ○) - - ▷ (with ▭)	A module or layer can provide an interface.
implement	—	Table row	A module can implement a conceptual element.
	Trace	- <<trace>> >	
assigned to	Association	Nesting	A module can be assigned to a layer.

Artifact	Representation
Conceptual-module correspondence	Table
Subsystem and module decomposition	UML Class Diagram
Module use-dependencies	UML Class Diagram
Layer use-dependencies, modules assigned to layers	UML Class Diagram
Summary of module relations	Table

Table 5.6. Summary of Module Architecture View *(continued)*

Figure 5.13 presents the meta-model for the module architecture view. It contains the elements and relations from Table 5.6, and shows how they can be combined.

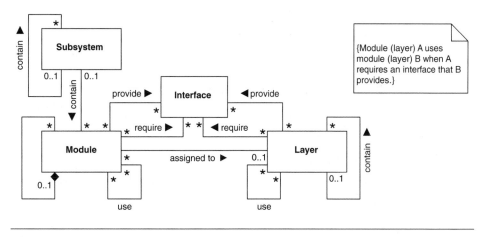

Figure 5.13. Meta-model of the module architecture view

We use the same notation for the "contain" and "composition" relations, but they are not quite the same. "Contain" relates subsystems and layers, which are based on UML packages, and "composition" relates modules, which are based on UML classes. Our convention is that subsystems and layers are simply containers; they have no implementation themselves. When a module is decomposed into other modules, the parent module is also just a container. Only the leaf modules are implemented eventually.

Interfaces are separate elements in the module view, and they can be provided or required by modules and layers. The "use" relation (also called *use-dependency*) is derived from the "require" and "provide" relations. One module uses another when it requires the interface provided by the other. This also holds for layers.

5.3.1 Traceability

Describing the relationships of the module view to requirements, external factors, and other views provides traceability. It is critical to relate the module view to the conceptual view, not just as an aid in designing the module view, but to have a complete architecture description. The following three items should be traceable in the module view:

1. *Critical requirements.* As we saw in the previous chapter, the factor tables and issue cards capture the product features and requirements that affect the architecture. Some of these can be traced to conceptual elements and others can be traced directly to modules or layers. This information can be used to determine the impact of changes in requirements to the module view. We can also use it to trace design decisions back to requirements to evaluate how well they are met.

2. *Organizational and technological factors.* Similarly, the organizational and technological factors are described in factor tables, and their impact on the architecture is

captured in issue cards. Tables like Table 5.5 show the strategies and factors used to make design decisions for the module view.

3. *Elements in the conceptual view.* The mapping of elements in the conceptual view to modules and subsystems should be recorded, for example, in a table such as Table 5.1.

Looking ahead to the next chapters, modules are assigned to runtime elements in the execution architecture view. Then, in the code architecture view, modules are mapped to source components.

5.3.2   Uses for the Module Architecture View

Once the module view is explicit, it becomes a starting point for reasoning about important system properties. The module view descriptions can be used for

- Management of module interfaces
- Change impact analysis
- Consistency checking of interface constraints
- Configuration management
- Effort estimation

The module view can be used for testing. Separation of function from communication simplifies function testing and enables unit testing of protocol implementations. The layer model can be designed to support independent building and testing of each of the layers.

Additional Reading

The work of DeRemer and Kron (1976) describes programming-in-the-large and the need for module interconnection languages. Prieto-Diaz and Neighbors (1986) provide a survey of the several variants of module interconnection languages that have been defined to support programming-in-the-large. Module interconnection languages of note include Intercol (Tichy, 1979), PIC (Wolf, 1985), and NuMIL (Narayanaswamy and Scacchi, 1987). This is similar to our module architecture view.

Parnas (1972) discusses the criteria to be used in decomposition. The criteria include changeability, among others, and are expanded in his article on software aging (Parnas, 1994).

A widely practiced convention for describing layers uses stacked rectangular boxes. Adjacencies between these boxes represent allowable interfaces between modules in different layers. Modules can only depend on modules in lower layers. Exceptions for crossing layers (for example, all applications access system services) are noted in text accompanying the diagram. Our description using arrows to represent the dependencies between layers is influenced by Selic, Gullekson, and Ward (1994). Buschmann et al. (1996) describe an architectural pattern for layers.

Kazman et al. (1996) describe the Software Architecture Analysis Method (SAAM), a scenario-based technique for evaluating the modifiability of an architecture based on structures in the module and code architecture views.

Chapter 6

Execution Architecture View

The execution architecture view describes the structure of a system in terms of its runtime platform elements (for example, operating system tasks, processes, threads, address spaces). It captures how the system's functionality is assigned to these platform elements, how the resulting runtime instances communicate, and how physical resources are allocated to them. It also describes the location, migration, and replication of these runtime instances.

Because this mapping will likely change over time (including during development), it is important to design the architecture to be easily adaptable to this kind of change. In addition, the resource decisions you make for a component will likely affect the resources available for other components. Because of this interdependency, it is easier to consider this aspect of the system separately from the others.

The driving forces behind the decisions for designing the execution architecture view are performance, distribution requirements, and the runtime platform, which includes the underlying hardware and software platforms. The execution view is used for performance analysis, monitoring, and tuning as well as for debugging and service maintenance.

The execution view is sometimes trivial; as, for example, when the system is a single-threaded, single process. However, as soon as the system has more than one process, the execution view diverges from the module view. An example of this situation is when an application and server are mapped to separate processes. The common practice is to provide a "client API library" with the server. Functionally, in the module view, the client API is part of the server. But physically, at runtime, the client API is part of the application process, not the server process. The execution view makes this runtime mapping explicit.

The execution view also captures replication. Suppose there are multiple client applications, each in its own process, and one server process to serve them all. In this case, the client API is instantiated multiple times, once in each client application process, whereas the server is instantiated only once, in the server process.

By making the replication explicit, you expose the concurrency requirements the server must meet. Concurrent requests must be handled not in the client API, but in the server itself. The execution view helps to pinpoint where protocols for things like interprocess communication and concurrency are needed.

Another important reason for having an execution view is so that you can better prepare for change. The execution view will likely change more often than the other views for the following two reasons. First, it has a strong dependency not only on the software platform, but on the hardware platform. Even if the user-level functionality of your system were to remain constant throughout its lifetime, you would most likely have to adapt to changes in the hardware and/or software platform due to advances in technology. Second, the execution view is tightly coupled with performance and distribution requirements. For systems with tight performance requirements, you will likely need to do some tuning of the execution view during development. A separate execution view helps isolate the effects of these kinds of changes.

6.1   Design Activities for the Execution Architecture View

The design tasks for the execution view are global analysis, runtime entities, communication paths, configuration, and resource allocation (Figure 6.1). Global analysis is the first task, but throughout the design you can expect some feedback from the later tasks. Similarly, resource allocation is the last task, but decisions made there may cause you to revisit earlier tasks. The middle tasks, the central design tasks, are much more tightly coupled, and one of these is an ongoing global evaluation. Figure 6.1 shows the design tasks of the execution view and their relations to other design tasks.

As in the other views, the issue cards from the global analysis task are input to the central design tasks. The components, connectors, and configuration from the conceptual view guide the design of the execution view, thus these are also input to the central design tasks. Another input to these tasks are the modules, which are mapped to runtime entities in the execution view.

During these central design tasks you may identify new factors, issues, or strategies that cause you to revisit the global analysis task. It is also possible that runtime constraints force you to modify some of the decisions in the conceptual view, or revise the module partitioning in the module view.

After the runtime entities, communication paths, and execution configuration are complete, you perform the final design task—resource allocation. This task could uncover resource constraints that require changes to some of the decisions you made earlier, but that should happen infrequently.

The hardware architecture is an important input to the design of the execution view. For global analysis you will likely have factors that describe aspects of the hardware for

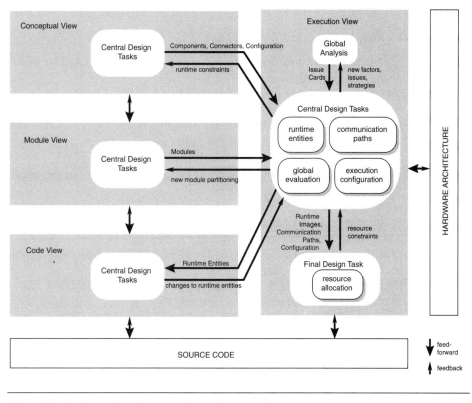

Figure 6.1. Design tasks of the execution architecture view

the system, and strategies related to the hardware architecture. During the central design tasks, the kinds of runtime entities and communication paths you use depend on the hardware. And the execution configuration should, in the end, be mapped to the hardware devices, which happens during resource allocation.

The results of the execution view, in particular the runtime entities, are input to the code architecture view. They also influence the implementation of the system in source code.

6.1.1 Global Analysis

In Chapter 3, we described how to perform the global analysis task. This task precedes all the other steps of the architecture design, and it must be revisited when designing each of the architecture views. You begin the global analysis for the execution view by reviewing the analysis for the conceptual and module views. Identify the factors that affect the execution view; for example, performance requirements and communication mechanisms.

If you haven't already done so, perform an analysis of the hardware platform and the software platform. For the hardware platform you need a list of the hardware components used in the system, and the topology or interconnection of these components. You also need to know which parts of the hardware platform could change, the likelihood of such a change, and when it could occur.

For the software platform you need to know the infrastructure software that is between your product and the hardware platform. Traditionally, this was the operating system. Today, it certainly includes the operating system, but you may also have additional software that is considered to be part of the software platform, such as networking software, other middleware layers on top of the operating system, or something like a DBMS. Often products within a company share a common custom software platform, particularly when they are part of a product line.

Once you've identified the software platform, list the platform elements that you plan to use in the execution architecture view. Figure 6.2 shows the meta-model for a platform element, which can be a process, queue, file, and so forth. You also need to know the basic characteristics of these platform elements. For both UNIX and NT platforms, threads and processes are platform elements. However, because of the difference in overhead for processes, you can expect to use processes more frequently on UNIX than on NT, where you're more likely to use threads.

As with the hardware platform, you determine what could change, and what kind of impact a change would have. Of course, your software platform may have to change as a result of a change in the hardware platform. With this information, you can make informed decisions about where to build in flexibility.

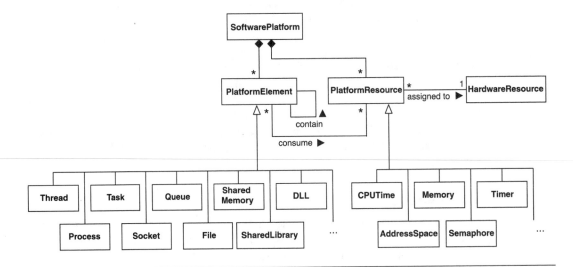

Figure 6.2. Meta-model for platform elements. DLL = dynamic link library.

After analyzing any new factors, record them in your factor tables. Look for new issues, particularly for those related to performance and dependability, and develop strategies for these. You should also eventually record as strategies the resource-sharing and scheduling policies, although you may not know these until the design of the execution view is nearly complete.

6.1.2 Central Design Tasks

Runtime Entities

During the global analysis task you identified the platform elements available on the software platform. Now you must decide how to map conceptual components and modules to these platform elements.

Ultimately the modules will be assigned to runtime entities. Figure 6.3 shows the meta-model for a runtime entity, which can have one or more modules assigned to it, whereas a module can be assigned to more than one runtime entity. A runtime entity is allocated to one of the platform elements defined for the software platform. You start by assigning conceptual components to platform elements for the first approximation of the runtime entities, then refine the partitioning by mapping modules to runtime entities. The end result is a set of runtime entities, their attributes, and the modules assigned to them.

There may also be runtime entities such as daemons or other server processes that have no direct correspondence to modules but are needed to support the other runtime entities. You should also identify and characterize these.

Next you must consider the resource sharing that is allowed or required among the runtime entities. Examples of resource sharing are the sharing of files, buffers, and servers. When definition of the runtime entities is complete, you know which of them will be replicated, and how they will be distributed across hosts. These decisions are recorded as the runtime characteristics of each runtime entity; for example, host type, replication, concurrency control mechanisms used, and other resource-sharing policies used.

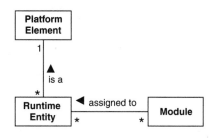

Figure 6.3. Meta-model for runtime entities

Communication Paths

In addition to defining the runtime entities, you need to identify the expected and/or allowable communication paths between them, including the mechanisms and resources used for that communication. Figure 6.4 shows the meta-model for a communication path, which uses a communication mechanism such as interprocess communication (IPC), RPC, the Distributed Component Object Model, and so on. A communication mechanism may use platform elements such as mailboxes, queues, buffers, and files.

The implementation of the protocols for communication paths is often distributed among the runtime entities participating in the communication. You may decide to introduce a new runtime entity if the complexity of the protocol warrants it (for example, links to special hardware).

Execution Configuration

At this point, the building blocks for the execution view are complete. The next step is to describe the system's runtime topology by characterizing the instances of the runtime entities and how they are interconnected.

We make a distinction between a runtime entity and its corresponding runtime instances. If each runtime entity has only one runtime incarnation, then this distinction isn't needed. However, a runtime entity is often replicated (multiple incarnations at runtime), and possibly distributed over multiple hosts. Each of these incarnations is a separate runtime instance. Under UNIX, runtime instances have unique process identifiers, even when they are instances of the same runtime entity.

You should determine each runtime instance and its attributes. These attributes include the corresponding runtime entity and host name. When appropriate, include infor-

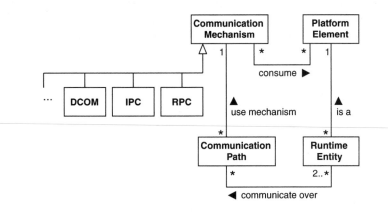

Figure 6.4. Meta-model for communication paths. DCOM = Distributed Component Object Model; IPC = interprocess communication; RPC = remote procedure call.

mation about the resource allocation of each runtime instance, and information about its creation and termination.

Next you need to describe the interconnection of the runtime instances. The interconnection should describe which runtime instances communicate, and it should include temporary as well as permanent communication paths. We do this with an execution configuration diagram. As in the conceptual view, the configuration diagram can contain types (runtime entities) or instances (runtime instances). It is more common for the execution configuration to contain runtime instances, but runtime entities can be useful for describing a set of configurations in a single diagram, as we did for IS2000's image pipeline.

The execution configuration is rarely static; most systems have start-up and shutdown phases in addition to the operating phase. Some systems have a configuration that changes throughout its operation. For example, in IS2000 a new image pipeline is created when an acquisition procedure is requested, and it is destroyed when the acquisition is complete. Thus you need to determine and describe how the configuration changes over time, and how those changes are controlled.

Global Evaluation

During the central design tasks you base your decisions on input from multiple sources. The global analysis gives you strategies for fulfilling performance and dependability requirements. The conceptual view design describes the concurrency among conceptual components, which the execution configuration must support. The modules and their dependencies constrain the runtime entities and how they communicate. The hardware architecture dictates the hardware resources and constrains the software platform, limiting your selection of platform elements and communication mechanisms. In addition, you must consider the implementation cost and try to avoid complex algorithms for implementing concurrency control, communication, and so forth. An ongoing evaluation task is to balance all of these guidelines and restrictions.

During global evaluation you may also need to do performance experiments and/or simulations for the evaluation; analytic techniques may not be sufficient. Based on the results of your ongoing evaluation you must then decide whether to adjust or to refine the boundaries of your runtime entities, and modify their characteristics accordingly.

6.1.3 Final Design Task: Resource Allocation

The remaining task is resource allocation. Here you take the runtime instances and budgets defined in the configuration task, allocate them to particular hardware devices, and assign specific values to the budgeted attributes (for example, by setting process priorities).

The resources to be allocated were identified during the global analysis task. Once the hardware and software platform was defined, you determined the resulting resources. The software platform may have a fixed number of each type of platform element, or this number may be configurable.

The allocation decisions made here are fairly localized, and are often made at build time. The intention is to use standard techniques and specific strategies from the global analysis to determine how resources are allocated. Example decisions are that these processes are assigned 256K of shared memory, or that rate monotonic scheduling (RMS) is used to assign priorities to the processes.

For larger, more complex systems, it is useful to deal with more than one resource or process at a time. For example, when there is a need to guarantee that a low-priority task eventually gets done, the set of processes responsible for this task may be assigned a common CPU time guarantee and budget (assigning them, in a sense, to a virtual CPU). Resources may be allocated to a collection of processes responsible for related functions, and therefore have a related cumulative need for processing resources. If it turns out that there are not enough resources, then you have to revisit the decisions made earlier during the central design tasks.

6.2 Design of Execution Architecture View for IS2000

Now that we have summarized the design tasks, let us return to the example system to show how to design the execution view for IS2000.

6.2.1 Global Analysis

The global analysis we've done so far hasn't produced many strategies that are directly applicable to the execution view. The few relevant strategies are the following:

Issue: Skill Deficiencies
Strategy: *Avoid use of multiple threads.*
Strategy: *Encapsulate multiprocess support facilities.*

Performance is a very important concern for the execution view. Because of the very high data rate of the probe hardware, let's add a new issue: High Throughput.

To keep the product costs down, let's use a single CPU and limit memory size to 64MB. Because of our real-time requirements, the processor is a high-end Pentium processor. However, if we can't meet our performance requirements with a single CPU, we have no choice but to add another. This second CPU can run UNIX, and the first CPU can be reserved for the real-time processes. We then need to add the strategy *Use an additional CPU* to the issue card.

A common technique to achieve higher performance is to increase concurrency by using multiple threads and/or multiple processes. In our case, the development team is deficient in the necessary skills, particularly in multithreaded processing, which caused us to create the strategy *Avoid use of multiple threads.* Another factor is that with UNIX, our selected operating system, it is relatively inexpensive to create and to destroy processes. So let's add another new strategy, *Map independent threads of control to processes.*

High Throughput

The system has high-performance probe hardware with a very high data rate, higher than for previous products. The processing rate must keep up with the data rate from the probe hardware, at least up to the point at which data is recoverable. Common techniques to achieve higher performance include the use of multiple threads and multiple processes. However, the development team is deficient in the necessary skills.

Influencing Factors

O2.3: There is only one developer with expertise in multithreading.

O2.4 There are only two developers with expertise in using multiple processes.

P7.1: The budget for the product is limited and there is very little flexibility in changing it.

T1.2: We don't know whether one CPU will be sufficient to meet system performance needs when fully loaded. It is possible to enhance the system performance by adding a CPU. However, this may exceed the budget for the product.

T3.2: The cost of creating/destroying operating system processes is low.

Solution

We know from experience that to achieve adequate performance we must maximize the use of the processor by maximizing concurrency. We need an approach for achieving this, given the skill set of the development team. If one processor is not sufficient to handle peak system load, there are a couple of options. We could add another processor running the same real-time operating system or a general-purpose operating system like UNIX. If additional processing power is needed, we must then determine what is technically feasible, the impact it will have on the cost of the unit, and how it affects the design.

Strategy: *Map independent threads of control to processes.*

To increase performance, take advantage of the low cost of process creation/destruction and map independent threads of control to processes. This strategy complements the strategy *Avoid use of multiple threads.*

Strategy: *Use an additional CPU.*

Perform experiments to determine whether one CPU is sufficient. If the processor load is too high, use a standard real-time operating system and consider a dedicated "real-time CPU." This further isolates the real-time requirements and allows a more general processor with more flexibility for the nonreal-time portion.

Continued

High Throughput *(continued)*

Related Strategies

Related strategies are *Encapsulate multiprocess support facilities* and *Avoid use of multiple threads* (issue, Skills Deficiencies).

Next let's revisit the Issue Real-Time Acquisition Performance, which has only one strategy so far, added during the design of the conceptual view. IS2000's real-time performance requirements are given as the maximum signal data rate, which is the rate at which the probe control can acquire data, and acquisition performance. Acquisition performance is measured by the size and number of images, and the acquisition response time measured in terms of end-to-end deadlines.

A common strategy is to run a simulation or other model of the system to estimate its performance. Although the results are only an estimate, they can provide valuable feedback at this early stage—during architecture design—rather than later, after many of the components have been implemented. Let's add the strategy *Use rate monotonic analysis (RMA) to predict performance.*

The strategies developed to support the issue High Throughput say that processes are the basic unit for the execution view, and that we may need to add a second CPU. Even with an analysis technique for predicting performance, we may still need to adjust process boundaries as the system is implemented. Therefore, let's add two more strategies: *Use flexible allocation of modules to processes* and *Develop guidelines for module behavior.* These should reduce the cost of adjusting process boundaries during development.

Real-Time Acquisition Performance

Meeting real-time performance requirements is critical to the success of the product. There is no separate source code for meeting the real-time performance requirements directly. The source code that implements functional processing must also meet the performance constraints.

Influencing Factors

T1: General-purpose hardware

T3: Operating system, operating system processes, and database management system

P3.1: Maximum signal data rate

P3.2: Acquisition performance

Continued

Real-Time Acquisition Performance *(continued)*

Solution

Partition the system into separate components for algorithms, communication, and control to provide the flexibility to implement several different strategies. Use analysis techniques to predict performance to help in the early identification of performance bottlenecks.

Strategy: *Separate time-critical components from nontime-critical components.*

To isolate the effects of change in the performance requirements, partition the system into components (and modules) that participate in time-critical processing and those that do not. This requires careful consideration at the interface between the real-time and nonreal-time sides of the system.

Strategy: *Develop guidelines for module behavior.*

Impose a set of guidelines on module behavior to help eliminate performance bottlenecks and to support correct behavior. For example, ensure that modules have a single thread of execution, are reentrant, and are nonblocking.

Strategy: *Use flexible allocation of modules to processes.*

Make it easy to change the module-to-process allocation so that the system can be tuned to achieve the required performance. This flexibility can also be used to group modules or threads with similar deadlines, periods, or frequencies, then assign the group to the same process to reduce scheduling and switching overhead.

Strategy: *Use rate monotonic analysis (RMA) to predict performance.*

Use RMA to make sure the project is on track for fulfilling performance requirements.

Related Strategies

See also *Separate components and modules along dimensions of concern* (issue, Skills Deficiencies) and *Encapsulate multiprocess support facilities* (issue, Easy Addition and Removal of Features).

Lastly, let's look at a related issue, Resource Limitations. These are driven mainly by budget and technological factors, and they have a large impact on the design of the execution view.

To provide support for meeting the real-time processing requirements, let's use QNX, a UNIX-like operating system that supports real-time processes. With the exception of

QNX proxies, we'll use only those features that are POSIX compliant. This means that the operating system could be replaced with another POSIX-compliant operating system.

The size of the memory is limited. Due to budget limitations, it is not likely to be increased. Operating system processes consume software resources such as memory, so too many active processes can degrade system performance. However, it is relatively inexpensive to create and to destroy processes on the selected operating system. Thus let's create a new issue card, for Resource Limitations, and add to it the strategy *Limit the number of active processes*.

Resource Limitations

To provide support for meeting the real-time processing requirements, a UNIX-like operating system that supports real-time processes is selected. The platform elements are processes, timers, shared memory buffers, and queues. It is relatively inexpensive to create and to destroy processes. Also, there are a fixed number of resources, such as sockets and timers.

The architecture design must cope with the limitations of these hardware and software resources. The strategies should provide guidance for making design choices that cope with resource limitations and make it easy to adapt the system when these limitations change.

Influencing Factors

T1.3: The size of the memory is limited. It is not likely to change drastically due to budget limitations.

T3.2: Operating system processes also consume software resources such as memory. Too many active processes may degrade system performance. However, it is relatively inexpensive to create and to destroy processes on the selected operating system.

Solution

Use a flexible approach for the usage of limited resources.

Strategy: *Limit the number of active processes*.

If memory requirements of active processes cause performance degradation, consider limiting the number of active processes that can run at the same time. We need to terminate and restart processes in this case. This is acceptable due to the low cost of process creation and destruction.

6.2.2   Central Design Tasks: Runtime Entities, Communication Paths, and Configuration

With the global analysis under way, let's turn to the central design tasks of the execution architecture view: defining runtime entities, communication paths, and configuration. As with the central design tasks of the conceptual and module views, these can't be done in a strict sequential order. Although there is potential feedback among many other analysis and design tasks, these central design tasks are even more tightly coupled.

In this section the central design tasks for portions of the example system are presented. You'll see how the results of one task feed back into the other immediate tasks, and sometimes into tasks in the other architecture views.

Begin Defining Runtime Entities

A good starting point for the central design tasks is to begin by associating each high-level conceptual component with a set of execution elements. In the case of the example system, let's avoid multithreaded processes if possible and, instead, put each thread in its own process. Thus we begin by drawing the picture shown in Figure 6.5. This shows the main conceptual components as sets of processes, and shows the main communication paths between them.

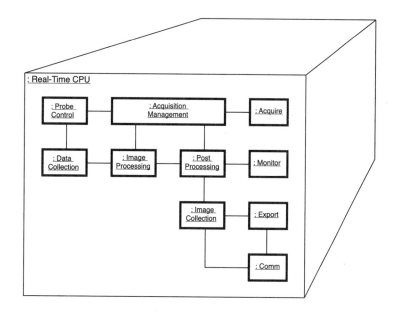

Figure 6.5. Overview of execution architecture view

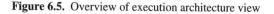

In Figure 6.5 we used a UML Deployment Diagram to show on which hardware resource these sets of processes will run. The hardware resource, in this case the real-time CPU, is shown as a node instance.

Next let's take each of these sets of processes in turn and go through the central design tasks for each. Let's start with the higher risk parts of the system first. For the example system, the ImageProcessing component is the computationally expensive part of the real-time portion of the system, so it should be examined early in the execution view design. In the rest of this chapter, we use the ImageProcessing component to explain the execution view design.

The heart of the ImageProcessing component, as we defined it in the conceptual view (Figure 4.6), is the ImagePipeline. In the module view we mapped the conceptual elements to modules and determined the decomposition relationships and use-dependencies. Figure 6.6 summarizes these relationships.

Although the imaging subsystem may contain many pipelines, they all follow the same pattern, so let's use just one to illustrate the design tasks. Recall that in the module view we mapped the first pipeline stage to MFramer and each of the later pipeline stages to a separate module, for example MImager. In this chapter we use MImager as a placeholder for the multiple, later stages that may be part of the pipeline.

We know that all modules in Figure 6.6 have to be mapped to a runtime element. There's no fixed rule for how to do this, but the approach we use here is a common one: We start with the assignments that are most straightforward, then let those decisions constrain the later assignments.

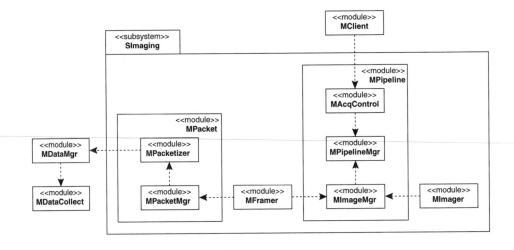

Figure 6.6. Modules in the imaging subsystem (from the module view)

When there is a simple one-to-one correspondence between conceptual components and modules in Table 5.2, we assign a module to a process or a thread. This is a straight-forward implementation of the concurrency expressed by the conceptual view. Because of the strategy *Map independent threads of control to processes*, let's create separate processes for each of the pipeline stages, and for the image pipeline client (MClient) and the data collector (MDataCollect).

Next let's examine the dependencies among these modules to determine the resulting communication paths and mechanisms between the processes. First let's look at the communication between the image pipeline client and the imaging subsystem. This takes place through MAcqControl. The MClient module accesses the MAcqControl module to initiate and to control the image pipelines. If MClient and MAcqControl were in different processes, they would have to communicate across process boundaries. Instead, let's link all of the MAcqControls into the process with MClient so communication is via a local procedure call.

These four processes are shown in Figure 6.7. We use a UML stereotyped class for a runtime entity, so these have the stereotype <<process>>. Because a process has a thread of control, it is modeled as an active class, which has a thick border. The modules assigned to each process are nested inside it. The EClient process contains module MClient and multiple MAcqControl modules, one for each image pipeline. Let's use UML multiplicities to show this, and use the convention that the multiplicity is 1 when none is shown. Thus the asterisk in the upper right corner of MAcqControl indicates that there are zero or more of this type of module linked to EClient.

Pipeline Manager

This brings us to the communication between individual pipeline stages, where performance is a major concern. We don't yet have any strategies that address this in the issue Real-Time Acquisition Performance. Because shared memory is available on our operating system, let's use it for sharing images between pipeline stages. This is a new strategy, so we need to add it to the issue card.

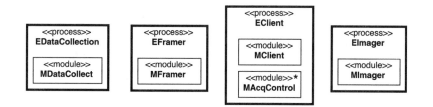

Figure 6.7. Initial processes for the imaging subsystem

Real-Time Acquisition Performance *(continued)*

Strategy: *Use shared memory to communicate between pipeline stages.*

Use shared memory between pipeline stages to eliminate any unnecessary data copying in the acquisition and processing pipelines.

In the module view, the responsibility for managing the image buffers was assigned to module MPipelineMgr. Shared memory is a runtime element—something that is visible to and managed by the operating system—so let's split the MPipelineMgr module into two parts: one for the management of the shared memory pipeline and another for the shared memory itself.

Next we have to go back and revise the module view, splitting the MPipelineMgr module into two modules: one called MPipelineControl for the image pipeline control and one called MImageBuffer for the image pipeline buffer. MPipelineControl coordinates the pipeline by controlling access to the shared memory MImageBuffer. These revisions are shown in Figure 6.8.

Next let's map these new modules to runtime entities. We could replicate the control module and link it to each process containing a pipeline stage. Because MPipelineControl coordinates the pipeline stages, this would force it to use a distributed control algorithm.

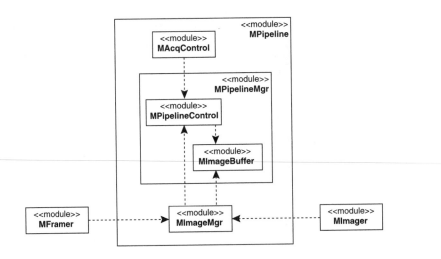

Figure 6.8. Revisions to the module view: MPipelineMgr

Distributed control requires a more complex handshaking protocol than centralized control, and because here the communication is between processes, distributed control is also more costly.

A simpler solution is to centralize pipeline control in a single process, separate from the pipeline stage processes. Because each image pipeline has its own manager, and active image pipelines run concurrently, each MPipelineMgr must be in a separate process. Thus let's create a new process, called EPipelineMgr, that contains MPipelineControl. Although it controls access to the shared memory area MImageBuffer, it does not read or write to MImageBuffer, so there is no communication path between them in the execution view.

Communication Paths for the Pipeline Manager

With the pipeline manager mapped to a separate process, let's use IPC for its communication with MAcqControl because the modules are in different processes. The same is true for communication between the MFramer and MImager modules and MPipelineControl.

This introduces a new technological factor, so we need to return to the global analysis to add this factor and analyze its impact. The use of IPC mechanisms requires resources such as sockets or mailboxes. Such resources are limited on a real-time operating system, so we may need to adjust our usage during development. Table 6.1 shows the new factor.

Technological Factor	Flexibility and Changeability	Impact
T3: Software technology		
T3.4: Interprocess communication (IPC) mechanism		
Use of IPC mechanisms requires resources such as sockets or mailboxes. Such resources may be limited on a real-time operating system.	These resource limitations are often based on memory size. Because memory size is not expected to change during development, the limitation is not likely to change. The IPC mechanism is likely to change every five years.	The impact on components is moderate at the process boundary. We may need to develop an approach to deal with the limitation. A change in IPC mechanism can have a large impact on design.

Table 6.1. Factor Added During Execution View Design

Because it uses other resources, we need to add this factor to the Resource Limitations issue card. Now we also need a strategy that addresses the resource limitations for IPC connections, so let's add a new strategy:

Resource Limitations *(continued)*

Strategy: *Use dynamic interprocess communication (IPC) connections.*

Make use of dynamic IPC connections between processes when possible. In this way, limited IPC resources such as sockets are used only when the processes are communicating. This strategy may degrade overall performance if the cost of creating and destroying IPC connections is too high.

Next let's apply the strategy *Encapsulate multiprocess support facilities* to reduce the burden of using IPC. As a result, we need to create a new module, called MCommLib (communication library), to handle the details of the IPC protocol. This module is linked to the processes EFramer, EImager, EClient, and EPipelineMgr, but to enhance readability it is not shown in the diagrams. Of course, this module must also be added to the module view.

The decisions we've made so far appear in Figure 6.9. We've used the UML association notation (a solid line) for communication paths. These are labeled to show the type of communication. Note that EImageBuffer, the shared data area, doesn't have a thread of control, so it doesn't have the thick border that the active classes have.

We should also consider resource-sharing policies and protocols. The MImageBuffer module, the shared memory for an image pipeline, is shared among the stages for that pipeline. Let's split the shared memory into multiple logical buffers, one for each stage in the pipeline. A pipeline stage has exclusive access (read and write access) to one of these logical buffers, and MPipelineControl controls this exclusive access.

These logical buffers must also be "passed" down the pipeline, and the pipeline stages initiate this transfer by requesting a new buffer, which also releases the old one. The MPipelineControl module accepts requests first come first served. The MPipelineControl module, because it knows the configuration of the pipeline, determines which buffer is to be allocated to the requesting stage. If the buffer is available, access is granted immediately. Otherwise, it continues to service new requests and releases buffers to pending requests as the buffers become available.

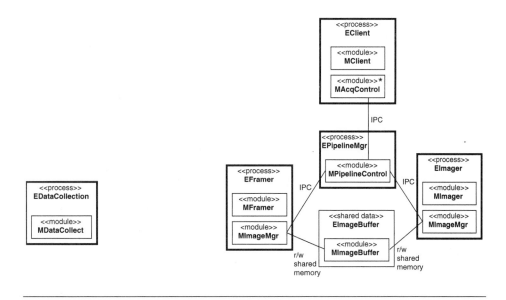

Figure 6.9. Processes and communication paths for the pipeline manager. IPC = interprocess communication; r/w = read/write.

Assigning Multiplicities to the Execution Configuration

Next we come to the question of exactly how many processes we expect to have at runtime. This is part of the configuration design task.

Because each image pipeline contains approximately 4 pipeline stages, and there are at least 10 image pipelines, the pipelines alone could use more than 40 processes. The strategy *Limit the number of active processes* indicates that, because of memory limitations and performance requirements, we can't keep all of these alive for all types of acquisitions and monitoring. The processes for an image pipeline must be created dynamically when the acquisition procedure is requested, and then they must be destroyed when the acquisition is complete.

For systems in which the configuration is fixed, it can be described in a single diagram. But you can also describe a set of configurations in a single diagram, as we did in the conceptual view. For IS2000's execution configuration, let's describe in one diagram all possible configurations of the imaging subsystem during normal operating mode.

Some of the processes have only one runtime instance and exist throughout the lifetime of the system. So far this includes only EClient and EDataCollection. In the configuration diagram (Figure 6.10), these processes have a multiplicity of 1, which is shown in the upper right-hand corner of the EClient and EDataCollection processes.

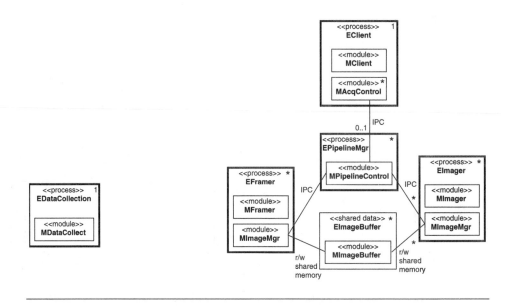

Figure 6.10. Adding multiplicities to the execution configuration for IS2000

Linked into the EClient process are multiple MAcqControl modules, one for each image pipeline that could be created during system execution. Each MAcqControl module creates an EPipelineMgr process, passing to it configuration information for the image pipeline. The MAcqControl module also configures the shared memory for its associated image pipeline.

The EPipelineMgr process in turn creates the pipeline stages. It launches a process for the stage, and binds the stage to the process group by putting it into the correct stage of the pipeline and giving it access to shared memory. We've used a UML Sequence Diagram to show this pipeline start-up (Figure 6.11). The objects in the diagram are runtime instances, and their vertical positions show the order in which they come into being. By looking at the line below each object, you can see its lifetime and the messages it sends. Active objects have a solid line, and passive objects, like the EImageBuffer shared memory, have a dotted line.

The imaging subsystem contains multiple EPipelineMgr processes, one for each image pipeline. Each image pipeline contains exactly one EImageBuffer, one EFramer process, and one or more additional EImager processes. These multiplicity relationships are summarized in Figure 6.10.

In a configuration diagram, the communication paths also have multiplicities. These are marked at each end of the communication path. If no multiplicity is shown, it is understood that it is 1.

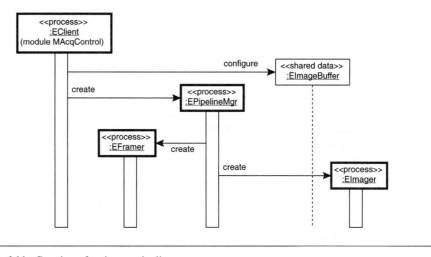

Figure 6.11. Creation of an image pipeline

Marking multiplicities on the communication paths constrains the configuration, so we must figure out how many of each process can exist relative to another. For example, there is exactly one EClient process, and it contains multiple MAcqControl modules. There are multiple EPipelineMgr processes, each containing exactly one MPipelineControl module. Next let's put multiplicities on the path between MAcqControl and MPipelineControl to show that each MPipelineControl communicates with exactly one MAcqControl, and each MAcqControl communicates with either zero or one MPipelineControl modules. The result of this constraint is that at any point in time there is at most one EPipelineMgr process for each MAcqControl module linked to the EClient.

EFramer and EImager both have a multiplicity of "*," which says only that there is zero or more of each of them. But by looking at the multiplicities on their communication paths, you can see that there is one EFramer and multiple EImager processes per pipeline.

Packetizer

Next let's look at the process for the Packetizer component, which passes data from the probe data collector (MDataCollect) to all existing image pipelines. In the module view we implemented its functionality with the MPacketizer module.

Again we must consider real-time performance constraints, so let's apply the strategy *Use shared memory to communicate between pipeline stages*, as we did for the image data within the image pipeline. Although the data is different, it is a very similar situation, in that the probe data is shared among multiple processes.

So we follow similar reasoning, and split the MPacketizer module into two modules: one for data control (MPacketControl) and one for the data buffer (MPacketBuffer). To keep the control algorithm simple, let's create a separate process—EPacketizer—for MPacketControl. Next we must add this to the list of processes that have only one runtime instance and that exist throughout the lifetime of the system.

The MPacketControl module controls access to the shared memory MPacketBuffer. This shared memory is written to by the EDataCollection process and it is read by the first pipeline stage of each image pipeline. MPacketControl must accept interrupts from EDataCollection as the probe data becomes available, and it must handle read requests from the image pipelines. These new modules must be added to the module view (Figure 6.12).

Communication between these processes is via IPC and shared memory. As before, the communication paths are derived from the dependencies shown in the module view. The resulting communication paths are shown in Figure 6.13.

However, access requirements for the shared memory MPacketBuffer are different than for MImageBuffer. Here we need to organize the shared memory into a queue of logical buffers. Buffers are queued by the probe data collector, but a buffer is dequeued only after all image pipelines have read it. The pipelines can read buffers concurrently, but MDataCollect must have exclusive access to a buffer in order to write. The MPacketControl module must enforce this protocol and ensure that each image pipeline receives the buffers in the correct sequence.

This protocol information is part of the definition of the communication path between EPacketizer and its users. A UML Sequence Diagram can be useful for showing this kind

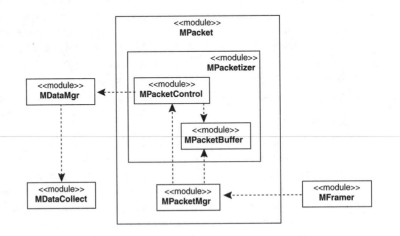

Figure 6.12. Revisions to the module view: MPacketizer

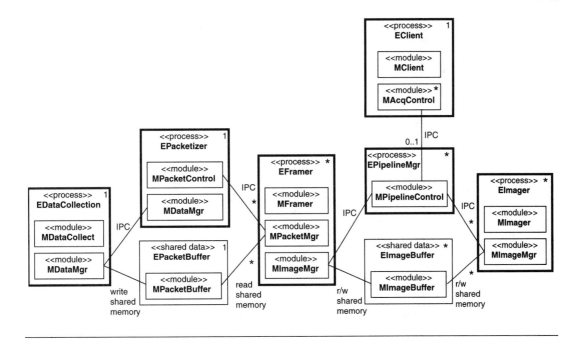

Figure 6.13. Final execution configuration for the imaging subsystem of IS2000. IPC = interprocess communication; r/w = read/write.

of protocol information. These diagrams are limited in that they can only describe a particular sequence rather than a more general pattern of repeated interactions; but often, an example of an interaction is very useful in communicating the protocol, as in this case for the interaction between EPacketizer and the other processes (Figure 6.14).

Now we have finished the central design tasks for the imaging subsystem. Only resource allocation remains.

6.2.3 Final Design Task: Resource Allocation

For the resource allocation task we need to use the global analysis results to allocate resources to the execution configuration. First we must allocate a slice of the CPU to each process by giving it a time budget and priority. Then we need to make decisions about how to allocate other limited resources (for example, address space, memory pool, timers, proxies, ports) to each process.

There are two global analysis strategies that are relevant to allocating processing time to each process. Initially we planned to use one CPU, with all processes assigned to this processor. After the configuration was complete, we applied the strategy *Use RMA to*

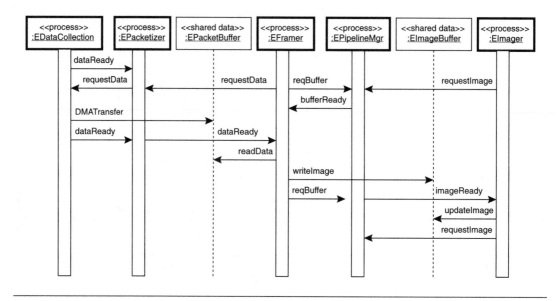

Figure 6.14. An example of EPacketizer's and EPipelineMgr's interactions. DMA = direct memory access.

predict performance, and discovered that the existing architecture design did not meet the real-time performance requirements. We had anticipated this possibility with the strategy *Use an additional CPU*, which we now apply.

Feedback to the Central Design Tasks

With the introduction of an additional processor, we have to redefine the hardware topology and decide how to assign processes to processors. We do this by returning to the diagram in Figure 6.5, which shows the initial sets of processes in the execution view.

The original CPU will handle the real-time processing, and the second CPU, which does not have a real-time operating system, will handle the applications and GUI. We can refine this partitioning by reexamining the processes and explicitly mapping them to processors. Figure 6.15 shows the first step: partitioning the initial sets of processes across the two CPUs.

We also need to introduce a hardware link, define the communication paths between the CPUs, and select the appropriate communication mechanisms. IPC can be encapsulated in the high-level MCommLib module we introduced earlier to handle the details of the IPC protocol.

Data that was passed from the image pipeline to the applications now has to be transferred between processors. One way to accomplish this is to introduce a data transfer ser-

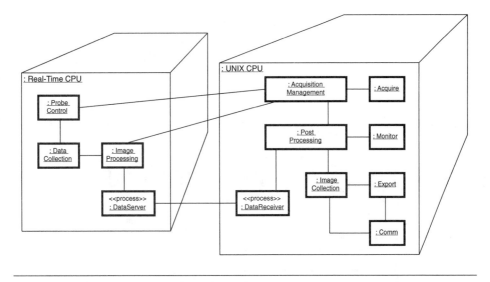

Figure 6.15. Overview of execution architecture view with two CPUs

vice. Such a service reads image buffers coming from the pipeline and sends them to the client running on a different processor.

Adding a data transfer service means introducing new modules to send and receive data between CPUs. We can put each of these in their own process or perhaps combine the data receiver with the client.

Now let's return to the execution configuration diagram and update it to show how it is mapped to the two processors (Figure 6.16). The EClient process is part of acquisition management, so it is mapped to the UNIX CPU. All the other processes in the imaging subsystem stay on the real-time CPU. The communication path between EClient and EPipelineMgr must be reexamined: Let's now use RPC because the path is between processors.

An important difference between these last two figures is that Figure 6.15 shows runtime instances on a particular machine and Figure 6.16 shows runtime entities on a type of machine. We used runtime entities for the second figure so we could describe in a single diagram how all image pipelines are structured. This is similar to the conceptual view, when we didn't want to draw a separate instance diagram for each possible image pipeline. The runtime instance information is better represented in a table than in diagrams.

You may have noticed that the multiplicities on this communication path are not the same as in Figure 6.13. This has nothing to do with the split across two CPUs. The multiplicity is different because in Figure 6.13 we show the communication path between the modules mapped to these processes, and in Figure 6.16 we show it between the processes themselves. There are multiple MAcqControl modules in EClient, and each of these com-

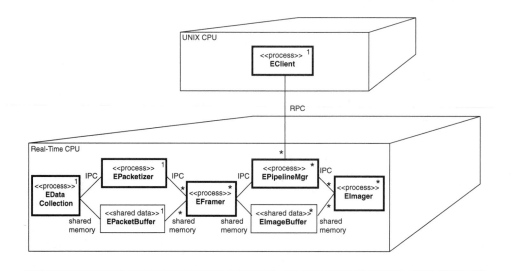

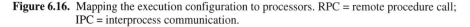

Figure 6.16. Mapping the execution configuration to processors. RPC = remote procedure call; IPC = interprocess communication.

municates with at most one EPipelineMgr. So EClient communicates with multiple (zero or more) EPipelineMgr processes.

Memory and Other Processing Resources

The total amount of memory we have to work with is 64MB. The packetizer and pipeline manager are the biggest memory users. Both use memory to implement buffers as circular queues. To simplify the algorithms for reading the buffers, they acquire memory as contiguous blocks, preallocated based on worst-case conditions.

For the pipeline manager, the size of the image buffer is dependent on the type of application. The number of buffers is typically one more than the number of pipeline stages. Buffers are preallocated to improve performance. Shared memory is shared only among the stages within a processing pipeline.

For the packetizer, the size of the packet buffer is important because it affects throughput and response time. If it is too large and the data arrival rate is low, then the transfer of buffers will be slow because a buffer has to fill before it is transferred. In this case there may be perceptible delays in the screen update. If the buffers are too small, CPU time is wasted servicing interrupts too frequently. Let's assign an initial size based on experience, and fine-tune the estimate as we analyze performance.

Some of the resources are not adequate for our needs, but we can design a system support service that extends the resource to meet the requirements. For example, the UNIX platform supports one real-time interval timer per executing process. The system time-out support requires capabilities beyond those services offered by the software platform. We can extend the capabilities by providing a timer service that allows users to create one or more concurrent timers and is easy to use: Users need not have platform-specific knowledge about signal handling and blocking.

6.2.4 Design Summary for IS2000 Execution View

When the design of the execution view is finished, we want to have made the implementation decisions for the dynamic aspects of the system, building in flexibility when we think it is needed. To accomplish this we first identified the runtime elements of the software platform, such as processes and threads. Then we related the conceptual components and modules to these runtime elements, first using a one-to-one mapping to get an approximation of the process boundaries, and then refining the process boundaries as the design progressed. Table 6.2 summarizes the design decisions discussed in this chapter.

Design Decision	Rationale
Global analysis	
Add a new issue: High Throughput.	The probe hardware has a very high data rate. Strategy: *Avoid use of multiple threads.*
Add strategies to the issue Real-Time Acquisition Performance: *Use flexible allocation of modules to processes. Develop guidelines for module behavior. Use rate monotonic analysis to predict performance.*	Strategy: *Map independent threads of control to processes.* Strategy: *Use an additional CPU.*
Add a new issue: Resource Limitations.	Strategy: *Map independent threads of control to processes.*
Begin defining runtime entities	
Each pipeline stage (e.g., EFramer, EImager) is a process. EClient is a process. EDataCollection is a process.	If there's a one-to-one correspondence between a conceptual component and a module, put the module in its own thread of control. Strategy: *Map independent threads of control to processes.*

Table 6.2. Sequence of Design Decisions for IS2000 Execution View

Design Decision	Rationale
Link MAcqControl to the client process.	Simplify the client's responsibility.
Pipeline manager	
Add new strategy to the issue Real-Time Acquisition Performance: *Use shared memory to communicate between pipeline stages.*	There is a high volume of data and real-time performance requirements.
Split MPipelineMgr into two modules—one for processing (MPipeline-Control) and one for data (MImageBuffer). Revise module view.	Shared memory is supported directly by the operating system.
Centralize pipeline control in a single process: EPipelineMgr. There is one EPipelineMgr per pipeline.	Keep the control algorithm simple.
Communication paths for the pipeline manager	
EPipelineMgr communicates with the pipeline stages via interprocess communication (IPC).	Use available technology.
Add a new technological factor, T3.4: IPC mechanism. Add a new strategy to the issue Resource Limitations: *Use dynamic IPC connections.*	Use IPC.
Introduce a new module (MCommLib) to provide higher level support for IPC.	Strategy: *Encapsulate multiprocess support facilities.*
Assigning multiplicities to the execution configuration	
Runtime entities for an image pipeline (EFramer, EPipelineMgr, EImage-Buffer, EImager) are created dynamically when the acquisition procedure is requested.	Strategy: *Limit the number of active processes.*

Table 6.2. Sequence of Design Decisions for IS2000 Execution View *(continued)*

Design Decision	Rationale
Packetizer	
The packetizer (EPacketizer) communicates with the pipeline (EFramer) via IPC, and transfers data via shared memory (EPacketBuffer).	Strategy: *Use shared memory to communicate between pipeline stages.*
One process for the packetizer (EPacketizer). One packetizer in the system.	Keep the control algorithm simple.
Resource allocation	
Introduce an additional CPU because performance is inadequate.	Strategy: *Use rate monotonic analysis to predict performance.* Strategy: *Use an additional CPU.*
Determine optimal image buffer sizes.	This depends on the number of pipeline stages in the acquisition procedure.
Determine optimal packet buffer size.	This depends on the data rate of probe hardware.
Preallocate a buffer from contiguous memory.	Keep the algorithm for accessing buffers simple.

Table 6.2. Sequence of Design Decisions for IS2000 Execution View *(continued)*

6.3 Summary of Execution Architecture View

The execution view describes the mapping of functionality to physical resources, and the runtime characteristics of the system. Table 6.3 summarizes the elements, relations, and artifacts to be used in this view. As in the other views, the elements and relations are the building blocks for the architecture view, and the artifacts are used to document or to describe the architecture.

The execution configuration describes how the runtime entities are instantiated as runtime instances, and describes the communication between runtime instances over the life of the system. A system usually has a different configuration at start-up and shutdown than it does during its normal operation. Sometimes a system has a configuration that changes throughout its lifetime.

Element	UML Element	New Stereotype	Notation	Attributes	Associated Behavior
Runtime entity	Process	—	<< ... >>	Host type, replication, resource allocation	—
	Thread	—			
	Class or active class	<<shared data>>, <<task>>, etc.			
Communication path	Association	—	————	—	Communication protocol

Relation	UML Element	Notation	Description
use mechanism	Association name	Name of communication mechanism; for example, IPC, RPC	A communication path uses a communication mechanism.
communicate over	—	□— (connection of class and association)	A runtime entity (or the module assigned to it) communicates over a communication path.
assigned to	Composition	Nesting (or ↑)	A module is assigned to zero or more runtime entities.

Artifact	Representation
Execution configuration	UML Class Diagram
Execution configuration mapped to hardware devices	UML Deployment Diagram
Dynamic behavior of configuration, or transition between configurations	UML Sequence Diagram
Description of runtime entities (including host type, replication, and assigned modules)	Table or UML Class Diagram

Table 6.3. Summary of Execution Architecture View

Description of runtime instances (including resource allocation)	Table
Communication protocol	Natural language description, or UML Sequence Diagram or State-chart Diagram
IPC = interprocess communication; RPC = remote procedure call; UML = Unified Modeling Language.	

Table 6.3. Summary of Execution Architecture View *(continued)*

The meta-model in Figure 6.17 shows the basic elements used in the execution view, and how they are related to the physical resources and to the modules from the module view. The basic elements are runtime entities and their communication paths. A module is assigned to zero or more runtime entities, and a runtime entity can have multiple modules assigned to it. Each runtime entity is mapped to exactly one platform element.

The runtime entities communicate with each other over communication paths. A communication path uses a particular communication mechanism, which in turn may consume additional platform elements.

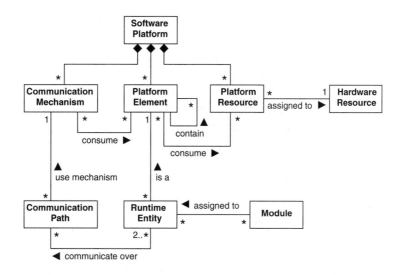

Figure 6.17. Meta-model of the execution architecture view

6.3.1 Traceability

Describing the relationships of the execution view to requirements, external factors, and the other architecture views provides traceability. The following three items should be traceable in the execution view:

1. *Critical requirements and organizational and technological factors.* Traceability between design decisions for the execution view and organizational, technological, and product factors helps you determine whether your design meets the requirements. It also helps you determine the impact of changes on requirements or factors.

2. *Elements in the module view.* To implement modules correctly, developers must know how they are mapped to elements of the execution view.

3. *Elements in the conceptual view.* Traceability between conceptual components and execution view elements can be done directly, or through the modules. In the case study of Chapter 8, traceability is used to determine the correctness of the automatically generated code. More commonly, it helps you determine whether the implementation is correct.

Looking ahead to the code architecture view, there is a correspondence between elements (for example, runtime components) in the code architecture view and the runtime elements in the execution view for the purpose of system building.

6.3.2 Uses for the Execution Architecture View

The execution view is used by

- Architects, to design the runtime aspects of the system so that it meets the requirements and can adapt to expected changes
- Developers, to provide a correct implementation
- Testers, who need to know the runtime aspects of the system to plan the testing (particularly unit testing)
- Maintainers, to determine how a change in the runtime platform affects the system or how changes in requirements affect the system's runtime aspects

Additional Reading

When systems become distributed, developers need to consider dynamic structure and communication, coordination, and synchronization. A number of interconnection languages have been introduced that address the issue of allocating components in a distributed environment. These include those cited by Barbacci, Weinstock, and Wing (1988); Magee, Dulay, and Kramer (1994); Purtilo (1994); and Royce (1990). These issues are addressed in the execution architecture view.

Hatley and Pirbhai (1988) and Schmidt and Suda (1993) emphasize the need for separate module and execution views and providing flexible assignment of modules to runtime elements.

Shaw et al. (1995) introduce a connector for real-time scheduling in their language for universal connector support (UniCon). Given the priority and period information, it is sufficient to schedule the processes. If the scheduling policy is set to rate monotonic, then UniCon can package the trace, period, execution time, and priority information and transmit it to the analysis tool for scheduling analysis.

Chatterjee et al. (1997) present a systems engineering tool kit for the design and analysis of real-time systems. This toolset was applied to the Healthy Vision case study, in which information from the execution architecture was used as input to the toolset to evaluate performance properties of the system.

Nord and Cheng (1994) use RMA (Klein et al., 1993) to evaluate the performance properties of a real-time system based on the execution architecture, and they demonstrate how this provides feedback to the architecture design decisions.

Kazman et al. (1999) have extended the work on SAAM to evaluate other quality attributes of a system such as performance and availability based on structures from the execution architecture view.

Chapter 7

Code
Architecture View

The code architecture view describes how the software implementing the system is organized. In this view, source components implement individual elements in the module view, and deployment components (for example, executables, libraries, and configuration files) in this view instantiate runtime entities in the execution view. The code architecture view describes how these components are related to each other through intermediate components, and how all of them are organized according to an organization's particular development environment. Lastly, this view describes the design decisions related to configuration management, multiple releases, and testing. Such decisions affect the effectiveness of the development team because of their impact on, for example, the turnaround time for the edit-compile-test cycle. The primary goal of the code architecture view is to facilitate the construction, integration, installation, and testing of the system while respecting the integrity of the other three architecture views.

By isolating the construction and development aspects of the system in a separate code architecture view, you can make the system more flexible. In the code architecture view you describe how a module, its interfaces, and its dependencies are mapped to language-specific components and dependencies. Such mappings and conventions can vary with the programming language, so by having a separate code architecture view, you can make the module and execution views independent of the programming language. In the code architecture view you also describe how source components and intermediate libraries are released to other teams for integration and testing, and describe how much of a module's functionality is implemented in each release. Because these decisions will change during and after development, it is important to design the code architecture view to make these kinds of changes easier.

Designing the code architecture view is straightforward when there is only one executable and a small development team. In this case, its structure will probably reflect the structure of the module view. However, when there are multiple executables, shared components, a large development team, or concurrent development, the code architecture view becomes more complex and usually diverges from the module and execution views. For example, as you design module implementations, you will discover opportunities to reuse code-level units, which often turn into new modules.

The code architecture view organizes code components to support

- Daily concurrent development tasks of developers (for example, edit, compile, build, and test)
- Constructing or building parts of the system and releasing them to different teams for installation, integration, and testing
- Ease of maintenance or change
- Enforcement of architectural design decisions such as encapsulation, abstraction, and allowed dependencies
- Configuration management of different versions of the system, including managing the versions of modules used to build different versions of the system

A good design of the code architecture view preserves architecture design decisions, streamlines development activities, and integrates smoothly with the development environment.

The module and the execution views are the inputs to the design of the code architecture view. The driving forces behind its design are the implementation language, development tools, development environment, and development process.

7.1   Design Activities for the Code Architecture View

Before describing how to design the code architecture view for the example system, we give an overview of the various design tasks. Figure 7.1 summarizes the code architecture design tasks and their relations to each other.

For the global analysis task you identify and review the inputs to the design process. These include the factors and strategies that influence the code architecture view. The goal is to develop strategies specifically for constructing the system and building in flexibility.

During the central design tasks you organize the source components, intermediate components (for example, object files and static libraries), and deployment components (for example, executables and dynamic libraries), making explicit their relationship to elements in the module and execution views. You evaluate your decisions continually with respect to the criteria and strategies established during the global analysis phase.

During the final design task you make detailed decisions related to the build procedures and configuration management, so that they support the decisions made during the central design tasks.

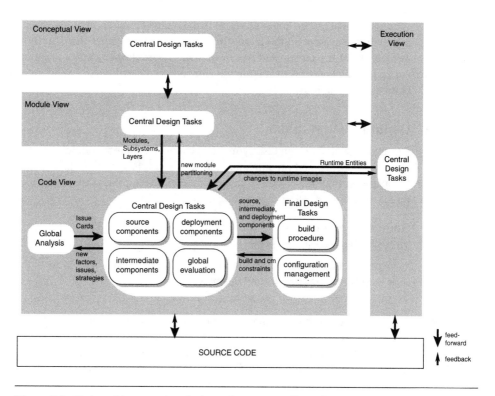

Figure 7.1. Code architecture view design tasks. cm = configuration management.

7.1.1 Global Analysis

You begin the global analysis for the code architecture view by reviewing the global analyses performed for the module and execution views. Review the factors and strategies to see whether they put additional requirements or constraints on the design of this view. Then, develop strategies to address these requirements or constraints. Consider factors related to the development platform, development environment, development process, and development schedule. For the development environment, you may want to list the capabilities of various tools. Pay particular attention to configuration management, and think about whether it is necessary or feasible to do cross-platform development. For the development process, identify the process and the testing requirements. With the development schedule, analyze whether the product will be released in stages, whether there are internal releases, and whether developers and testers will be working on multiple releases concurrently. Identify whether multiple versions of components will be developed, and note the commonalities and differences among them.

Also, consider the target platform and the target environment. Analyze the support for installing the system on the target platform. Analyze whether there are limitations on the availability of the target platform or hardware. Develop strategies to guide the design of the code architecture view, taking advantage of the development environment while overcoming its limitations.

7.1.2 Central Design Tasks

During the central design tasks you map elements from the module and execution views to code components, and organize them according to the criteria established during the global analysis. Figure 7.2 shows the meta-model for the basic elements of the code architecture view and the relationships among them.

Source Components

To design the source components, you

- Identify source components and map elements and dependencies from the module view to the source components and dependencies

- Organize the source components using storage structures such as directories or files

    Typically you have source components for language-specific interfaces and modules or for components that generate them. For languages such as C and C++, language-specific interfaces are files with names like *.h, *.H, whereas language-specific modules have names like *.c and *.CPP. For languages like Ada, the source components are package specification and package implementation.

    Source components are related to each other by two kinds of language-specific dependencies. A source component may need to import another source component for a successful compilation. This "import" relation is a compile-time dependency between the two. An include dependency between a source file and a header file in C++ is an example of an import dependency. The second type of dependency—generate—applies when a source component is generated from another source component (for example, by preprocessing).

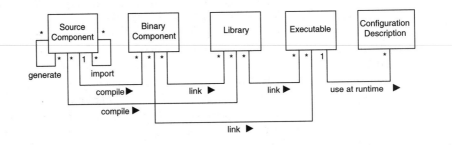

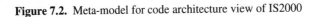

Figure 7.2. Meta-model for code architecture view of IS2000

Elements from the module view are mapped to the language-specific source components that implement them. In a simple mapping in C++, the interface provided by a module is mapped to a .H file, and the code implementing it is mapped to a .CPP file. For large systems implemented in C or C++, code size and compilation time are usually important issues. For reducing code size, a common solution is to distribute the code defining an interface over several .H files so that common definitions can be reused. Some compilers allow header files to be precompiled, which may improve the compilation time.

For larger, more complex modules, you may want to distribute the implementation code across several files for easier editing and rebuilding, or for reusing existing source components. In exceptional cases, implementation code for several tightly coupled modules can be combined into one file to improve performance. You shouldn't consider this alternative except for very time-critical modules, because the larger files can degrade the time of an edit-compile-link cycle.

After you have identified source components, the next activity is to organize them so they can be developed and tested by individual developers. Many development tools use a directory hierarchy to organize components in the code architecture view, whereas other development environments organize them in a database or a shared repository. For these approaches and any others, we use the UML package hierarchy to describe how components are organized in the code architecture view.

For a simple system with only a few modules, this organization can be very easy. You may decide to organize the components based on criteria such as similarity of functionality (for example, GUI components) or developer responsibility.

For a larger system with concurrent development, you need to consider additional issues such as ease of accessing interface components, or organizing related source components such as test drivers and test data. You need to support the release process for your system, including partial releases.

You should also consider the time for an edit-compile-link cycle. This time depends on your language and the development tools, and on the organization of source components. For systems in which a build is measured in minutes, this is not a major concern. For systems in which a build is measured in hours or days, the organization of source components can affect productivity and cause schedule delays.

Intermediate Components

To design the intermediate components you

- Identify intermediate components, such as binary components and libraries, and their dependencies on source components and each other
- Organize them using storage structures, such as directories or files

Intermediate components are specific to the implementation language and the development environment. For example, for C++, each .CPP file has a corresponding binary component or .obj file. For a language such as Ada, the resulting binary components are compiled into one or more program libraries.

In Figure 7.2, binary components are intermediate components, and so are static libraries. The binary components are related to their respective source components by a compile dependency. Static libraries and binary components are related by a link dependency. Using static libraries can reduce link time because one unit is created for all binary components (for example, object files) linked to it.

You need to organize the intermediate components to facilitate sharing so that the time for an edit-compile-link cycle is reduced. Static libraries are one way to facilitate sharing, by grouping related binary components. For example, you may want to link components in a layer, producing one or more libraries for use by components in the higher layer.

Deployment Components

To design the deployment components, you

- Identify and map runtime entities and dependencies in the execution architecture view to deployment components and their dependencies
- Organize the deployment components

The deployment components are deployed at runtime to instantiate the runtime entities. They include executables, dynamic libraries, and configuration descriptions (Figure 7.2). A configuration description can describe processes and/or resources, such as storage for data and shared memory. Executables and dynamic libraries are related to binary components and static libraries by a link dependency. Executables are also related to the dynamic libraries by a link dependency. Using dynamically linked libraries can reduce your link-time dependencies and give you more flexibility to change implementations at a later date, but they also increase start-up time.

For a small system, the organization of deployment components can be very simple, requiring only a package or two containing files for an executable and its configuration descriptions. For a large, complex system with many executables, the organization can be very complex. For example, you may need to establish a separate file system for storage of data and for shared memory areas. You may want to separately organize each executable and associated components such as required resources and test data.

Global Evaluation

The code architecture view plays a very important role in the development activities. Its definition gets input from strategies in the global analysis, from design decisions in the module and execution architecture views, and from the development environment and execution platform. The major evaluation criteria are preserving the integrity of the architectural decisions, streamlining the development activities, and integrating smoothly with the development environment and external components. Other criteria are consistency, simplicity, and uniformity of your design decisions.

Global evaluation includes evaluating all design decisions against these criteria. You need to make or to reevaluate continually the trade-offs needed to satisfy the various evaluation criteria. Global evaluation may lead you to change decisions made in the module and execution views, and as changes are made to these views, be prepared to propagate them to the code architecture view.

As development proceeds, you should look for additional factors, issues, and strategies, and make adjustments in the organization of source and intermediate components to improve the edit-compile-link cycle time. You may need to partition or to combine header files. You also may need to reevaluate configuration management decisions as new developers join, responsibilities are reassigned, or the release schedule changes.

7.1.3 Final Design Tasks

During the final design tasks you add detail to the decisions made in the central design tasks. This phase involves two tasks:

1. **Build procedure**—Design the procedure for building and installing the intermediate and deployment components.

2. **Configuration management**—Determine design decisions related to management of versions and releases of components.

Build Procedure

During this task you design the procedure for building the system. The procedure is based on the components and dependencies identified during the centralized design tasks, the release process identified during the global analysis, and the design decisions related to configuration management.

Configuration Management

During this task you design how the versions and releases of components and the system are managed. Concurrent development implies that several versions of the components and systems are active or used at a time. A flexible configuration management environment can reduce the complexities of managing multiple versions of source code and intermediate releases of parts of the system. Such a system would allow you to define role-specific views of components and their organization, to be used by developers and testers of particular parts of the system.

7.2 Design of Code Architecture View for IS2000

Now that we have introduced the design tasks, let's return to the example system and show how to design its code architecture view.

7.2.1 Global Analysis

Let's first analyze those factors relevant to the code architecture view that have not yet been analyzed. Then we'll analyze these factors using the steps described in Chapter 3.

Review Global Analysis

Several strategies that we used earlier for other architecture views also have an impact on the code architecture view. The following strategies are useful here:

Issue: Easy Addition and Removal of Features
Strategy: *Separate components and modules along dimensions of concern.*
Strategy: *Encapsulate features into separate components.*

Issue: Real-Time Acquisition Performance
Strategy: *Use flexible allocation of modules to processes.*

Issue: Aggressive Schedule
Strategy: *Make it easy to add or remove features.*

The first two strategies encourage separation of components and modules along the dimensions of concern. We need to adapt this strategy of separation and apply it to the code architecture view as well. In particular, we need to design the components in the code architecture view so that they can be linked to different executables without modifying them. Otherwise the advantages of applying these strategies in other architecture views are lost.

The strategy *Use flexible allocation of modules to processes* implies that the modules assigned to processes or other runtime entities may change as the system is tuned for performance. The strategy *Make it easy to add or remove features* requires greater flexibility in the code architecture view because many of the features, such as acquisition procedures, make use of either the same modules or modules that implement the same interfaces. A new strategy that supports both is to separately organize the deployment components and the source components that are linked to them.

Analyze Factors

Table 7.1 summarizes the new organizational factors added for the code architecture view. The development will take place in a cross-platform environment with a mix of UNIX and real-time UNIX platforms (factor O3.1). The two development platforms offer different levels of tool support. Compiler features are also slightly different. Tool support on the real-time UNIX platforms is not as good as that on the UNIX platform.

The configuration management tool for the organization is ClearCase, which facilitates definition of a variety of roles (for example, developer and tester) and corresponding views on the code architecture (factor O3.2).

The release process calls for three internal releases with concurrent development, integration, and testing of several releases at a time (factor O3.3). The impact of this factor is moderate and requires the code architecture view to be flexible.

The testing process calls for three levels of testing: module testing to be performed by the module developer, integration testing at the level of subsystems and layers, and system testing at the product level (factor O3.4). The impact of this factor is moderate to large. The code architecture view must support builds for different types of testing.

Organizational Factor	Flexibility and Changeability	Impact
O3: Process and development environment		
O3.1: Development platform		
Use UNIX and real-time UNIX.	Components that use real-time features can only be developed on the real-time UNIX platform.	There is a moderate impact on the productivity for development of real-time features.
O3.2: Configuration management		
Facilitates a variety of roles and views of the code architecture.	There is a lot of flexibility.	Facilitates concurrent development and flexible releases of software components.
O3.3: Release process		
Three internal releases are required. Concurrent development, integration, and testing are also envisioned.	There is no flexibility.	The configuration management process and the code architecture view must be designed to support concurrent development and testing.
O3.4: Testing process		
Three levels of testing are required: module, integration, and system.	There is no flexibility.	There is a moderate impact on the configuration management process.

Table 7.1. Organizational Factors Added During Code Architecture View Design

Organizational Factor	Flexibility and Changeability	Impact
O4: Development schedule		
O4.3: Release schedule for probe hardware		
There is limited availability of probe hardware in the early stages of development.	The functionality supported by the probe prototype releases may change.	There is a large impact on the schedule and features for internal releases. There is a moderate impact on time-to-market.

Table 7.1. Organizational Factors Added During Code Architecture View Design *(continued)*

The release schedule for the probe hardware indicates its limited availability during the early stages of development (factor O4.3). The first probe prototype with limited functionality will be available only after six months, and then two additional probe prototypes will be available the following year. As more functionality is added to the probe hardware, the probe prototypes available for development will be upgraded. The functionality supported by the probe prototypes may change as development proceeds.

Table 7.2 contains the new technological factors added for the code architecture view. The implementation languages for the system are C and C++ (factor T3.5). For these languages, language-specific modules and interfaces are characterized by source (*.c or *.CPP) files and header (*.h or *.H) files. Module interfaces are mapped to one or more of the header files, and module implementations are mapped to source files. A large logical module may be split into several body files, and additional header files are used to define data types or classes that are shared among these files but are private to the module.

There are several coding conventions and techniques to improve the quality of code and to improve management of its development and change (factor T5.6).

Develop Strategies

As we review the analysis, we identify the following new issues:

Issue: Architectural Integrity

Architectural decisions and principles must be preserved and enforced in the code architecture. Their violation needs to be detectable.

Technological Factor	Flexibility and Changeability	Impact
T3: Software technology		
T3.5: Implementation language		
C and C++ will be the implementation languages.	There is no flexibility.	There is a moderate impact on module implementations.
T5: Standards		
T5.6: Coding conventions		
Standard coding and naming conventions are required. They have not yet been defined.	There is some flexibility.	There is a moderate impact on the organization and quality of source components.

Table 7.2. Technological Factors Added During Code Architecture View Design

Issue: Concurrent Development Tasks
Developers may be working concurrently on different component versions for multiple internal releases.

Issue: Limited Availability of Probe Prototypes
The limited availability of probe prototypes will adversely affect the developers' ability to test many components.

Issue: Multiple Development and Target Platforms
The use of multiple development and target platforms must be considered and facilitated.

Architectural Integrity

Architectural design decisions related to layering, encapsulation, abstraction, or separation of concerns can be violated in code. This eventually leads to degradation of the architecture. It is the architect's responsibility to ensure architectural integrity in code.

Influencing Factors

O3.2: The configuration management tool can be used to define restricted views of the code architecture view for predefined roles. This approach reduces degradation of the architecture.

T3.5: It is possible, though undesirable, to circumvent the module encapsulation and abstraction decisions through techniques such as inclusion of private header files and use of untyped conversions. Similarly, it is easy to create disallowed module dependencies. The decomposition of header files also has a significant impact on the time to execute the compile-link-test cycle.

T5.6: Standard coding conventions and techniques will be used. There is some flexibility in selecting, combining, or adding conventions.

Solution

Making architectural decisions explicit in the code can go a long way toward detecting violations. There is tension between the goal to make editing more convenient by reducing the number of header files and between reducing compile-time dependencies by separating header files into public and private ones.

Strategy: *Preserve module view hierarchies.*

Reflect module and layer hierarchies explicitly in the code architecture view by hierarchically mapping each layer and module into a separate package. This preserves previous decisions related to component separation, improves traceability between module and code architecture views, and thus makes violation of architectural decisions easier to detect. This also makes it easier to assign responsibility for particular modules and layers to a single person. Note that this strategy does not mean that the code architecture view should be made identical to the module architecture view.

Strategy: *Separate organization of public interface components.*

Organize public interface components in separate directories. In particular, create a public interface package for each layer and subsystem. This makes it easier to restrict the use of private header files through build scripts and search paths, thus enforcing certain architectural decisions such as encapsulation and abstraction, and detecting their violation.

Concurrent Development Tasks

Because there are three intermediate releases, the development team will be working on several versions of the source components simultaneously. While one version of a component is being released or tested, another version is being designed and developed. Using the wrong component version introduces expensive errors and schedule delays. Periodic intermediate builds can be used to detect and to correct errors as development proceeds for a particular release. It may become necessary to make changes to detailed definitions of interfaces or include files. Frequent changes to interfaces and implementations of commonly used modules require recompilation and relinking of the entire system, which slows down the development cycle. Implementation errors in commonly used modules also slow down the development and testing of the rest of the system.

Influencing Factors

O4.2: The development schedule for the delivery of features in various internal releases has a moderate impact on the code architecture view and the build process, and a moderate impact on change management and bug fixing of internal releases.

O3.4: The testing process calls for three levels of testing: module testing to be performed by the module developer; integration testing at the level of subsystems, layers, and system; and system testing at the product level. The impact of this factor is moderate to large. The code architecture view needs to support builds for different types of testing.

Continued

Concurrent Development Tasks *(continued)*

Solution

Make the different releases of source components transparent to developers, and organize the released deployment components to reflect the execution view.

Strategy: *Separate organization of deployment components from source components.*

Many of the acquisition procedures share pipeline stages and other modules, so the corresponding binary components are linked to many executables. By organizing the source components separately from the executables that use their derived binary components, we can support this.

Strategy: *Preserve execution view.*

Reflect the execution view explicitly in the code architecture view by putting each executable and shared resources into separate directories. This improves traceability between the execution and code architecture views, and facilitates the tasks of integration and testing.

Strategy: *Use phased development.*

Use phased development of the release version of a set of components (for example, in the OperatingSystem layer) to be one or two versions ahead of the release versions for the set of components using them. This shields individual developers from day-to-day changes made by other developers and minimizes their effect on the development cycle.

Strategy: *Release layers through static libraries.*

Release components in a layer linked to one or more separate static libraries to encapsulate changes and to improve linking performance.

Related Strategies

Use a flexible build procedure (issue, Limited Availability of Probe Prototypes) and *Make it easy to add or remove features* (issue, Aggressive Schedule).

Limited Availability of Probe Prototypes

Only a limited number of probe prototypes will be available during development. This decreases the time available for testing by individual developers or testers. It also limits the ability to test certain functionalities of components.

Influencing Factors

O3.2: The configuration management environment makes it possible to build executables with different releases of components.

O3.3: The development schedule calls for three internal releases.

O3.4: System testing requires the use of the probe hardware. Testing of acquisition procedures may need to be carried out before probe prototypes with sufficient functionality are available.

O4.3: The release schedule of the probe prototypes cannot promise sufficient functionality for initial releases of the software.

Solution

Use a probe simulator while the probe hardware is not available and create flexible build scripts to use the simulator transparently.

Strategy: *Develop an off-line probe simulator with an appropriate abstraction.*

It is necessary to reduce our dependence on the probe hardware for testing. Although the probe hardware is needed to test performance and throughput of image pipelines, their error-free operation can be tested without the hardware. By implementing an off-line probe simulator to act as a data source, we can check the functionality of various image-processing pipeline stages. Use an appropriate abstraction for this module so that executables and libraries are not affected.

Strategy: *Use a flexible build procedure.*

Use a flexible build procedure to build executables and libraries for off-line or on-line testing. Also use them to build different releases and to install deployment components.

Related Strategies

Separate and encapsulate code dependent on the target platform (issue, Multiple Development and Target Platforms).

Multiple Development and Target Platforms

There are at least two target CPUs and three development platforms. We need to take advantage of productivity tools.

Influencing Factors

T1.1, T1.2: The UNIX and real-time target platforms can share some executables. However, executables that use real-time features of the operating system can only be tested on the real-time platform.

O3.1: Two development platforms are available with different levels of support and features. Compiling and linking modules and layers that use real-time operating system features is not possible on nonreal-time platforms.

O3.2: The configuration management environment has a moderate impact on the ability to do cross-platform development.

Solution

Create the source components to separate code dependent on the target hardware; for example, by using additional procedures.

Strategy: *Separate and encapsulate code dependent on the target platform.*

By decomposing the modules so that code dependent on the target platform is separated, we can share and test platform-independent code on the development machine that is most convenient for the developer. Examples of platform-dependent code are user interface code and code that uses the real-time capability of the operating system. One way to separate such code is to encapsulate it and make a different implementation available for each target platform. In some cases, it may be advantageous to make this change in the module architecture view itself.

Related Strategies

Use a flexible build procedure (issue, Limited Availability of Probe Prototypes).

7.2.2   Central Design Tasks: Source Components, Intermediate Components, and Deployment Components

After having accomplished the global analysis, let's now begin the central design tasks of identifying and organizing source, deployment, and intermediate code components. In this section, we discuss only the central design tasks for selected parts of the example system. Let's use the results of the module and execution views as inputs, and the global strategies to guide these tasks.

Source Components

One way to start the task of mapping elements of the module view to source components is to start with the layers defined in the module view. Let's first apply the strategy *Preserve module view hierarchies* to create a structure for organizing source components. Figure 7.3 shows code groups (modeled with a UML package), each of which contains the set of related source components for a layer. Let us apply the strategy *Separate organization of public interface components* and create a code group named "include" to copy and organize the public interface components that are commonly used by all of the layers.

After having selected a layer-based organization of source components, let us look closely at the modules and subsystems of the ImageProcessing layer. In particular, let's look at the SImaging subsystem as defined in the module view (Figure 7.4).

First let us map some of the supporting modules and interfaces in the subsystem to source components. We can capture the traceability of this mapping with the help of a naming convention. For example, the module named MPacketMgr can be mapped to CPacketMgr.CPP. Similarly, the modules MPacketizer, MImageMgr, MAcqControl, and MPipelineMgr can be mapped to CPacketizer.CPP, CImageMgr.CPP, CAcqControl.CPP, and CPipelineMgr.CPP respectively.

Next let's map the interfaces of modules of the SImaging subsystem to respective language-specific components. For this purpose, let's apply the strategy *Separate organization of public interface components*. For example, the interface IPacketMgr, for the module MPacketMgr, can be mapped to its public header file CPacketMgr.H. Then the pri-

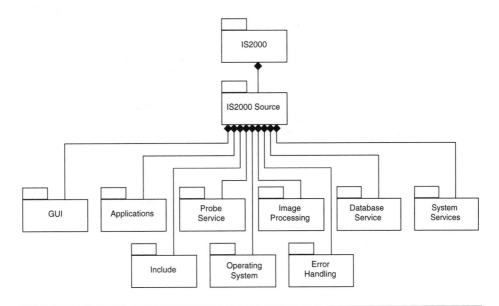

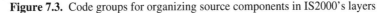

Figure 7.3. Code groups for organizing source components in IS2000's layers

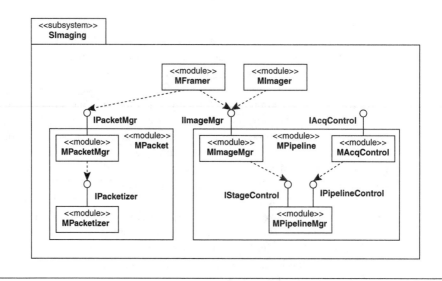

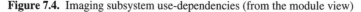

Figure 7.4. Imaging subsystem use-dependencies (from the module view)

vate declarations of the components can be separated into one or more .H components. For the time being, let's use only one such private component for each of the interfaces and name it CPacketMgrPvt.H. This helps us check that components only use program units defined in public header files. Interfaces for the modules MPacketizer, MImageMgr, and MAcqControl (IPacketizer, IImageMgr, and IAcqControl respectively) are mapped to the code architecture view. Because the module MPipelineMgr has two interfaces—IStage-Control and IPipelineControl—they are mapped to CStageControl.H and CPipelineControl.H respectively.

The modules and interfaces discussed so far are mapped to the source components shown in Figure 7.5. In our diagrams we use the UML component to render source components.

Now it is time to map the dependencies among the modules. There is an import (include) dependency between the public and the private header files. Similarly, there is an import dependency derived from the relationship between a module and its interfaces. For example, there is an import dependency from CPipelineMgr.CPP to CStageControl.H and CPipelineControl.H because these two components correspond to the two interfaces IStageControl and IPipelineControl. In Figure 7.4, modules MImageMgr and MAcqControl require the interfaces IStageControl and IPipelineControl respectively of the module MPipelineMgr. These two dependencies are mapped to the import dependencies from CImageMgr.CPP to CStageControl.H and from CAcqControl.CPP to CPipelineControl.H respectively. The result of completing this task for all the supporting modules in the SImaging subsystem is shown in Figure 7.5. Note that if elements in the module view get further refined, the corresponding source components also need to be refined.

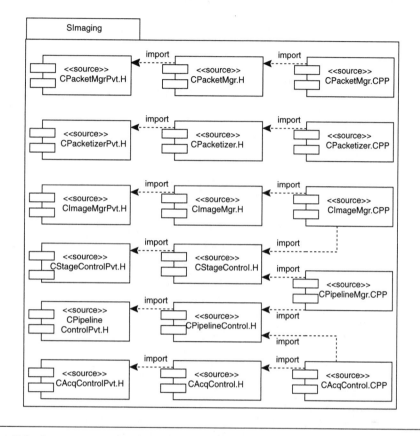

Figure 7.5. Source components and dependencies for the image-processing subsystem

Next let's look at the modules MFramer and MImager in Figure 7.4. As we said in Chapter 5, there are several instances of these modules, depending on various acquisition procedures. We can map the individual instances of these modules to source components as we did earlier. Figure 7.6 shows how two specific instances of MFramer and MImager—named MFramer_2D and MImager_2D—can be mapped to corresponding source components. Their use-dependencies from Figure 7.4 have been transformed to import dependencies in a manner similar to that for other modules. We need to create such source components and dependencies for each instance of MFramer and MImager.

Now it is time to organize these source components. Because it is likely that the source components corresponding to each module may be further decomposed, let's apply the strategy *Preserve module view hierarchies* and organize them in separate packages as shown in Figure 7.7. Notice that each instance of MFramer and MImager has been organized in its own package. Notice also that there are packages corresponding to MPacket

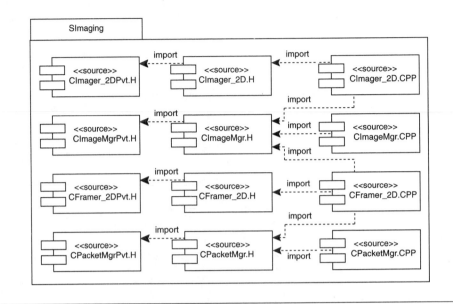

Figure 7.6. Mapping MFramer and MImager to source components

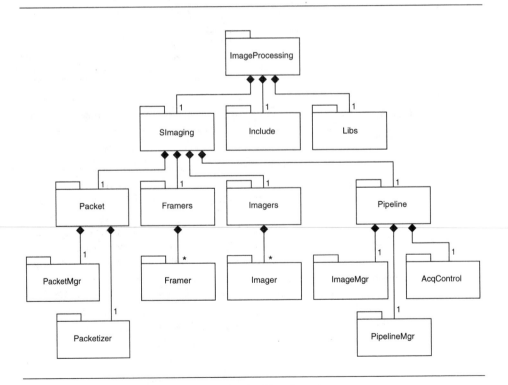

Figure 7.7. Organizing source components for the SImaging subsystem

and MPipeline, even though we have not identified any source components for these modules. It is quite likely that source components common to their subcomponents are organized in these packages.

Next, let us take a look at the ProbeService layer as decomposed in Figure 5.9. The strategy *Develop an off-line probe simulator* suggests that the MDataCollect module may be replaced with the MDataCollectSimulator module. Let's support this decision by mapping the interface of MDataCollect to CDataCollect.H, and moving it to a separate package. A flexible build procedure allows us to use the source components for either MDataCollect or MDataCollectSimulator transparently.

Source components corresponding to the data collection functionality of the ProbeService layer, and their dependencies, are shown in Figure 7.8. Source components and dependencies for the probe control functionality (modules MDataAcq and MProbe-Control) can be similarly identified, although these aren't shown in the figure. Identifying and organizing these components is carried out in a similar manner for all of the layers.

Intermediate Components

Let us start the task of identifying and organizing the intermediate components by first identifying the strategies that are applicable: *Develop an off-line probe simulator, Separate and encapsulate code dependent on the target platform, Use phased development,* and *Release layers through static libraries.* Let's use these strategies to allow developers to work independently on the target and development platforms of their choice and to work concurrently with each other. Another goal is to improve development cycle time for individual developers.

Because the main source components for IS2000 are C++ language code components, for each .CPP component (for example, CDataCollect.CPP) there is a .obj binary compo-

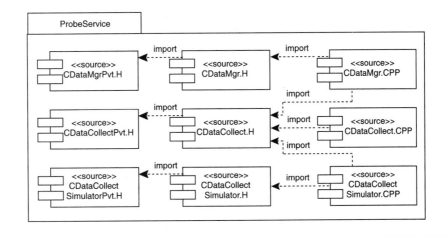

Figure 7.8. ProbeService source components and their dependencies

nent (for example, CDataCollect.obj). By default, the compiler creates the .obj files in the same package as the source component. Instead, let's organize these .obj files into a separate subpackage for each target platform. This allows a developer to change the target platform easily without having to recompile everything. Note that the build procedure may need to transform the intermediate components into a format suitable for the particular target platform.

Guided by the strategy *Release layers through static libraries,* let's create one static library for each of the OperatingSystem, ErrorHandling, and SystemServices layers. We name these libraries OperatingSystem.lib, ErrorHandling.lib, and SystemServices.lib.

In line with the strategy *Develop an off-line probe simulator,* ProbeService offers two different libraries: ProbeService.lib and ProbeSimulatorService.lib. The first of these libraries provides services of the real probe hardware and the second provides services of the probe simulator.

The MImager and MFramer modules are internal to the SImaging subsystem in the ImageProcessing layer. Thus the library for the subsystem need not contain intermediate components corresponding to these modules. Recall that MPacketMgr, MAcqControl, and MImageMgr are linked to many processes, whereas MPacketizer and MPipelineMgr are not. Also, because there may be many different kinds of image data flowing through the image-processing pipeline, MPacketizer may become very large. Therefore, let's offer five separate libraries for the ImageProcessing layer: PacketMgr.lib, Packetizer.lib, AcqControl.lib, PipelineMgr.lib, and ImageMgr.lib. Let's use a simple organization for the libraries and locate them in a subpackage called libs, under the package for each layer.

Deployment Components

Let us start the task of identifying and organizing deployment components for the example system by mapping executables, configurations, and resources. Let's restrict our focus to the set of processes required for the imaging subsystem, as presented in Figure 7.9. For each process in the execution architecture view, we need to identify an executable in the code architecture view.

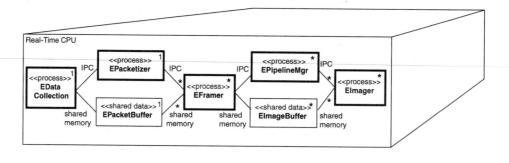

Figure 7.9. Execution configuration of the imaging subsystem. IPC = interprocess communication.

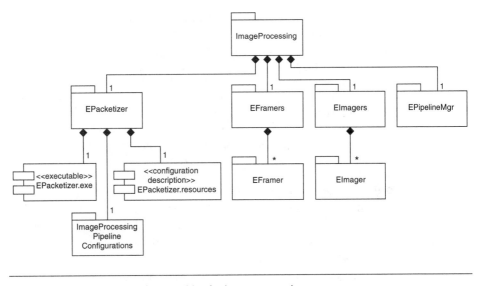

Figure 7.10. Organization of executables for image processing

The link dependencies of each of the executables to the binaries and static libraries can be identified based on the modules that are assigned to each of the runtime entities (for example, as shown in Figure 6.13). Each executable needs to link with intermediate components derived from all the modules that are assigned to its corresponding process.

Figure 7.10 describes the organization and deployment components for the processes used in image processing. Deployment components related to various layers and subsystems are clustered into their own packages. There is also a package to organize shared memory for communicating among processes. The following three points should be noted:

1. There is a package for each executable that contains the executable and the supporting files that describe how each process is to be configured and the resources it uses.

2. Executables for different EFramer and EImager processes are organized hierarchically.

3. The configurations for each of the possible pipelines corresponding to acquisition procedures are mapped to configuration files organized in the Configurations package.

7.2.3 Final Design Tasks: Build Procedure and Configuration Management

Build Procedure

When performing the central design tasks of source, intermediate, and deployment components, we identified all of the components, how they are organized, and the dependencies among them. We now need to design a build procedure that builds the entire system or parts thereof in an efficient manner, avoiding unnecessary production of derived components.

The design of the build procedure includes the order in which derived objects are built or rebuilt, how the dependencies are expressed in build scripts (for example, makefiles), and the installation procedures used to install and to organize deployment components on appropriate processors.

For convenience, it is common to use hierarchical build procedures to perform the required tasks. The decisions we have made so far have standardized the organization of layers, subsystems, and components. Thus the nested build procedures will all be very similar except for component-specific information. You may want to add a variety of build targets to rebuild a component, subsystem, or a layer for module testing, internal release, or release for a particular target platform.

Configuration Management

During the configuration management task we need to design how versions and releases of components are managed. Let's divide the intermediate components into categories based on the source components from which they are derived:

- Source components developed by the developer
- Source components developed by other team members
- Source components developed by other teams

For the IS2000 project, the teams are organized based on layers and subsystems. Using the strategy *Use phased development*, let's decide that each team will release its components first internally for use by other team members. The frequency of these internal releases is left to individual teams. At regular intervals, components being developed by a team should be relatively stable and released to other teams. Thus each developer minimizes the effect of changes made by other developers through selective use of these releases.

Different configuration management tools offer version naming schemes to distinguish between different releases of components. More sophisticated tools (ClearCase) also allow individual developers to define their own views by selecting appropriate released versions of components.

7.2.4   Design Summary for IS2000 Code Architecture View

To design the code architecture view, we identified source components corresponding to the elements of the module view. Next we translated decomposition and use-dependencies among the module view elements to source components and dependencies among them. We also organized the source components into directories.

In the next step we identified all the components derived from the source components and organized them based on release procedures and team organization. Similarly, we identified and organized deployment components corresponding to the elements in the execution view.

Lastly, we designed the build procedure and made several configuration management decisions related to the release procedures and the team organization. Table 7.3 summarizes the design decisions we discussed in this chapter.

Design Decision	Rationale
Global analysis: Review global analysis	
Preserve separation of components and modules in the code architecture view.	Strategy: *Separate components and modules along dimensions of concern.*
Preserve encapsulation of features.	Strategy: *Encapsulate features into separate components.*
Separate organization of executables from source components.	Strategy: *Make it easy to add or remove features.*
Global analysis: Develop strategies	
Add a new issue: Architectural Integrity.	Maintain architecture integrity.
Add a new issue: Limited Availability of Probe Prototypes.	Overcome limited availability of probe prototypes.
Add a new issue: Multiple Development and Target Platforms.	Provide for easier use of multiple development and target platforms.
Add a new issue: Concurrent Development Tasks.	Support concurrent development tasks transparently.
Identify and organize source components	
Group source components in each layer into a separate package.	Strategy: *Preserve module view hierarchies.*
Group common .H files in a package named "include" at the system level as well as for each layer.	Strategy: *Separate organization of public interface components.*
Map each interface in the module view to a public and a private .H source component.	Strategy: *Separate organization of public interface components.*

Table 7.3. Sequence of Design Decisions for IS2000 Code Architecture View

Design Decision	Rationale
Organize packages hierarchically according to module decomposition and layer assignment.	Strategy: *Preserve module view hierarchies.*
Identify and organize intermediate components	
Separate packages to group intermediate components related to the target platform.	Strategy: *Separate and encapsulate code dependent on target platforms.*
Provide one or more static libraries for each layer, organized in a separate package.	Strategy: *Release layers through static libraries.* Reduce development cycle time.
Use several libraries for the ImageProcessing layer.	Manage the size of static libraries.
Identify and organize deployment components	
Organize deployment components for various process sets identified in the execution view.	Strategy: *Preserve execution view.*
Group pipeline configurations and shared resources separately from those for process sets.	Strategy: *Separate components and modules along dimensions of concern.*
Address build procedure	
Use a hierarchical build procedure. Parameterize the build procedure to select desired released versions of components.	Strategy: *Use flexible build procedure.*
Address configuration management	
Use appropriate levels of product, team, and team-internal releases to stabilize the release process.	Strategy: *Use phased development.*

Table 7.3. Sequence of Design Decisions for IS2000 Code Architecture View *(continued)*

Design Decision	Rationale
Categorize source components based on development responsibility.	Manage versions and releases in a flexible manner.

Table 7.3. Sequence of Design Decisions for IS2000 Code Architecture View *(continued)*

7.3 Summary of Code Architecture View

Table 7.4 summarizes the elements, relations, and artifacts of the code architecture view. As in the other views, the elements and relations are the building blocks for the architecture view, and the artifacts are the descriptions or documentation of the architecture.

Element	UML Element	New Stereotype	Notation	
Source component	Component	<<source>>	▤<<source>>	Examples of source components are .H and .CPP files for C++.
Binary component	Component	<<binary>>	▤<<binary>>	These are intermediate components.
Library	Library	—	▤<<library>>	Static or program libraries are intermediate components. Dynamic libraries are deployment components.
Executable	Executable	—	▤	These are deployment components.

Table 7.4. Summary of Code Architecture View

Configuration description	Component	<<configuration description>>		Describes execution configurations as well as resources.
Code group	Package	—		

Relation	UML Element	Notation	Description
generate	Dependency	generate	Source components can generate other source components.
import	Import	import	Source components can import other source components.
compile	Dependency	compile	Source components are compiled to binary components or libraries.
link	Dependency	link	Binary components link statically to form libraries or executables. Dynamic or shared libraries link dynamically with and are loaded into executables.
use at runtime	Usage	use at runtime	An executable uses configuration descriptions at runtime.
trace	Trace		A code group may trace to a subsystem or layer. A source component may trace to a module or interface.
instantiate	Instantiate	Table row	At runtime, an executable instantiates a runtime entity (as a runtime instance).

Artifact	Representation
Module view, source component correspondence	Trace dependency, tables
Runtime entity, executable correspondence	Instantiation dependency, tables
Description of components in code architecture view, their organization, and their dependencies	UML Component Diagrams or tables

Table 7.4. Summary of Code Architecture View *(continued)*

Description of build procedures	Tool-specific representations (for example, makefiles)
Description of release schedules for modules and corresponding component versions	Tables
Configuration management views for developers	Tool-specific representation

Table 7.4. Summary of Code Architecture View *(continued)*

The elements and their relationships for the code architecture view are described in the meta-model (Figure 7.11). The meta-model contains three kinds of components produced during the central design tasks. Source components are, in general, the language-level modules that implement elements in the module view. Language-specific interfaces or modules may be generated from other source components. For example, a parser can be generated from a more abstract grammar description such as Backus-Naur form. These source components are different for different languages: They are .H and .CPP files for

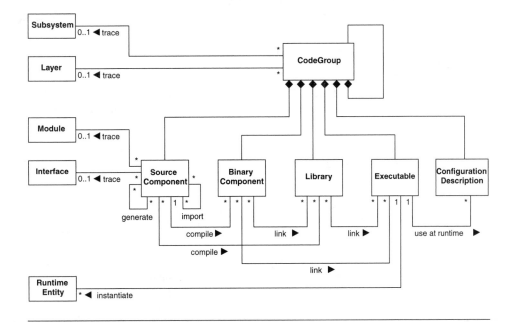

Figure 7.11. Meta-model of the code architecture view

C++, specification and body files for Ada, or interfaces that may be implemented by several classes in Java, corresponding to <InterfaceName>.java and <ClassName>.java files.

Intermediate components are derived from the source components. They consist of the binary components (for example, object files) that are compiled from the language-specific modules, and the static libraries to which binary components are linked statically. For languages such as Ada and CHILL, source components are compiled into a program library that manages the corresponding binary components.

The deployment components are those that are needed to form an executable system, such as executables, dynamic libraries, process descriptions, and resource descriptions. The "link" relation is an abstraction for both static and dynamic linking. The trade-off of which to choose is one of performance versus flexibility. A compiled component is linked statically to an executable. A dynamic library (for example, .DLL) is dynamically linked with and loaded into an executable.

Configuration descriptions are used at runtime to instantiate runtime entities from the execution view. The operating system or a central utility of the system may use a configuration description to start executables with the appropriate parameters (for example, loading them from permanent storage into memory). An instance of an executable is instantiated as a runtime entity (for example, process), and a resource configuration is instantiated as a resource entity (for example, shared memory) in the execution view.

Although we used UML diagrams to describe dependencies between components, it may be easier to document these dependencies in tables. In Chapter 11 you will see an example of a system in which the large number of components and dependencies requires the use of tables.

7.3.1 Traceability

Describing the relationships of the code view to requirements, external factors, and the other architecture views provides traceability. The following three items should be traceable in the code view:

1. *Critical requirements and organizational and technological factors.* Traceability between design decisions for the code architecture view and the influencing factors helps determine whether the design meets the requirements. It also helps determine the impact of changes in the influencing factors on the code view. Traceability to the release schedule is maintained by explicitly recording the schedules of the developers responsible for implementing their work packages of components.

2. *Elements in the module view.* To implement source components correctly, developers must know how they are mapped to elements of the module view. Traceability is maintained by describing the correspondence of modules and interfaces to source components, using naming conventions, and reflecting the module view hierarchy of layers and modules in the hierarchy of packages. These relationships, along with the development environment, determine many of the other components and dependencies.

3. *Elements in the execution view.* To implement deployment components, developers must know how they map to elements in the execution view. Traceability is maintained by describing the correspondence between runtime entities and deployment components, using naming conventions, and reflecting the execution view hierarchy by putting executable and shared resources into separate packages.

7.3.2 Uses for the Code Architecture View

Once the code architecture view is explicitly described, it can be used for a variety of purposes:

- Traceability to elements of the module and execution architecture views
- Transparent access to all the components needed for a particular development task
- Building parts of the system
- Managing versions and releases of components
- Preserving architecture design decisions and detecting their violations

Additional Reading

Lakos (1996) discusses engineering trade-offs for the development of large systems, and provides rules and guidelines for the physical design (his term for code architecture design). He discusses how physical design may affect the logical design (for example, module architecture). Issues include when and how much to insulate and to encapsulate. He addresses code architecture-level issues such as compile- and link-time dependencies; physical design of files, directories, and libraries; and other important issues (such as testing and testability) that are beyond the scope of this chapter.

Make build scripts (Feldman, 1979), configuration management (Feiler, 1991), and systems building techniques (Lange and Schwanke, 1991) are used to describe and manipulate the file-level organization of source code. Cohen et al. (1988) and Schwanke et al. (1989) describe various version and configuration management issues related to construction of systems in large development teams. These papers describe the compile-time, link-time, and runtime relationships between components in the code architecture view, and how they affect the design of build procedures. More information on the UML elements component and package on which the code architecture elements are based is contained in *The Unified Modeling Language Reference Manual* (Rumbaugh, Jacobson, and Booch, 1999) and the *UML Toolkit* (Eriksson and Penker, 1998).

Weiser (1987) discusses the motivation for relating design to concrete programming artifacts. Royce (1990) describes the software architects lifecycle environment (SALE). SALE depicts the process configuration and generates the corresponding Ada or C++ source code.

Lakos (1996) also discusses evaluating design for maintainability, and uses measures such as cumulative component dependency and average/normalized component dependency for incremental regression testing. The architecture trade-off analysis method (Kazman et al., 1999) uses information from the code view to evaluate modifiability and security attributes of the architecture.

PART III

Software Architecture Best Practice

In Part II we used the IS2000 system as a running example to explain how to design software architecture using the four views approach. To do this we went deep into the details of parts of IS2000, and gave a broad overview of the rest. In Part III we present four additional systems, although not in the same depth as IS2000. These systems were previously designed within Siemens and are advanced in their use of software architecture.

You can learn a lot from the concrete details of these systems, rather than trying to learn from more abstract explanations of the concepts. We present more examples of what goes in each view, which engineering concerns it addresses, and how the notation is used to describe it. We present more examples of the kinds of things you should consider during architecture design, which will help you understand the scope of architecture concerns. And we present the design decisions and the design trade-offs made by different architects to solve a variety of architectural design issues.

These four systems were not originally designed using the approach described in Part II. The approach is too new to have results from its application to systems of the size and/ or complexity of these. Such a retrospective analysis is useful for validating that these views are generally applicable and useful. Because the four views approach is based on existing practice, it is not surprising that it works well for describing these systems. You may notice that some naming conventions in Part III differ from those in Part II. This is because we followed the naming conventions of the particular system.

Not all the systems used all four views to the same extent. Sometimes the conceptual view was not explicit, and sometimes the views were not well separated. By reading these chapters, you'll learn some of the reasons for this, and the impact it had on architecture design.

These systems come from a variety of domains, they vary in size and complexity, and they have different system characteristics (Table III.1). All of these differences have an effect on the software architecture design.

System	Application Domain	Size*	Important System Characteristics
Safety Vision	Instrumentation and control	Large	Fault tolerance, multiprocessing, safety critical
Healthy Vision	Signal processing	Large	Monitoring, real time, safety critical
Central Vision	Central monitoring	Medium	Monitoring, real time, open system
Comm Vision	Communication	Very large	Distributed, heterogeneous, multiprocessing
*Medium = 100–500 KLOC; large = 500 KLOC–1 MLOC; very large = more than 1 MLOC.			

Table III.1. The Example Systems Described in Part III

Safety Vision

The Safety Vision product line is a set of digital I&C systems for nuclear power plants. Because the I&C systems control safety-related and safety-critical functions, they must meet the highest quality standards, as defined by the regulatory agency. These safety I&C systems must be fault tolerant, redundant, and distributed, and must have real-time response.

Each safety I&C system is custom designed for an individual plant, so Safety Vision provides a complete toolset for creating them. An I&C engineer uses a domain-specific graphical language to design the I&C system, then Safety Vision automatically generates the implementation. In software architecture terms, the I&C engineer designs the conceptual view of an I&C system. The toolset uses rules about mapping the conceptual view to the module, execution, and code architecture views to generate the code for the application.

Safety Vision is like a product line in that the software architecture defines a standard set of components, rules for interconnecting them, and implementations. It is not a typical product line because a product (an I&C system) is specified in the conceptual view, and the Safety Vision toolset generates the implementation. It still has module, execution, and code architecture views, but the rules for generating these views are embedded in the tools. Another difference from a typical product line is that the specification language for the conceptual view is a domain-specific graphical language, and the specification of the product is done by domain experts.

Healthy Vision

Healthy Vision is an embedded, real-time patient monitoring system. It is a stand-alone bedside unit that obtains and displays a patient's vital signs, or sends them to a central unit for display. The bedside unit can be transported along with a patient, so physical size and cost limitations impose severe hardware constraints on Healthy Vision. Healthy Vision has different configurations to produce a set of medium to high-end patient monitors, so it's actually a small, homogeneous product line.

Previous products started the software architecture design with the execution view, which then dominated the architecture and limited the evolution and portability of the products. To support Healthy Vision's planned configurations and additional ones in the future, the architects made an explicit module view that was separate from the execution view. Healthy Vision did not originally have an explicit conceptual view, although it was implicitly there. This use of multiple views (including an explicit code architecture view) proved critical in meeting the requirements of building an extensible, portable, and configurable system. Another interesting aspect of Healthy Vision is its use of new RMA technology for early performance analysis (during architecture design).

Central Vision

Central Vision is a central patient monitoring station designed to interact with systems like Healthy Vision. It can display patient data from multiple bedside monitors, and can also control these units remotely.

For future extensibility and because it must interact with a variety of systems, the architects designed it as an open system using off-the-shelf hardware and software. They also decided to use object-oriented technologies: C++, object modeling technique, and design patterns. Previous central station products used embedded, proprietary solutions and a procedural programming language, so the use of new technologies added considerable risk to the project. To mitigate this risk, they designed the software architecture carefully.

The investment in making an extensible, open system has paid off. New products have since been built on the Central Vision platform using the same basic architecture design and sharing as much as 90 percent of the source code. Thus Central Vision has grown into a product line, although a somewhat heterogeneous one. In addition, because of the success in using new technologies, some of Central Vision's design concepts and even some code is being used by other organizations to develop products in the medical domain.

Comm Vision

Comm Vision is a product line of computer-controlled, digital communication switching systems. Because of widely varying customer requirements, each Comm Vision system is a custom product, configured from standard Comm Vision modules and new customer-specific modules. This is the largest and the most complex of the systems described in Part III. Its size, complexity, and use of multisite development presented unique technical and coordination challenges.

Comm Vision uses hardware redundancy and software fault recovery to provide highly reliable systems that can be upgraded without interruption in service. The systems can also interoperate with a variety of existing communication platforms through uniform, standard services. A Comm Vision system has a long lifetime of 20 years or more. During its lifetime, new software upgrades are integrated regularly. Even its hardware may be upgraded every few years to take advantage of faster processors and new telecommunication hardware or technologies.

To support its key architecture principles directly, Comm Vision has extended an existing programming language and developed an in-house operating system and tools. This is similar to the approach taken in the Safety Vision product line. In contrast, for Healthy Vision, support of architecture principles takes the form of coding conventions that developers must follow.

When choosing systems for Part III from our original set of case study systems, we didn't look for product-line architectures. However, it's not just coincidence that these four systems with well-designed architectures all have product-line aspects. For product lines, weaknesses in the software architecture multiply because they show up in each product and they can limit the applicability of the product line. Thus an early investment in a good software architecture is especially important. For Central Vision, although it wasn't originally intended for multiple products, the success of the architecture has led to its use in other products.

Chapter 8

S afety Vision

with Contributions by
Stephan Stöcker

Instrumentation and control of nuclear power plants can be divided into three main categories: operational I&C, safety-related I&C, and safety-critical I&C. The Safety Vision product line supports parts of operational I&C (such as closed-loop control of the reactor coolant temperature or pressure), but it mainly supports safety-related and safety-critical I&C systems. Examples of these are reactor limitation systems and reactor protection systems. These I&C systems interface with sensors and actuators in the plant, and interact with monitoring and control systems in the control room.

The Safety Vision product line differs from most product lines in that the products (the safety I&C systems) are not predefined; instead, they are custom designed for each new power plant. For this reason, Safety Vision is generally referred to as an engineering system. It defines the product-line architecture and it provides an engineering toolset that is used to create individual I&C systems, or projects, for each plant.

Most safety-related and safety-critical I&C systems today still use hardwired analog devices. Some vendors have introduced digital technology for these safety I&C systems, but they have encountered difficulties with verification and licensing of these software-intensive systems. The Safety Vision product line uses digital technology, so a critical goal was to avoid these verification and licensing problems by considering them at the beginning of the design of the product line.

The Safety Vision engineering system supports the design of a wide range of safety I&C systems, from simple, single failure-tolerant one-out-of-two systems to large two-out-of-four systems with enough functional diversity to accommodate common cause failures. In a one-out-of-two system, an activation command (for example, to open a valve or start a pump) is carried out if either of two redundant subsystems issues the command. A two-out-of-four system requires two of the four redundant subsystems to issue the activation command.

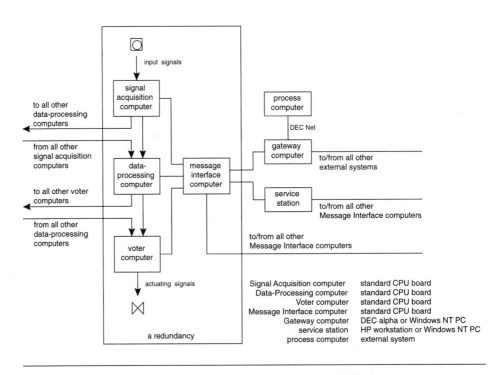

input signals

signal
acquisition
computer

to all other
data-processing
computers

from all other
signal acquisition
computers

data-
processing
computer

to all other voter
computers

from all other
data-processing
computers

voter
computer

actuating signals

a redundancy

process
computer

DEC Net

gateway
computer

to/from all other
external systems

service
station

to/from all other
Message Interface computers

message
interface
computer

to/from all other
Message Interface computers

Signal Acquisition computer	standard CPU board
Data-Processing computer	standard CPU board
Voter computer	standard CPU board
Message Interface computer	standard CPU board
Gateway computer	DEC alpha or Windows NT PC
service station	HP workstation or Windows NT PC
process computer	external system

Figure 8.1. Hardware topology of a redundancy in a typical safety I&C system

An I&C system, or project, is a distributed, redundant computer system. Typically it consists of four independent, redundant data-processing paths (redundancies). Figure 8.1 shows the topology of a single redundancy within a typical project. A redundancy is not just a separate data-processing path; it is also physically isolated in a separate room. It contains four computers, each serving a different processing role and communicating via networks.

The main processing path is the path of data from the input signals through the signal acquisition, data-processing, and voter computers to the actuators.

The signal acquisition computer in each redundancy acquires analog and binary input signals from transducers in the plant (for example, temperature, pressure, and level measurements). Each signal acquisition computer acquires its input signals and performs preprocessing, such as filtering. It then distributes the signals to all four data-processing computers in all four redundancies. Thus each data-processing computer is provided with the same set of input information.

The data-processing computers perform signal processing such as limit value monitoring and closed-loop control calculations. The results are actuating signals destined for actuators like pumps, valves, or control rods, but first these signals pass through the voter computers.

In the voter computers, the results of the four redundancies join together. A voter computer controls a set of actuators. Each voter receives the redundant actuation signals from the four data-processing computers. It compares this redundant information and computes a validated (voted) actuating signal, typically using a two-out-of-four voting scheme. The voters then output these signals to the switchgear system to actuate the assigned actuators. To increase reliability, a voter computer itself can be built as an inherent redundant and fault-tolerant computer.

In addition to the computers in this main processing path, each redundancy typically has a message interface computer. The message interface computer is connected via local area networks (LANs) to the signal acquisition, data-processing, and voter computers in its redundancy. It serves as a gateway between the computers of the automatic path and other, nonsafety-relevant systems, such as the service station, gateways to process control computers, or monitoring and control computers.

Each computer consists of one or more racks mounted in cabinets. It contains one or more processor boards for performing the signal processing. Communication is handled by dedicated communication processors. Communication links within a cabinet are electrical, and communication links between cabinets are optical. Signal acquisition and output are performed by a set of input and output boards for analog and binary signal types.

8.1 Global Analysis

The key characteristics that must be met by the Safety Vision engineering system can be classified into product factors, technological factors, and organizational factors.

8.1.1 Analyze Product Factors

Table 8.1 shows many of the product factors for the Safety Vision engineering system. Four of the product factors directly affected the hardware selection. Although each project has its own distinct hardware configuration, it is built from the hardware components that Safety Vision supports. The components have to provide high communication performance and be impervious to seismic disturbances (for example, from earthquakes; factors P3.1, P4.2). In addition, these components must provide sufficient computing power and competitive product pricing (factor P7.1). Because the projects must be fault tolerant, they generally have a configuration that is distributed and physically separated into redundancies, so Safety Vision must support these configurations (factor P4.1).

Safety Vision must also be scalable to support diverse project architectures (factor P1.3). Safety Vision provides specific support for redundancy and fault tolerance so that project designers can build projects with these properties (factors P1.4, P1.5). Safety Vision provides this support through a set of engineering tools. These tools have to be easy to use for I&C engineers when designing and implementing a project, and for process engineers when validating the design (factor P2.1).

Product Factor	Flexibility and Changeability	Impact
P1: Features		
P1.1: External system interoperability		
Projects need to communicate with third-party systems (for example, process computers, service stations, and operating and monitoring computers).	New third-party systems may need to be accommodated.	There is a potentially large impact at the boundaries of the system.
P1.2: Hardware portability		
Projects must be portable to new hardware platforms.	New hardware platforms must be accommodated.	There is a potentially large impact on the software platform.
P1.3: Scalable architecture		
The engineering system must be scalable to support a large range of products.	Projects range from a simple stand-alone CPU and input/output board to a large distributed system with more than 100 CPUs.	The impact affects primarily the conceptual view.
P1.4: Redundancy in projects		
The engineering system must support redundant structures within projects.	This is fairly stable.	There is a moderate impact.

Table 8.1. Product Factors for Safety Vision

Product Factor	Flexibility and Changeability	Impact
P1.5: Fault tolerance in projects		
The engineering system must provide projects with fault-tolerant mechanisms (for example, for error/exception handling).	This is fairly stable.	There is a small impact.
P1.6: Hardware-independent simulation		
The engineering system must support simulation of I&C functionality without requiring a target hardware installation.	This is stable.	There is a moderate impact.
P2: User interface		
P2.1: Accessible engineering tools		
The engineering system must provide tools for I&C engineers to create projects and communicate results easily to process engineers. It must also make it easy for them to perform verification.	This is stable.	There is a localized impact.

Table 8.1. Product Factors for Safety Vision *(continued)*

Product Factor	Flexibility and Changeability	Impact
P3: Performance		
P3.1: High-speed communication		
Projects require a high communication performance of as many as 200 messages at 500 bytes per second.	Flexibility could increase in the future.	This affects hardware selection.
P3.2: Deterministic execution times		
The execution timing of the I&C systems must be deterministic. They must have guaranteed maximum computing and reaction times, and constant communication loads.	There is no flexibility.	There is a pervasive impact.
P4: Dependability		
P4.1: Physically distributed projects		
The engineering system must support the physical distribution of the projects' hardware and software.	All projects will be distributed physically, but their configurations will vary.	This affects primarily the module and execution views.

Table 8.1. Product Factors for Safety Vision *(continued)*

Product Factor	Flexibility and Changeability	Impact
P4.2: Withstand seismic disturbances		
The I&C systems must be impervious to seismic disturbances (from earthquakes, plane crashes, and so on).	There is no flexibility.	This affects hardware selection.
P4.3: Software quality		
Projects must conform to regulatory agency requirements for software quality.	There are different ways this could be fulfilled.	This affects nearly all design decisions.
P4.4: Simple implementation		
The implementation of projects must be as simple as possible, as required by the regulatory agency.	There are different ways this could be fulfilled.	This affects primarily the module and execution views.
P7: Product cost		
P7.1: Hardware costs		
Hardware costs for projects must support competitive product pricing.	There is little flexibility.	This rules out custom components.

Table 8.1. Product Factors for Safety Vision *(continued)*

Product Factor	Flexibility and Changeability	Impact
P7.2: Project development costs		
The cost of verifying, validating, and licensing projects must not prohibit competitive product pricing.	It is prohibitively expensive to verify, validate, and license each project independently.	Strategies are needed for reducing these costs.
I&C = instrumentation and control.		

Table 8.1. Product Factors for Safety Vision *(continued)*

At runtime, the execution times of the I&C systems must be deterministic. A project must have guaranteed maximum computing and reaction times, and constant communication loads (factor P3.2). It must also be possible to simulate the I&C functionality of a project without requiring a target hardware installation (factor P1.6). Projects also must be able to interoperate with third-party systems (for example process computers, service stations, and operating and monitoring computers; factor P1.1).

Additional properties of the Safety Vision engineering system are that projects must be portable to new hardware platforms (factor P1.2), and the cost of developing new projects must be competitive (factor P7.2). The regulatory agency requires that the software of safety I&C systems be of the highest quality (factor P4.3), and that their implementation be as simple as possible (factor P4.4), in part to support the quality requirement.

8.1.2 Analyze Technological Factors

Table 8.2 contains some of the important technological factors for Safety Vision. Innovation cycles in digital automation systems are rather short compared with the typical lifetime of a nuclear power plant, which is as long as 40 years. On the other hand, the expected number of components to be sold is rather low compared with other standard industry application fields. There are, however, standard components available for digital automation systems (factor T2.1). To meet national and international regulatory standards for reactor control systems, these hardware components are subjected to a certification process called *type-testing*.

Functional diagrams are a standard I&C documentation notation: They are well-understood by I&C and process engineers, and can be independent of the implementation method (factor T5.1). This is a well-established, stable notation.

Technological Factor	Flexibility and Changeability	Impact
T2: Domain-specific hardware		
T2.1: Input/output and CPU boards for digital automation systems		
There are standard hardware components for digital automation systems. Relatively few components are sold for nuclear power plants.	Innovation cycles are short; thus, new components should be incorporated as they become available.	There is a large impact on hardware-dependent components.
T5: Standards		
T5.1: Functional diagram notation		
Functional diagrams are a standard I&C documentation notation.	This is stable.	There is a large impact on all components.
T5.2: Standard hardware protocols		
There are standard protocols for certain hardware (for example, local area networks).	This is stable.	There is a large impact on hardware-dependent components.

Table 8.2. Technological Factors for Safety Vision

8.1.3 Analyze Organizational Factors

Table 8.3 contains the main organizational factors for Safety Vision. The development of the Safety Vision engineering system was scheduled for a period of 10 years, starting from the first conceptual and feasibility studies to the delivery of the first project in a nuclear power plant. This reflects the enormous effort needed to develop and to qualify a computer-based digital I&C system for safety-critical applications in nuclear power plants. It also reflects the organization's commitment to the Safety Vision product line, by providing sufficient time and resources (factor O4.1).

The Safety Vision project also had access to people with a wide range of training (factor O2.1). At the start of development, four major working groups were formed. One

Organizational Factor	Flexibility and Changeability	Impact
O2: Staff skills		
O2.1: Range of training		
The Safety Vision project requires expertise in process engineering, I&C engineering, electrical engineering, and software engineering.	Other staff can be transferred to the Safety Vision project as needed.	There is a large impact.
O2.2: Access to hardware platform engineers		
Engineers from the supplier of the hardware platform are available.	These engineers can act as consultants throughout the Safety Vision project.	There is a large impact on receiving regulatory agency certification of the operating system.
O2.3: Training in software engineering analysis techniques		
The process engineers and I&C engineers who design individual projects are not trained in software engineering analysis techniques.	Training engineers in these techniques is possible.	There is a high cost to training all users of the system.
O4: Schedule		
O4.1: Time and resources		
The organization is committed to dedicating the time and resources for a product line.	The business climate could change.	This could kill the project.
I&C = instrumentation and control.		

Table 8.3. Organizational Factors for Safety Vision

group worked on the overall product-line concept and was responsible for overall system design. It consisted of an experienced senior I&C engineer and an electrical engineer. The group was reinforced on a case-by-case basis by additional I&C experts.

A second group worked on methods for specifying requirements for individual I&C projects. This group consisted of approximately five experienced process engineers. The project requirements specification is typically prepared by process engineers using informal methods such as textual descriptions, diagrams, and mathematical notation. Using this specification, I&C engineers design and implement the I&C system. The results of the design phase must be reviewed by the authors of the requirements specification. Normally, neither party is an expert in software engineering, so an approach using classic software engineering techniques like data flow diagrams, extended Backus-Naur form notation, or entity-relationship diagrams is not suitable (factor O2.3). A more domain-specific specification method had to be used for designing individual projects.

A third group worked on evaluating algorithms for signal validation and error propagation barriers, and developed a failure model. Initially, this group consisted of one electrical engineer. After making the decision to use functional diagrams (FDs) for specifying an I&C system (see the Usability issue and the strategy *Use FDs for specification*), two computer scientists and an electrical engineer were added to form the software development group. Their task was to develop the engineering tools needed (graphical editor, code generators, function blocks). Later, when additional on-line software components had to be developed, another electrical engineer and a technical assistant were added to the group. For a limited period, as many as three additional in-house software developers were involved on a contract basis.

After the hardware platform had been selected, it became clear that its standard off-the-shelf operating system software had to be redeveloped (see the Quality of Software issue and the strategy *Create custom operating system*). The primary reason for this was to obtain certification from the regulatory agency. This was done by a fourth group, which consisted of five to six engineers from the supplier of the hardware platform (factor O2.2).

During the development phase of the Safety Vision system software, in addition to the internal quality assessment measures, there were two independent external institutes inspecting and qualifying the software components for conformance to national and international standards. As stipulated in the development phase model, the results of the external assessors were fed back into the development, which led to corrections and improvements in the software development documents.

8.1.4 Develop Strategies

The factors, requirements, and standards listed so far led to particular strategies and design guidelines, summarized below.

Evolution

The project designer specifies instrumentation and control (I&C) functions to control the safety aspects of the plant, and specifies the hardware these functions use. Projects should be able to use state-of-the-art hardware, now and in the future, at a reasonable cost. Each project has a distinct hardware configuration.

Influencing Factors

P1.1, P1.2: Projects interoperate with external systems, and must be portable to new hardware.

P1.3, P1.6, P4.1: The system must be scalable and must support simulation and distribution.

P7.1: Hardware costs for projects must be reasonable.

T2.1, T5.2: Standard hardware components and protocols are available.

Solution

Safety Vision has strategies to insulate projects from changes in the hardware platform, and to support the projects' diverse hardware configurations. It uses standard components and protocols when possible, and maintains a strict separation between the software and the hardware.

Strategy: *Use standard hardware components.*

Use standard hardware components for digital automation systems. The input/output and CPU boards are standard for the I&C domain: The CPU board uses the Intel 486 and special I&C integrated circuits. The Ethernet and Profibus network components are industry standard.

Strategy: *Use standard local area network (LAN) protocols.*

Use standard LAN protocols whenever possible. This makes it easier to communicate with external systems and to incorporate new hardware (provided it uses the standard protocol).

Continued

Evolution *(continued)*

Strategy: *Separate hardware and software specifications.*

When designing projects, put hardware and software specifications on different diagrams. Traditionally, these were intermingled, which made the I&C functionality difficult to understand. By separating them, the software specification is independent from the target system (hardwired analog systems, digital systems, or any other). The I&C functionality can then be tested on a simulator. In addition, a software specification can be mapped to different hardware configurations, including configurations that contain new hardware components.

Strategy: *Produce target-independent code.*

Keep the code that implements the I&C system independent of the target system platform. Although the project designer assigns a CPU number specifying where each part of the I&C functionality executes, the resulting code should be independent of the particular CPU type.

Strategy: *Use a highly configurable runtime environment (RTE).*

Provide a target-specific execution platform for directly executing the generated code. This execution platform is called the RTE, and it acts as a "virtual" CPU for application execution. This means that projects can run on other target platforms without porting. The RTE itself should be easily portable to new target platforms. It should also be highly configurable, because each project has its own distributed hardware configuration.

Usability by Target Audience

Projects are designed and implemented by I&C engineers according to specifications written by process engineers. These process engineers also verify that a project design meets the specification. The Safety Vision engineering system must be easy to use for these domain experts.

Influencing Factors

P1.2: Projects must be portable to new hardware platforms.

P1.3: The system must be scalable to support diverse project architectures.

P1.4, P1.5: The system must support redundancy and fault tolerance for projects.

P2.1: The system must provide engineering tools for I&C engineers to create projects, communicate results to process engineers, and perform verification easily.

P4.2: Projects must be impervious to seismic disturbances.

P4.3: Projects must conform to regulatory agency requirements for software quality.

P7.2: The cost to develop projects must be reasonable.

T5.1: Functional diagrams are a standard I&C documentation notation.

O2.1: People with a wide range of training are available as needed to support the project.

O2.3: The process engineers and I&C engineers are not trained in classic software engineering analysis techniques.

Solution

Have domain experts (I&C engineers, process engineers, electrical engineers) set the basic software architecture concepts for Safety Vision.

Strategy: *Have the architecture designed by domain experts.*

The I&C, process, and electrical engineers have extensive knowledge of domain-specific notations that can be used to design projects. They are familiar with the variety of configurations these I&C systems can support, and are familiar with their distributed nature. They understand the real-time, fault-tolerant, and regulatory requirements of projects, and have experience building systems that fulfill these requirements. All of these project characteristics have a profound impact on the design of Safety Vision.

Continued

Usability by Target Audience *(continued)*

Strategy: *Use functional diagrams for the specification.*

Use functional diagrams for the project design. Functional diagrams are a standard I&C notation, so they are well understood by both I&C and process engineers.

Related Strategies

The strategy *Generate code automatically* is primarily motivated by the Quality of Software issue, but it also makes the system easier to use. The project designer is an expert in the I&C domain, but is not necessarily an expert software engineer. With automatically generated code, the I&C experts can concentrate on the project design instead of on the software engineering challenges.

Quality of Software

Safety I&C systems must meet the highest quality standards, as defined by the regulatory agency for nuclear power plants. The regulatory agency specifies a process for verifying the design of a project and for certifying the quality of its software implementation. However, each project is a custom I&C system, and it is prohibitively expensive to certify each project independently.

Influencing Factors

P1.3: The system must be scalable to support diverse project architectures.

P2.1: The system must provide engineering tools for I&C engineers.

P4.3, P4.4: Projects must fulfill regulatory agency requirements (software quality, simplicity).

P7.2: The cost to develop projects must be reasonable.

O2.1: People with a wide range of training are available, as needed by the project.

O2.2: Engineers from the supplier of the hardware platform are available as consultants.

Continued

Quality of Software *(continued)*

Solution

Implement each project using only certified software components and code that is generated and validated automatically.

Strategy: *Develop type-tested software components.*

Use prefabricated and type-tested software components. The notion of type-testing was originally developed for hardware components: A type-tested component has been tested under varying conditions and is certified to operate according to its specification. A similar concept is applied to software components.

Strategy: *Generate code automatically.*

An I&C system's functionality is designed by selecting function blocks from a library and interconnecting them. The implementation is then an interconnection of pre-defined, type-tested software components. This interconnection code is generated automatically, so it is implemented consistently over all projects. It is free from the variations and errors that can occur when code is implemented manually.

Strategy: *Validate code automatically.*

Although the code generators are certified, this cannot guarantee that they are error free. To increase confidence in the generated code, it is supplemented with tracing information for recreating the functional diagram. The recreated diagram is automatically compared with the original to verify consistency between the functional diagram and the implementation.

Strategy: *Create a custom operating system.*

The off-the-shelf operating system is not certified. By redeveloping the portions needed by Safety Vision and by following an approved development process, the result can be certified. This is feasible because a member of the team has extensive knowledge of a similar operating system. A benefit of this approach is that the operating system software can be tailored to the needs of Safety Vision. Unneeded functionality can be removed, and the operating system kernel can be simplified.

Real-Time Performance

The I&C systems must have adequate overall performance and deterministic timing behavior during execution. On a functional diagram, the engineer can schedule I&C functions to be executed with an assigned period, and the resulting implementation must meet this schedule.

Influencing Factors

P1.1: The system must support a project's interoperability with external systems.

P3.1: Projects require communication performance of as many as 200 messages of 500 bytes per second.

P3.2: The execution timing of the I&C systems must be deterministic.

P4.1: The system must support the physical distribution of projects' hardware and software.

P4.2: Projects must be impervious to seismic disturbances.

P4.4: The implementation of projects must be simple, as required by the regulatory agency.

P7.1: Hardware costs for projects must be reasonable.

T2.1: Standard hardware components are available for digital automation systems.

Solution

The two keys to this solution are to select the appropriate hardware and to design an execution model that guarantees that applications meet their scheduled deadlines.

Hardware Selection

The hardware had to meet both the real-time performance needs and additional safety requirements for nuclear power plants. Because of the low volume of hardware components sold for nuclear power plants and the short innovation cycles for standard digital I&C hardware components, it made sense to use standard components. Three hardware platforms came under close examination, but only one could fulfill all of the requirements for communication performance, diskless operation, and computing power. The selected platform uses an Intel 486 processor board, with 1MB RAM, 512KB flash-erasable programmable read-only memory (FEPROM) for storing program code, and a 32KB electrically erasable programmable read-only memory (EEPROM) for storing project-specific data. The input and output boards are standard automation components; such boards are widely used in other technological fields. Communication processor boards are available for the LAN standards Ethernet and Profibus. These boards are mounted in racks and communicate via a

Continued

Real-Time Performance *(continued)*

32-bit multimaster-capable parallel backplane bus. Other LAN components like electrical to optical transducers and starcoupler components are also standard industry components.

Strategy: *Follow a simple processing model.*

Follow a simple processing model for the execution of the function diagrams. Execution is cyclic, with a predefined cycle time. There is a fixed sequence of processing steps, and there is no conditional execution of function blocks. This means that control flow is static; it does not depend on runtime data. Message size and communication rates are fixed, resulting in constant communication loads.

Fault Tolerance

The I&C systems must be fault tolerant. They must have high availability, with redundant structures that can take over if a fault occurs. They must be able to detect faults and have fail-safe behavior, meaning that in case of failure the system fails in a predefined way.

Influencing Factors

P1.4: The engineering system must support redundant system structures within projects.

P1.5: The engineering system must provide projects with fault-tolerant mechanisms; for example, for error/exception handling.

Solution

Although the project designer is responsible for designing fault tolerance into the project, the Safety Vision engineering system must support it.

Strategy: *Provide function blocks for signal validation.*

Provide support for signal validation in the function diagrams via special function blocks.

Strategy: *Provide message and signal statuses.*

Each message and each signal has a status. Faulty signals or signals from a missing or corrupted input telegram are marked as faulty and are disregarded by the function blocks used for signal validation. All outputs are set to a defined error state after a fault occurs.

8.2 Conceptual Architecture View

The conceptual view for the Safety Vision product line defines how the designers of an individual project specify an I&C system. The three strategies that had the most impact on the conceptual view are the following:

1. *Have the architecture designed by domain experts* (issue, Usability by Target Audience)

2. *Use FDs for specification* (issue, Usability by Target Audience)

3. *Separate hardware and software specifications* (issue, Evolution)

The requirements specification for a project is usually prepared by process engineers. It defines the project in terms of functional units and their dependencies.

These functional units are then analyzed by I&C engineers and transformed into a formal software specification using FDs. This analysis includes, for example, evaluating the input and output signals of the system, identifying common submodules in different functional units, and partitioning functional units into several FDs. These FDs are understood by both process and I&C engineers, thus facilitating the verification of the software specification.

The FDs used in Safety Vision are independent from the target system technology. They specify the signal processing but impose no other implementation restrictions. The signal processing is specified by selecting predefined function blocks, then interconnecting them to define the signal flow. An FD can import and export signals from and to other FDs or input/output boards.

Figure 8.2 presents an example of an FD. The center area is used for placing and connecting function blocks. The left side contains an area for importing external signals from other FDs or input boards, and the right side is used for exporting signals to other FDs or output boards. Signal import and export is based on a naming scheme that uniquely identifies each FD and each signal. The bottom area of an FD is used for additional information like project name, author's name, date of last modification, and FD name.

Although the hardware specification is not strictly part of the conceptual view, in Safety Vision the I&C engineers prepare it along with the software specification. It serves as the definition and documentation of the hardware structure and system architecture of the I&C system. It defines

- All hardware components used in the I&C system, such as processor boards, communication processors, LAN components, racks, and cabinets

- The logical interconnections (communication connections) between processor boards

- The systemwide communication cycle, which defines the rate at which telegrams are exchanged between processor boards

- The physical arrangement of hardware components in racks, cabinets, and rooms

This information is used for preparing hardware orders, for setting up the hardware during system assembly, and for documentation during operation and maintenance. It is also used during automatic code generation for evaluating possible communication links, defining telegrams, and generating the configuration information for each processor board.

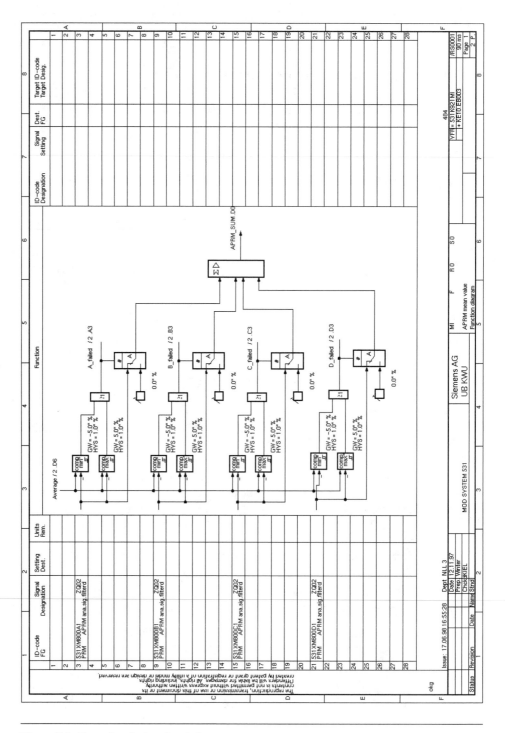

Figure 8.2. Example of a functional diagram

The software/hardware assignment is also completed using the hardware specification diagrams. To simplify the later automatic code generation, an FD must be processed by one processor unit; it cannot be distributed over several processing units. Thus for each processor board, the I&C engineer lists all FDs that are to be processed on that board.

The hardware specification uses diagrams similar to those for the software specification, but they contain hardware blocks instead of function blocks. Each hardware block represents a specific hardware component. Logical connections and physical arrangements are defined in separate diagrams but both are defined by interconnecting the hardware blocks. For logical connections, the hardware blocks are connected by lines, indicating communication connections like a common backplane bus or LAN. For physical connections, the hardware blocks are connected to each other; for example, a processor board is "plugged" into the backplane bus of a rack, or a communication processor is connected to a starcoupler unit. Figure 8.3 presents an example of a hardware specification diagram showing the logical connections of the components.

One of the Safety Vision engineering tools is a graphical editor, which is used to create these FDs and hardware diagrams. The editor supports horizontal and vertical navigation. Horizontal navigation means that signal flow through different FDs can be followed automatically. Vertical navigation allows the user to navigate from overview diagrams to detailed diagrams.

Each project has its own relational database, containing both project-specific and general information, such as the characteristics of function blocks and hardware blocks. The project database is used to configure the graphical editor (by defining the function blocks and hardware blocks the I&C engineer can use), and to store the contents of the project diagrams.

In the rest of this section we focus on the underlying model of the software specification. This is the conceptual view of Safety Vision's software architecture.

8.2.1 Components for Software Specification

The building blocks for the conceptual view are components and connectors. For the Safety Vision product line, the components are function blocks and FDs.

A set of well-defined function blocks is provided by the Safety Vision engineering system. For each function block, the functionality, input/output ports, parameters, and start-up behavior are precisely defined. The function blocks are composed of ten categories, as shown in Table 8.4. Although the number of function blocks should be limited for ergonomic reasons, the set of function blocks can be easily expanded with new function blocks if needed.

An FD, the other type of component in Safety Vision, is used to group and to connect function blocks. It serves primarily as a functional grouping, but there are also runtime implications to grouping function blocks in a diagram: The CPU assignment and the cycle time for execution apply to the entire FD.

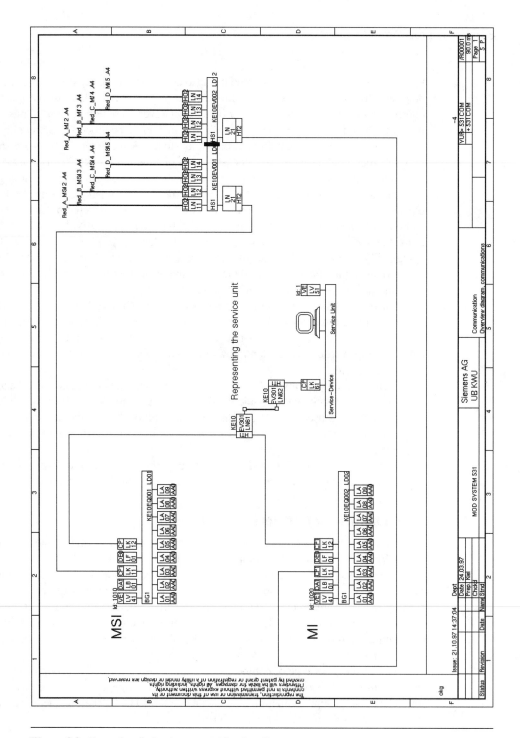

Figure 8.3. Example of a hardware specification diagram

Category	Examples of Function Blocks
Arithmetic operations on analog signals	add, sqrt, abs
Analog signal processing	Unit delay, PT1, differentiation, integrator, controller, digital filter, ramp generator
Selection of analog signals	Switches, min/max value selection, sorting
Mixed analog/binary signal processing	Limit switch
Logical operations	and, or, xor
Binary signal processing	Unit delay, pulse with specified duration, on and off delays, flip-flops
Selection of binary signals	Switches, three-out-of-four voting, two-out-of-four-voting, two-out-of-three voting, one-out-of-two voting
Domain-specific actuator interfaces	Interfaces to control rod drives, pressurizer heating elements
Interface to the runtime environment	Acquire operation-mode permission, pass error flags
Decode message signals into binary signals	One for each function block module that generates a message signal

Table 8.4. Categorization of Function Blocks

A meta-model for a software specification is shown in Figure 8.4. A software specification contains multiple FDs, which in turn contain multiple function blocks and FB_connectors. An FD can have multiple input ports (FD_input_signal) and multiple output ports (FD_output_signal). These are the signals listed in the left and right sides of an FD respectively.

Function blocks also can have multiple input ports (FB_input_port) and multiple output ports (FB_output_port). Each port has an associated protocol, Signal_type, that defines the type of signal that can be connected to it. Three types of signals are defined: those for analog (float value) signals, binary (Boolean value) signals, and message (binary code) signals.

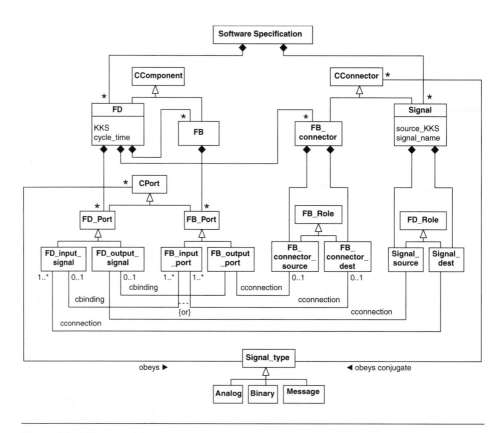

Figure 8.4. Meta-model for software specification. FD = function diagram; FB = function block.

8.2.2 Connectors for Software Specification

The conceptual connectors in Safety Vision are FB_connector, for connecting function blocks within an FD, and Signal, for interconnections between FDs. Both of these types of connectors have exactly two roles each—a source and a destination. They simply transmit a signal from one end of the connector to the other, so the protocol Signal_types is associated with the connector rather than the role.

A port can be connected to a role only as allowed by the meta-model: FD_Ports can only be connected to FD_Roles, and FB_Ports can only be connected to FB_Roles. Similarly, bindings are only allowed between FD_Ports and FB_Ports. The other constraint for connections and bindings is that the signal types must be compatible. These constraints are checked by the Safety Vision graphical editor when an FD is created or modified.

The meta-model in Figure 8.4 is a specialization of the general conceptual view meta-model in Figure 4.16. For Safety Vision, there are only two levels of decomposition for components (FDs and function blocks), and no decomposition of connectors. In addition, as we said earlier, the Safety Vision connectors are simple, with a single source and destination, so that the protocol is associated with the connector rather than with individual roles.

8.2.3 Conceptual Configuration

Although the components, connectors, and their relationships are defined in the product-line architecture of Safety Vision, it is the I&C engineer who defines the configuration of a particular project. This is the software specification.

During a typical software specification process, the I&C engineer creates a set of FDs using the Safety Vision graphical editor. To connect function blocks in different FDs, the engineer exports the connecting signal in the source FD and assigns it to a unique signal name. Next the engineer opens the target FD and creates an import signal, which is connected to the corresponding function block port. Finally, the engineer assigns the imported signal to the signal name of the previously exported signal, thus defining the connection. At specification time, the editor automatically checks whether the import/export signal exists and whether the connected function block ports are of the same signal type. If the source, target function block, or FD is deleted, the signal is automatically marked as "open ended" in the connected FDs. By connecting the different FDs with signals, the complete software specification is created.

8.2.4 Resource Budgeting

The specification of a complete I&C system must include its hardware structure and the assignment of FDs to processor boards. In Safety Vision, the resource budgeting task consists of assigning FDs to hardware components, and specifying certain runtime characteristics of the FDs.

The hardware specification diagrams are also used for the hardware/software assignment. For this, each processor board contains a list of the FDs that are to be processed by it. Each FD is assigned to one processor board.

Each FD has an individual cycle time, which specifies how frequently it must be processed. The FD's cycle time is specified by the I&C engineers based on required response times or bandwidth considerations. A typical value is 50 msec, although values from 5 msec to several hundred milliseconds are possible.

Each processor board can handle FDs with as many as two different cycle times (although this could easily be changed to three or more different cycle times). The ratio of the two different cycle times must be an integer. The faster cycle time determines the rate of operation of the processor board. The ratio between this cycle time and the communication cycle must also be an integer (although either could be the faster cycle time).

8.3 Module Architecture View

Safety Vision's module view must describe how the conceptual view maps to abstract software modules. It must also describe the support software that does not appear in the conceptual view. The strategies *Use a highly configurable runtime environment (RTE)* (issue, Evolution) and *Create a custom operating system* (issue, Quality of Software), address two kinds of support software that first appear in the module view: the RTE and the operating system software.

The module view of the software for an I&C system is divided into three layers: ApplicationSoftware, PlatformSoftware, and OperatingSystemSoftware. Figure 8.5 provides an overview of these layers.

The ApplicationSoftware layer implements the I&C functions of an individual project using three types of modules: function block modules (FB_module), FD modules (FD_module), and FD group modules (FDG_module). Because this layer depends only on the interface to the RTE, all modules in this layer are completely independent from target system specifics.

The PlatformSoftware layer consists of the RTE, the IO_Driver, the exception_handler, and the self-test module. All of these have dependencies on the OperatingSystemSoftware layer and/or the target system hardware.

The RTE acts as an abstract machine for the application software (I&C functions). It contains a SYSTEM module that encapsulates the OperatingSystemSoftware layer and the target system hardware. This insulates the other modules in the RTE from changes in the target system.

The bottom layer is the OperatingSystemSoftware layer, which consists of the real-time operating system (real_time_OS), communication software (comm_sw), and the hardware organization tool (HOT). This layer has the strongest dependencies on the target system platform.

8.3.1 ApplicationSoftware Layer

Figure 8.6 describes the modules in the ApplicationSoftware layer.

Each function block from the conceptual view has a corresponding function block module (FB_module) in the module view. Due to the simplicity of most function blocks,

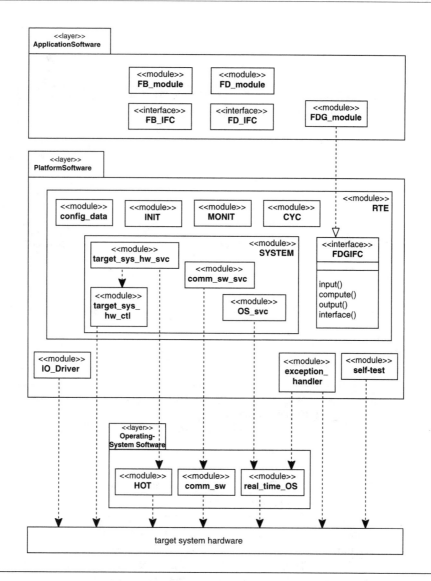

Figure 8.5. Layers of a project's software

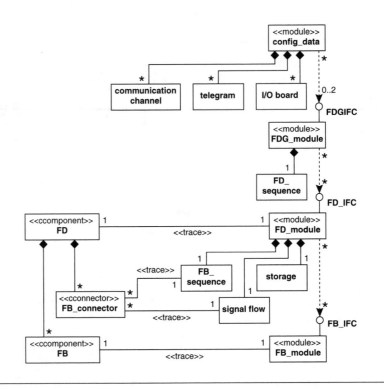

Figure 8.6. Modules in the ApplicationSoftware layer. I/O = input/output; FD = function diagram; FB = function block.

an FB_module is generally implemented by a single function, although in some cases there can be more. The FB_modules are prefabricated and type-tested. They form a library of reusable software components.

Each FD from the conceptual view is implemented in one FD module (FD_module). Unlike the FB_modules, which are reusable, the FD_modules are generated. An FD_module consists mainly of a set of data structures that implement the signal flow between the FB_modules within the FD, storage for parameters and state variables of the FB_modules, and internal signals of the FD_module. It also contains a sequence of function calls to the FB_modules that implements the signal processing of the FD. This sequence is automatically determined by the code generator by topological sorting, based on the signal flow between the FD's function blocks.

The FB_connectors have no direct counterpart in the module view. The entire group of connectors in an FD is implemented by the sequencing of function block calls and the signal flow between them.

An FB_module provides its associated interface (FB_IFC). This can be required by any number of FD_modules, depending on in which FDs the function block appears. An FD_module requires the interface of each function block used by the FD.

An FD_module provides a predefined interface (FD_IFC), defined by a set of global functions and data structures. Strict naming conventions for all symbols used in an FD_module (functions, variables, data types) have been defined. Additional comments in the code preserve all information needed to reconstruct the initial database representation of the FD_module, even its graphical layout. This supports the automatic validation of the generated code.

The FD group module (FDG_module) serves as a wrapper for the FD_modules contained in it, and it has no corresponding component in the conceptual view. The FDG_module calls the compute functions of its assigned FD_modules in a sequential order, which is automatically determined during code generation by topological sorting, based on the signal flow between the FD_modules.

The FDG_module provides the interface FDGIFC, which is required by the module config_data (in module RTE). An FDG_module is basically a set of functions called by the RTE. The interface contains functions for input, compute, output, and accessing the internal data of the FDG_module and its contained FD_modules. This interface hides the internals of the FDG_modules from the RTE. The RTE is unaware of the particular FD_modules contained in the FD group or their sequential processing order. The dependencies within the ApplicationSoftware layer are summarized in Figure 8.7.

8.3.2 PlatformSoftware Layer

The primary module in the PlatformSoftware layer is the RTE module. Its purpose is to give a unified environment for execution of the FDG_modules. The RTE hides target specifics such as hardware, operating system, communication media, communication protocols, and input/output boards from the FDG_modules.

As many as two FDG_modules can be assigned to the RTE. The cycle times of these two FDG_modules must have an integer ratio. The RTE controls the cyclic processing of the FDG_modules and the transfer of signals via telegrams or directly by input/output boards. The basic sequence is to read input signals from input boards and/or telegrams, compute the assigned FD modules, and send output signals to output boards and/or telegrams.

The RTE has four operational modes. Mode OPERATION is the normal operation mode for cyclic processing of the FDG_modules. Mode PARAM is the same as OPERATION, except parameterization of FB_modules and definition of trace data are also supported. The TEST mode is used for functional testing. It supports processing FDG_modules in single-step mode, inserting external input signals from the service station, and tracing internal and external signals. The fourth mode, DIAGNOSIS, gives the service station direct memory access so that it can download special diagnostic programs

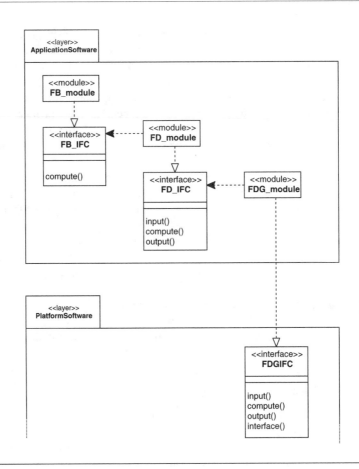

Figure 8.7. Dependencies in the ApplicationSoftware layer

into RAM. In this mode the target system's debug functions are also activated, so that debugging with an external debugger is possible.

Interface FDGIFC defines the interaction between the FDG_modules and the RTE. It contains the input, compute, output, and interface functions.

- The input function is used to pass input signals (from telegrams and/or input boards) to the FD_modules contained in the FDG_module.

- The compute function is used to initiate the computation for the FDG_module. It calls the associated FD's compute functions in the correct order, which in turn call the function blocks of each FD in the required order.

- The output function is used to pass the calculated output signals of the FDG_module to the caller. The signals are then sent via telegrams or to output boards.

- The last function is a universal interface for read-write access to all FDG_module internal data structures, such as parameters, state variables, and signals. The RTE uses this interface function for accessing signals when a trace or parameterization of FDG_modules is required by the external service station.

The RTE accesses interface FDGIFC using function pointers. The function pointers and the associated data structures and data types are defined in the RTE config_data module, which is generated by an automatic code generator.

The RTE also provides a monitoring and control interface that can be accessed by external service stations (for example, to trace signals, read error messages, switch operation modes, or parameterize FB_modules).

The RTE's decomposition and internal dependencies are shown in more detail in Figure 8.8. The RTE contains three modules that control the major functions of the RTE: INIT for initialization, CYC for cyclic processing, and MONIT for monitoring.

Module INIT controls the start-up of the RTE. After initialization has been successfully completed, control is branched to the modules CYC and MONIT. If the initialization fails, the cyclic operation is not achieved and module INIT ends in an endless loop.

Module CYC controls the cyclic operation of the RTE. CYC uses services of underlying modules like FDGIFC (for interface to the FDG_modules), MODE (for handling operation mode transitions), or ERRORMSG (the central error message-handling module).

Module MONIT controls the RTE's interface to an external service station. MONIT accepts a set of basic control commands, like reading an error message buffer, request for a change of operating mode, or setting a new parameter value.

Module SYSTEM of the RTE insulates the other modules of the RTE from the OperatingSystemSoftware layer and from the target system hardware, so that porting the RTE to another platform can be accomplished easily by adapting the module SYSTEM to the new platform. It contains the following three modules:

1. Operating system services (OS_svc) provides a minimal set of services. No other operating system services are used by the RTE. In particular, there is no dynamic allocation of resources like memory heap or dynamic task definitions. The services provided are real-time-related services (pause, task end, and resume after specified time interval), semaphore services, and event-flag services.

2. Communication software services (comm_sw_svc) provide a unified set of services for sending and receiving telegrams via communication channels. This is independent of the medium used. (Media supported by the communication software are 32-bit parallel backplane bus, 16-bit parallel local extension bus, Ethernet 802.2/3 LAN, and Profibus Fieldbus Data Link LAN). The communication services provided are creating communication channels, sending and receiving data via communication channels, and requesting the communication channel status.

3. Target system hardware services (target_sys_hw_svc) provide access to certain components of the target system hardware, either by direct access or by functions provided by HOT. This includes access to light-emitting diodes on the processor board's front plate, EEPROM programming services, and watchdog services.

By adapting only the module SYSTEM, the RTE has been ported successfully to other platforms, such as a standard personal computer with the OS/2 or Windows NT operating system. In every case, the porting effort took only a few days.

In addition to the RTE module, the PlatformSoftware layer includes three other modules: IO_Driver, exception_handler, and self-test.

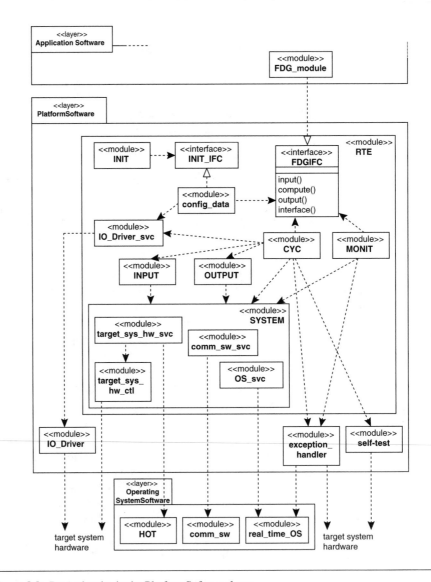

Figure 8.8. Dependencies in the PlatformSoftware layer

For every type of input/output board, an IO_Driver module is provided. It serves to transfer input/output signals between the RTE and the specific input/output board. The IO_Drivers also take care of initialization of the input/output boards and detection of errors.

The exception_handler module handles unexpected situations, like time-out, and watchdog or unexpected operational code exceptions. Information about the exception and its context is saved in RAM. Depending on the type of exception, the exception handler then either restarts the processor board (by a software-activated reset) or shuts down the processor board in a defined state. Information saved by the exception handler can be read from the service station using the services of the RTE, or can be read directly via a serial line connection from the processor board's front plate.

The self-test module performs a sequence of self-test checks on the various hardware components of the processor board, like RAM test, FEPROM test, watchdog test, and so on. The self-test is performed during time intervals when no cyclic processing of the FDG_modules is active. It is repeated continuously, and its cyclic processing is monitored by the RTE. Any errors found are reported to the exception_handler, which stores the information and takes care of error handling.

8.4 Execution Architecture View

In Safety Vision, an I&C system is a distributed computer system with several independent processor boards operating in the same or different racks. It communicates via telegrams using LAN or backplane bus communication links. Thus the execution of the FDs is distributed over several processor boards. This distribution is specified by assigning the FDs to processor boards during hardware specification. The execution structure within one processor board is fixed and is described next.

8.4.1 Processes

The designers considered splitting the process for one processor board into two processes, one containing only the operating system software and platform software, and the other containing only the application software. This would mean that after a change in the FD_modules, only the application software process would have to be loaded onto the target system. However, this approach was not implemented because of the additional effort required to resolve address references between the two independently located processes. Also, the benefits of this approach would have been small, due to the relatively short loading times needed.

As a result, one process is created for each processor board. The process contains all software modules (operating system software, platform software, and application software). These components are linked and located to give one "loadable" file for each processor board.

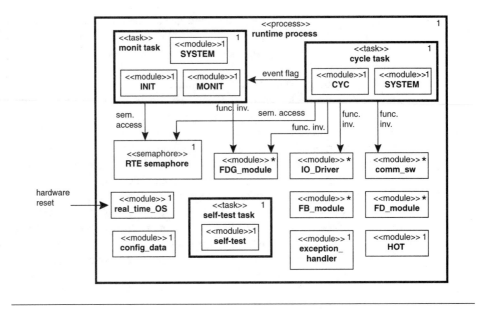

Figure 8.9. Execution structure of runtime process

Because of the requirements for simplicity and deterministic behavior, a simple and straightforward task organization is used in the runtime system's execution structure, as shown in Figure 8.9.

The runtime process contains three tasks: the monitoring task, the cycle task, and the self-test task.

The monitoring task contains modules INIT and MONIT. Control starts in module INIT, which controls the complete initialization phase of the RTE. After successful initialization, control is permanently passed to module MONIT, which processes control commands received via telegrams from the external service station.

The cycle task contains module CYC, and operates with a predefined, constant cycle time, equivalent to the cycle time of its fastest FDG_module. The cycle task handles all communication via telegrams and the input/output boards, and it does the cyclic processing of the FDG_modules.

The cycle task and the monitoring task share a set of functions for accessing commonly used data. Coordination between the two tasks is done by protecting critical regions of control flow with a mutual-exclusion semaphore.

The self-test task contains the self-test module, which continuously performs tests of all relevant hardware components of the processor board (RAM test, ROM checksums, watchdog test, and so on).

The design decision to put the CYC and MONIT modules into two separate tasks was made for the following reason. MONIT processes the control commands received via telegrams from the service station. Processing of these commands requires additional computing time, depending on the command and its parameters. For example, programming the EEPROM might take up to 2 msec per byte. By separating MONIT and CYC into two tasks, the computing time for the cyclic operation is decoupled from the computing time needed for command processing. In this way, deterministic behavior (in other words, nearly constant computing time) can be achieved for FDG_module processing, and maintaining the required cycle time is guaranteed.

The start-up behavior of the runtime process is shown in Figure 8.10. The runtime process itself is activated by a hardware reset. The runtime process contains the real_time_OS module, which activates the monitoring task and self-test task. The cycle task is activated by the monitoring task after successful completion of the initialization phase. The self-test task is automatically started by the operating system after each reset. It has the lowest priority of all tasks, and is only scheduled when the monitoring and cycle tasks are not active.

The cycle task is the highest priority task, thus ensuring that the cyclic operation of the FDG_modules always happens with the specified cycle time. Its behavior is described in the state diagram in Figure 8.11. On activation, the cycle task requests the semaphore. When the semaphore is available, it holds it from the start of its operating cycle until its end. Thus the monitoring task cannot access (and change) common data when the cycle task is active. If the semaphore is not immediately available because it is held by the monitoring task, the cycle task is suspended to avoid deadlock.

During the processing of an FD group operation, the cycle task may receive a control telegram from the service station. In this case, it sends an event_flag to the monitoring

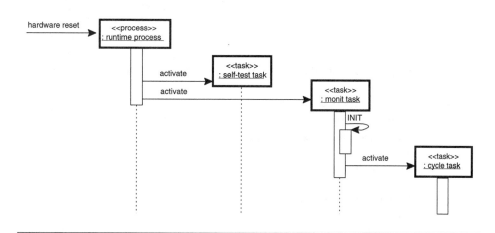

Figure 8.10. Start-up of runtime process

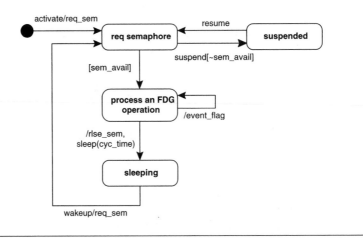

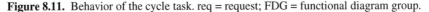

Figure 8.11. Behavior of the cycle task. req = request; FDG = functional diagram group.

task, which processes the command. After the control commands have been processed, the cycle task takes over the results and sends the command responses to the service station with the next message telegram.

At the end of its operating cycle, the cycle task releases the semaphore and notifies the scheduler that it will sleep until the start of the next cycle. It passes the cycle time along with this notification.

The monitoring task has medium priority. Its behavior is described in Figure 8.12. After being activated, the monitoring task performs the initialization and activates the cycle task. Then the monitoring task sleeps until an event_flag arrives, indicating that it must process a control command. It does not begin processing the command until the cycle task has finished its current operation. In addition, if the next cycle begins before it has finished processing the command, then it is suspended so that the cycle task can do its work. This means that it may take multiple execution cycles for the monitoring task to process a command.

During the course of processing a command, the monitoring task may acquire the semaphore to access a common datum. It holds the semaphore only for short time intervals (less than 1 msec) (for example, for writing a new a parameter value) and then immediately releases it. This guarantees that the start of the cycle task cannot be delayed indefinitely by the monitoring task.

The behavior of the self-test task, the lowest priority task, is very simple (Figure 8.13). Once it is activated, it is immediately suspended. If the cycle task completes an operation before the cycle time is up, then the remainder of the cycle time goes first to the monitoring task. The self-test task gets scheduled only if the monitoring task has no commands to process.

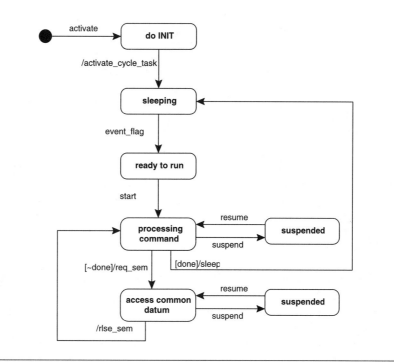

Figure 8.12. Behavior of the monitoring task

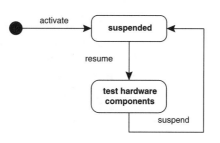

Figure 8.13. Behavior of the self-test task

8.4.2 Communication Paths

Communication between different processors is done using telegrams. These telegrams can contain

- Signals from FDG_modules (signal telegrams)
- Control commands from the service station (control telegrams)
- Error messages, trace data, and command responses to the service station (message telegrams)

To achieve a deterministic timing behavior, all communication is strictly cyclic using the systemwide unique communication cycle. No event-driven communication is used. All telegrams have an individual but fixed telegram length. This makes communication loads constant under all circumstances.

The communication protocols for sending telegrams do not expect acknowledgment from the receiver. Thus the telegram receiver cannot interfere with the sender's operation.

Several communication media are supported by the communication software. Processor boards in the same rack communicate directly via backplane bus using shared dual-ported communication RAM. Processors in different racks communicate via Ethernet or Profibus LAN. For LAN communication, dedicated communication processors are used; they handle all tasks related to the specific LAN protocol. These communication processors work autonomously so that the processor boards processing the FDG_modules are not burdened with LAN communication. Telegrams between the processor boards and the communication processors are exchanged using shared dual-ported random access memory (DPRAM). These shared DPRAM channels use a handshake protocol: The sender can only send when the channel is empty; the receiver can only read when the channel is nonempty.

8.4.3 Execution Configuration

A fixed operating system software configuration is used for all processor boards. No project-specific configuration is needed or possible. The runtime process described earlier is loaded onto all computers in each redundancy (signal acquisition, data-processing, voter, and message interface computers), and onto the gateway computers (Figure 8.1).

However, the platform software in the runtime process must be configured individually for each processor board. This is done by the RTE configuration module (config_data), which is generated by an automatic code generator based on the hardware and software specification in the project database. The configuration module defines a unique processor identifier, the operating and communication cycle times, the interface to the FDG_modules to be processed, configuration data for the IO_Drivers, and the complete list of all telegrams and communication channels.

The project-specific software (FDG_modules and FD_modules) are completely generated by an automatic code generator, so no additional configuration is needed. During linking of the target system software, the FB_modules used by the specific FD_modules are taken from the function block module library, so that only the FB_modules actually used are included in the target system code.

8.5 Code Architecture View

Figure 8.14 shows the directory structure for the software of an individual project. It contains all generated code for the project, and the runtime loadable file (which corresponds to the runtime process in the execution view). This structure is automatically generated the first time code is generated from a project database. The directory structure of the prefabricated software modules for the operating system and platform software is not shown here.

Each project has subdirectories for FD group files and runtime files. In the FDG Files directory, there is a subdirectory for each FD group (named with the unique identifier for the FD group). Each of these FD group directories has three subdirectories: c, h, and obj.

Directory c contains one generated source code file for the FDG_module and one for each of its FD_modules. Directory h contains the corresponding header files with the external interface definitions. Directory obj contains an automatically generated makefile

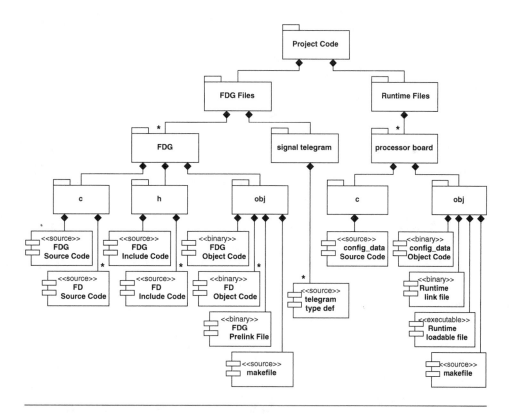

Figure 8.14. Directory structure for project-specific code. FDG = function diagram group.

for compiling and linking the FD group code. After compilation and linking, this directory also contains the object files for the FDG_module and its FD_modules, and the FD group prelink file. The prelink file contains the FD group object code, the FD object code (for those FDs in the directory), and compiler and linker listing files.

The directory FDG also contains a subdirectory for the signal telegrams, which in turn contains header files for the signal telegram data-type definitions of all signal telegrams used in the system. A header file is included by the FD group source code when its corresponding FDG_module sends or receives a signal telegram.

The directory Runtime Files contains a subdirectory for each processor board of the system, named with the processor's unique identification number. Each of these processors will have a separately configured runtime process running on it. The processor board directory contains two subdirectories: c and obj.

Directory c contains the generated source code for the config_data module for this processor board. Directory obj contains an automatically generated makefile for compiling the config_data source and linking it with the operating system software, the platform software prelinks, and the prelinks for the FDG_modules assigned to this processor board. The resulting link file is then located to absolute addresses to get a target system loadable file. After executing the makefile, the obj directory contains the config_data object code, the link file for the runtime process, its target system loadable file, and the listing files generated by the compiler, linker, and locator.

8.6 Software Architecture Uses

During the development of the Safety Vision engineering system, the software architecture was used to identify the subsystems and tools needed, and for planning schedules and work assignments. The software architecture also helped to clarify the Safety Vision concept to managers and external assessors.

The concepts of Safety Vision's software architecture are embedded primarily in the engineering tools it provides for developing an I&C system.

Safety Vision graphical editor—Although the graphical notation used in Safety Vision's editor is domain specific, its underlying model is the meta-model of the conceptual view. This ensures that the specification of an I&C system conforms to the conceptual architecture view.

Automatic code generation—One of Safety Vision's code generators interprets the contents of an I&C specification and automatically generates its source code. It generates the high-level language program code for each FD. It also generates the communication between diagrams by interpreting the hardware specification and software/hardware assignment. Thus it contains the rules for mapping the conceptual view to the module and execution views, then to the code view.

The other code generator creates the configuration data for each processor board. This configuration data describes the FDs to be processed, their cycle time, and the relevant telegrams, communication channels, and input/output boards. This code generator also uses the specification and the mappings between the architecture views to generate the configuration data.

Automatic validation of code—To validate that the generated code matches the specification of the I&C system, Safety Vision provides tools to parse the generated code, transform it into an internal representation, and compare this representation with the information stored in the project database. Supporting this traceability had some influence on the code architecture view, for example by causing the FD group and FD source files to be structured with data in one contiguous memory area. Embedded in these tools is knowledge of the code architecture view, and its mapping to the module view then the conceptual view.

Project database—In addition to containing the specification of an I&C system, each project database contains a complete definition of the function blocks, including their graphical representation, input and output ports, parameters, and state variables. When a function block is added or changed, only its definition in the database is changed. This is done via Structured Query Language (SQL) script files. Each function block, as well as each hardware block, has its own SQL script containing its database definition data.

In contrast to the definition of FB_modules, the IO_Driver_svc modules are not completely defined by definition tables in the database. The result is that to add a new type of input/output board and its associated IO_Driver modules to the system, the code generators have to be adapted. Although the changes are rather straightforward and small, the documentation must be updated and test suites must be repeated. A better solution would have been to define completely the IO_Driver_svc modules in database definition tables, as was done for the FB_modules. With this approach, adding a new input/output board would mean simply adding its definition data to the database without adapting the code generators.

The FDs and hardware specification diagrams in a project database are also used as forward documentation for the project. These diagrams are used not only as software specification documentation but are also used during commissioning and plant operation. Because the project database is the sole source for the project software, this documentation is always up to date.

8.6.1 Software Process for Projects

To conform to regulatory agency requirements, the software development of each safety I&C system should follow a standard phase model, with a requirements specification phase, a design phase, and a coding phase. The results of each phase must be verified against its inputs. Because Safety Vision supports a formal graphical specification method with its graphical editor, a modified phase model was defined for developing project software. In this modified phase model, the requirements specification phase and the design phase are replaced by the formal software specification process using FDs. Verification of the software specification is done partly automatically based on rules (syntax conventions), and partly manually by verification with the system engineers. The coding phase is replaced by automatic code generation for the FDs. The results of the code generation phase can be automatically verified by applying the inverse code generation rules and comparing the results with the original information stored in the project database.

8.6.2 Testing of Projects

Both the module and the execution views explicitly address self-supervision and self-testing. The fault-tolerant architecture facilitates on-line testing of any processor board (one or more) in a redundant system. The inputs (outputs) to (from) function blocks are marked as being one of normal, under testing, or faulty. Thus, processor boards not under test can disregard these signals by using special validation or voting function blocks (for example, second maximum, second minimum, two-out-of-four voting, and so forth).

8.7 Summary

Safety Vision's product-line architecture and engineering toolset has an important impact on the development of digital safety I&C systems. It provides

- A high degree of support for the specification of these systems using existing domain-specific graphical notations
- Reuse of certified components
- Automatic generation of the implementation
- Automatic validation of the implementation against the specification

Using the Safety Vision engineering system, engineers can develop high-quality I&C systems at a significantly lower cost than they could without this product-line support.

A project specification is decomposed into a software and a hardware specification phase, both of which are supported by the Safety Vision graphical editor. The software specification is a domain-specific formal specification that defines the signal processing used to implement the functional units defined in the system requirements specification.

The hardware specification defines the hardware structure of the target system, with all of its hardware components. To specify the software/hardware assignment, each FD created in the software specification is assigned to one processor board.

All of this specification information is stored in the project database. The specification is prepared by I&C engineers using notations and methodologies that have become common practice in the I&C community and are well-known to them. The software specification remains independent from specific details of the target system. Verification of the specification by the process engineers who prepared the system requirement specification is supported by using a commonly understood notation.

The hardware specification is not considered part of the software architecture, but the software specification and the software/hardware assignment are supported by a well-defined conceptual view for the Safety Vision product line. This conceptual view defines a software specification as a network of FDs, each composed of interconnected function blocks. The function blocks are standard Safety Vision components.

Having a separate, well-defined conceptual view facilitates the design, analysis, verification, reconfiguration, and update of I&C functions by process engineers and I&C engineers. The conceptual view is preserved and/or traceable in the code, supporting on-line diagnosis of FDs.

A project specification is formal in the sense that all information needed to implement the final code running in the distributed target system is available from the project database. On the basis of the formal specification and a set of predefined rules, the target system code is generated automatically, thus improving code quality and reducing costs. Automatic code generation greatly reduces the probability of coding errors, and reduces coding time significantly.

Then, by applying the inverse rules, the generated target system code is analyzed by independent tools and compared with the original database representation. Thus, high-quality verification of the generated code is performed automatically by independent tools, improving quality and reducing costs.

In the module view, the ApplicationSoftware layer implements the I&C functions. The adjacent layer, the PlatformSoftware layer, provides a "virtual" execution platform for the I&C functions. This insulates them from the OperatingSystemSoftware layer and the target hardware. Although the PlatformSoftware layer must be configured for each processor board, this is done by automatically generating a single configuration module.

Due to the fact that a formal specification method with automatic code generation is used for the Safety Vision application software, the only software modules that change in a specific project are the configuration module, the FD modules (which implement interconnections within the diagram), and the FD group modules (which implement interconnections between diagrams).

All other software components in the PlatformSoftware layer, all those in the OperatingSystemSoftware layer, and the function block modules are the same across all projects. These software components were developed once using a development and quality assurance process that conforms to the requirements of the regulatory agency. They have been type-tested by external assessors to prove their qualification for safety applications.

By separating the ApplicationSoftware layer from the PlatformSoftware layer, Safety Vision has managed to separate I&C functionality completely from the complex protocols related to communication, fault tolerance, on-line monitoring, and on-line testing. This approach has made the introduction of digital technology to safety I&C of nuclear power plants both tractable and feasible.

Separating the complex protocols makes them amenable to formal modeling techniques, and simplifies their implementation and verification. These protocols were modeled using state charts and other appropriate notations. This separation also simplifies the manual implementation of function blocks and the RTE, because the code to support these protocols is eliminated from the application software. It also allows early and intensive module testing at a phase when errors can be detected more easily than during integration testing.

Lastly, separation of the execution view facilitates reconfiguration of FDs into FD group modules and their processor board assignments. It also makes it easier to change the operating system software (for example, operating system and communication) without affecting the application software.

Safety Vision—Lessons Learned

- The conceptual view played a key role in complete software development. Close attention should be paid to a careful analysis phase so that a reasonable conceptual view is designed. Engineers with experience within the domain and with software techniques should be involved.

- The conceptual view should be well documented and completely understood by all participants of the project to avoid misconceptions and later dilution of the concepts.

- A layered module view should be used to keep the system portable and adaptable to future foreseen and unforeseen changes and extensions. Care should be taken when analyzing influences of the different layers. Some influences on the interfaces might be hidden and difficult to see, like the byte order used by the processor, or the specific maximum telegram length used by different LAN protocols.

- Standards should be used whenever possible. Additional layers (wrappers) should be used to wrap these interfaces because even standards might change or be replaced by others, or might not be supported by another platform.

- Common design and coding standards should be used by all participants. Design reviews, code inspections, and module testing help to increase software quality and save time, money, and nerves during system integration testing.

Chapter 9

Healthy Vision

with Contributions by
Tony Lanza

Healthy Vision is an embedded real-time patient-monitoring system. Healthy Vision is used in hospitals for monitoring a patient's vital signs. It is a stand-alone bedside unit that obtains a patient's data via pods attached to the patient or to other monitoring devices, and communicates via a network to a central station such as the one described in Chapter 10.

Figure 9.1 depicts a Healthy Vision system in which the base unit is attached to a docking station, which is the usual case when a patient is in a hospital room. When the patient is being transported, the base unit can be detached from its docking station and it travels with the patient. This means that the base unit must be compact, light, and must have its own two-hour battery supply.

The base unit has a liquid crystal display (LCD) screen that displays the patient's physiological data as waveforms, parameter values, and alarms (Figure 9.2). For example, heart rate and pressures are discrete, intermittent parameter values, whereas an electrocardiographic (EKG) recording of heart activity or arterial pressure is a continuous waveform sample. Hospital personnel use Healthy Vision's menus to select the kind of data to be displayed and the display format. They can configure the alarms to go off when values fall outside the range they specify. Healthy Vision can also display as much as 24 hours of trend data.

The following are some of the most important marketing requirements for Healthy Vision:

- Integrated parameter set of EKG, pulse oximetry, respiration, temperature, and cardiac output

- Optimized patient data display for easy patient assessment and for the user to view required parameters and waveforms "at a glance"

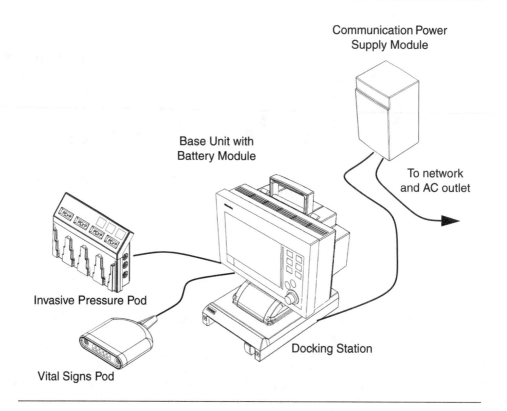

Figure 9.1. Healthy Vision hardware configuration

- Organized monitoring operations for easy, quick access
- Alarms that are easily seen and heard
- Integrated mounting system plus automatic network and power connection
- Two-hour battery life for portability
- Minimized downtime and failures
- Easy software upgrades
- Competitive pricing
- Ability to meet the needs of a wide range of critical-care monitoring customers
- Compatibility with the current product line
- Ability to meet the standards for quality, safety, and manufacture as set forth by the company, appropriate regulatory agencies, and patient-monitoring standards organizations

In this chapter we describe the software architecture for Healthy Vision. The software must fit inside the base unit, and it must acquire and display the patient data in real time. It

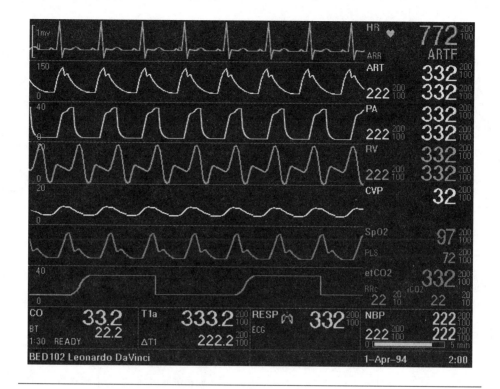

Figure 9.2. Healthy Vision home screen

also has to support the menu-driven interface for hospital personnel to set up the unit. It must store 24 hours of patient data and it must send patient data over the network to a central station or another external device.

In addition, Healthy Vision is not a single product, but a small range of medium to high-end products. Each installation of Healthy Vision can be customized with a different set of pods, external devices, and user features. The software architecture must support this range of products.

9.1 Global Analysis

First we summarize the global analysis for Healthy Vision's software architecture. After listing some of the important product, technological, and organizational factors, the main strategies that were used in designing this architecture are described.

9.1.1 Analyze Product Factors

The relevant product factors for Healthy Vision are listed in Table 9.1.

Product Factor	Flexibility and Changeability	Impact
P1: Features		
P1.1: Application policy rules		
Support customized user settings and application policy rules.	New settings and rules are added regularly.	There is a large impact on all components.
P1.2: Transportable base unit		
The monitor is transportable (two hours of battery life).	The monitor must adjust dynamically to transport or network mode.	This affects signal acquisition and processing.
P1.3: Network connection		
The monitor can be moved to a different network.	The monitor must handle dynamically changing features based on network type.	This affects the user interface.
P1.4: Heterogeneous input/output devices		
The monitor must communicate with third-party devices.	New devices are being added.	This affects acquisition components.
P1.5: Dynamic detection of input/output devices		
The software must detect the presence of input/output devices.	The monitor must handle dynamically changing features based on connected devices.	This affects acquisition components.

Table 9.1. Product Factors Influencing Healthy Vision

Product Factor	Flexibility and Changeability	Impact
P3: Performance		
P3.1: Real-time performance		
There must be real-time display of patient data. Each type of patient data has a maximum delay specified.	The maximum delays are not negotiable.	There is a large impact on signal acquisition and processing components.
P3.2: Processing deadlines		
Several processing priority levels are needed to support multiple processing deadlines.	Deadlines and priority levels could change based on changes to the requirements or the platform.	There is a large impact on all components if process partitioning changes.
P4: Dependability		
P4.1: High availability		
The system must display correct information, 24 hours a day, 7 days a week.	Requirements are stable.	There is a moderate impact on all components.
P6: Service		
P6.1: Software options		
One version must support multiple levels of functionality for a variety of user-purchased options.	Packaging of software is likely to change in response to market conditions.	There is a moderate impact on all components.

Table 9.1. Product Factors Influencing Healthy Vision *(continued)*

Product Factor	Flexibility and Changeability	Impact
P7: Product cost		
P7.1: Product cost		
Cost of CPU and memory is fixed.	There is no flexibility.	There is a moderate impact on signal acquisition and processing.

Table 9.1. Product Factors Influencing Healthy Vision *(continued)*

The features factor provides the product requirements visible to the user. The product supports hundreds of customized user settings and thousands of application policy rules. These policy rules apply to features like EKG processing, parameter processing, alarms processing, patient admission, patient setup, display of patient information, two-channel local recording, network support, and acquisition and display of waveform and parameter information from other devices such as ventilators and anesthesia systems.

The application policy rules are expected to change over time. They are likely to become more complex in the future, driven by changes in hardware, software, and the monitoring domain. Examples of policy rules for alarm volume are as follows:

- Alarm volume can be set between 0 and 100 percent in steps of 10 percent if the monitor is actively communicating with a central station.

- Alarm volume can be set between 10 and 100 percent in steps of 10 percent if the monitor is not actively communicating with a central station.

- If the monitor detects an alarm and is communicating with a central station, it will send the alarm to the central station and expect an acknowledgment. If the monitor does not receive an alarm acknowledgment, a network alarm condition has occurred. Part of processing a network alarm is to set the alarm volume of the monitor to 100 percent and to remember the alarm volume in effect when the network alarm occurred.

- If processing a network alarm, and all alarms clear either on their own or by the user clearing the alarms through an alarm silence or an "all alarms suspend" request, the alarm volume should return to the alarm volume setting in effect when the network alarm was detected.

The monitor is transportable and can be moved to other networks. This means the monitor must be able to dynamically adjust to differences in monitor processing based on whether it is in transport or network mode. Because not all networks support all of the user features, the monitor must also dynamically adjust to the availability of user features based on the connected network type. The monitor must be able to support legacy as well as new-generation network protocols in the same device.

The monitor can be connected to third-party devices. New types of devices can be added and the monitor must be able to detect automatically the presence of new devices while the monitor is running. Although they are heterogeneous, the input and output devices generate or require a similar set of information, including signal data, parameter data, alarm data, and screen layout information.

The product factors related to performance refer to the real-time processing requirements of the system. These requirements are given in terms of the maximum allowable delay for displaying waveforms, and audio and alarm information. Table 9.2 presents examples of a few of the system's processing deadlines.

Processing Deadline	Maximum Delay
Local waveform display delay	200 msec
Local pulse detect blip/beep delay	1.2 sec
Drift in blip/beep stream	50 msec
Alarm annunciation delay	500 msec

Table 9.2. Examples of Performance Requirements

9.1.2 Analyze Technological Factors

The relevant technological factors for Healthy Vision are listed in Table 9.3.

Technological Factor	Flexibility and Changeability	Impact
T1: General-purpose hardware		
T1.1: Processor type		
The base unit has a signal processor, a standard processor, and a graphics processor.	For the standard processor, the CPU type is likely to change in the future.	There is no impact, unless the operating system changes.

Table 9.3. Technological Factors Influencing Healthy Vision

Technological Factor	Flexibility and Changeability	Impact
T1.2: Processor number		
There is one signal processor, one graphics processor, and one to three standard processors.	The number of standard processors is likely to increase.	There is a need to support distributed computing.
T1.3: Memory		
Fixed 8MB code and 8MB data space are required.	There is no flexibility.	This places restrictions on implementation.
T1.4: Diskless system		
1MB of data is stored in battery-backed memory.	There is no flexibility.	This places restrictions on implementation.
T2: Domain-specific hardware		
T2.1: Device management		
There are many types of input and output devices.	New types and upgraded versions need to be supported.	There is a large impact on acquisition components.
T3: Software technology		
T3.1: Distribution		
The selected operating system may not provide support for client/server applications.	If the operating system doesn't support this, the product must provide these services.	Additional components are needed.

Table 9.3. Technological Factors Influencing Healthy Vision (*continued*)

Technological Factor	Flexibility and Changeability	Impact
T3.2: Reentrant code		
The selected operating system may not provide full support for multiprocessing.	If the operating system doesn't support this, portions of the software must be written as reentrant code.	It is extremely difficult to write correct reentrant code.
T3.3: Code portability		
The product must be ported to different platforms, which could force a change in software platform. These software platforms may not provide the same services or have the same interfaces.	A change in hardware platform is likely. This could force a change in the software platform.	On the standard processor, there is a large impact on everything using operating system and interprocess communication services. On the graphics processor, there is a large impact on everything using graphics services.

Table 9.3. Technological Factors Influencing Healthy Vision *(continued)*

The technological factors related to general-purpose hardware reveal some of the issues for building software for an embedded system. The space and power budgets were very limited, and the system has no disk. The performance of algorithms to date has been hampered by available processing resources. Compared with previous generations of patient monitors, future generations will need far more processing power to handle new processing algorithms.

Thus the number of processors is likely to increase in the future. This means that the real-time operating system must be supplemented with support for a distributed computing environment. Data is distributed over the network to other Healthy Vision units and to central monitoring stations. Within Healthy Vision, data is distributed across the three types of processors (digital signal processor, graphics processor, and standard processor).

For domain-specific hardware, there are many types of input and output devices that the base unit must support. These include third-party monitoring devices, multigas monitors, anesthesia workstations, local LCD displays, independent surgeon displays, overflow displays, chart recorders, laser printers, legacy and new networks, and clinical information systems.

9.1.3 Analyze Organizational Factors

The last set of factors is the organizational factors, and these are listed in Table 9.4.

Organizational Factor	Flexibility and Changeability	Impact
O1: Management		
O1.1: Support for reuse		
There is a preference for in-house software. There is no particular support for reuse.	Reuse of domain-specific components built in-house will be considered.	There is a moderate impact on meeting the schedule.
O2: Staff skills		
O2.1: Patient monitors		
Two prior generations of monitors have been built.	There is a bias toward what has worked well in previous products.	Designers favor static task and memory allocation.
O2.2: Software design		
Half of the team has skills in structured design.	It is feasible to mentor junior-level staff.	There is a low impact on meeting the schedule.
O2.3: Multiprocess systems		
One fourth of the team is competent in these skills.	Training can be supplemented with software abstraction.	There is a large impact on being able to meet performance requirements.
O4: Schedule		
O4.1: Time-to-market		
Time-to-market is extremely aggressive.	There is no flexibility.	There is a large impact on all design choices.

Table 9.4. Organizational Factors Influencing Healthy Vision

Organizational Factor	Flexibility and Changeability	Impact
O4.2: Delivery of features		
Features are prioritized.	Features are negotiable; product requirements change often.	There is a large impact on meeting the schedule.
O5: Budget		
O5.1: Head count		
There are 25 programmers, 4 supervisors, and 1 manager.	Engineers can be transferred to the team as needed.	There is a low impact on meeting the schedule.

Table 9.4. Organizational Factors Influencing Healthy Vision *(continued)*

The organization has had limited success integrating third-party software into its embedded systems because the software size and quality are not often compatible with its requirements. However, existing in-house software for physiological algorithms is reused on a regular basis.

For factors related to staff skills, one fourth of the team had a solid patient-monitoring background because the organization built two generations of patient monitors. Half of the team had structured design skills and all were experienced with C programming. Only one fourth of the team was familiar with the concepts of object technology, but no one had developed a large object-oriented design-based product. This made an object-oriented approach less appealing. One fourth of the team was extremely competent in building multiprocess systems, and all the other team members had some exposure to these systems. It was feasible to use a combination of training and software abstraction so that extensive multiprocessing experience was not necessary for all personnel.

The product schedule was extremely aggressive, even though there were frequent changes in product requirements. Although this continued as the organization determined the scope and market of the new product, the features were prioritized, and their delivery was somewhat negotiable.

9.1.4 Develop Strategies

Next we summarize the main architecture design issues and the resulting strategies for the architecture design. During the design process, there were constant trade-offs regarding when to build more flexibility, and thus complexity, into the software and when to implement something in a more straightforward, less flexible manner. A guiding principle was to separate the how-to-do-it processing from the application policy rules, which dictated what needed to be done. In practice the separation of "what to do" from "how to do it" was achieved by defining and implementing a set of changeable attributes that could be manipulated as necessary by the what-to-do parts of the software.

Changes in Hardware Technology

Changes in the general-purpose and domain-specific hardware are anticipated on a regular basis. The goal is to reduce the effort and time involved in adapting the product to new hardware.

Influencing Factors

T1.1, T1.2: The processor speed is likely to change frequently, even during development. As technology improves, the goal is to take advantage of faster processors or to change the allocation of processors.

T2.1: Many types of input and output devices need to be supported.

T3.1: Support is needed for client/server applications in a distributed computing environment.

P7.1: The processor speed needs to be balanced against memory size and other factors to meet the fixed product cost.

Solution

Encapsulate and separate software and components related to hardware.

Strategy: *Encapsulate general-purpose hardware.*

Encapsulating the system hardware allows changes to be made to the hardware with little or no impact on the applications. This is provided by layers for the operating system and communication mechanisms.

Continued

Changes in Hardware Technology *(continued)*

Strategy: *Use a naming service.*

A distributed computing environment is essential for distributing data over different types of processors. The goal is to be able to use either a single general-purpose processor, three different processors for signal processing, general processing, and graphics processing, or some other combination. The central concept underlying the distributed computing environment is a naming service.

Strategy: *Create a device manager interface.*

Develop a standardized POSIX-like interface to all devices. Create a virtual device manager that implements this interface between the device managers and the applications. The device manager interface provides access to devices that exist on the same processor or on a different processor than the application using the device. The device manager interface also provides a service that can notify device users asynchronously of the availability of a device.

Strategy: *Encapsulate device communication.*

Encapsulate details of communicating with devices into device-specific managers.

Changes in Software Technology

The software platform consisting of the operating system, communication mechanisms, and graphics commands is likely to change when the applications are ported to new platforms.

Influencing Factors

T3.1: Support is needed for client/server applications in a distributed computing environment.

T3.3: Portability requirements are that the system must operate on different graphics environments, operating systems, and processors.

Solution

In addition to the operating system, add infrastructure software between the product applications and the hardware platform. This includes the networking software, communication mechanisms and interfaces, data management mechanisms and interface, and timer interface.

Continued

Changes in Software Technology *(continued)*

Strategy: *Encapsulate operating system and communication mechanisms.*

Encapsulate operating system dependencies into an operating system library and interprocess communication library that include software timer support.

Strategy: *Encapsulate graphics.*

Create a generic graphics interface and encapsulate dependencies in a library so that display software can be easily ported to different graphics environments.

Strategy: *Use a reentrant repository for data sharing.*

Create a reentrant repository that serves as the dominant mechanism by which applications share data.

Related Strategies

The *Use a naming service* strategy identified in the issue Changes in Hardware Technology is supplemented by the reentrant repository. Distribution is supported by the naming service and explicit data manager connections combined with asynchronous replies to data requests.

Easy Addition of Features

Application policy rules change over time and are likely to become more complex in the future. The monitor must present different features to the user, depending on the transport mode, the connected network, and the connected input/output devices. This adaptability is complicated by the fact that these changes can occur while the monitor is running.

Influencing Factors

P1.1: There are hundreds of customized settings and thousands of application policy rules.

P1.2, P1.3: The monitor adapts to transport versus network mode.

P1.4, P1.5: The monitor communicates with third-party devices and adapts to connected devices.

P6.1: Different levels of functionality are provided depending on the user-purchased options.

Continued

Easy Addition of Features *(continued)*

Solution

Build applications from loosely coupled software components, called *entities*. They communicate using a central repository and a publish/subscribe protocol that provides immediate change notification. Each component owns or is responsible for publishing information (for example, waveforms, alarms) that is available to other components in the system. Other components can subscribe to the information.

Strategy: *Use a central data manager and repository to exchange information.*

Decouple applications by using a central data manager and repository to transfer information among the different applications. Information is exchanged much like a bulletin board.

Strategy: *Separate monitor functionality into loosely coupled components.*

Separate monitor functionality into software components that represent a logically related set of application features. The application policy rules place requirements on the software components (entities) regarding the actions they perform, the information they need, and the information they produce.

Strategy: *Use publish/subscribe communication.*

Using a data registration feature allows a software component to ask for notification whenever a data item changes. Software components do not poll. The monitor's processing model is event or data driven in almost all cases. All graphical applications must dynamically accept and display updates to information, even while the menu is being displayed.

Related Strategies

The *Use a reentrant repository for data sharing* strategy identified in the issue Changes in Software Technology and the *Do not allow applications to share global memory directly* strategy from the Quality Assurance issue also contribute to this loosely coupled software component model. The publish/subscribe protocol complements these strategies. The component model makes the physical location of other components transparent, decouples data producers from consumers, allows consumers to register for data dynamically, provides asynchronous access to data, and makes the physical location of data transparent to consumers.

Quality Assurance

An embedded system is difficult to debug and to test code.

Influencing Factors

O2.3: One fourth of the team is extremely competent in building multiprocess systems whereas the remaining three fourths of the team only have exposure to these skills.

T1.4: A diskless operating system places restrictions on multiprocessing and the amount of data that can be logged.

T3.1: A mechanism is needed for sharing global data across processors.

T3.2: Reentrant code is extremely difficult to write correctly

Solution

Place design constraints on software components to alleviate certain risks. Provide support for diagnostics.

Strategy: *Do not allow applications to share global memory directly.*

All information shared among applications should be shared via interprocess messages or via the data manager. The replies to the data manager requests are asynchronous to prevent blocking among applications.

Strategy: *Create RAM-based error logging.*

Create RAM-based error logging and an execution trace system to support debugging of the target platform.

Strategy: *Create tasks at start-up.*

Create tasks at start-up to avoid exception conditions with respect to resource management and task communication.

Strategy: *Use static memory allocation when possible.*

Use static memory allocation to be less susceptible to memory leaks.

Related Strategies

Use a central data manager and repository to exchange information (issue, Easy Addition of Features).

High Availability

Ensuring high availability of the product is critical to its success.

Influencing Factors

P4.1: Correct information must be provided to the user 24 hours a day, 7 days a week.

Solution

Implement mechanisms to alleviate certain risks.

Strategy: *Implement watchdog mechanisms.*

Implement hardware and software watchdog mechanisms to ensure software is not in an infinite loop.

Strategy: *Implement recovery mechanisms.*

Implement recovery mechanisms in the data manager to ensure the integrity of the data in the repository, even if monitor power was lost during a data write operation.

Related Strategies

Use a central data manager and repository to exchange information (issue, Easy Addition of Features).

High Performance

Meeting the real-time performance requirements is critical to the success of the product.

Influencing Factors

O.2.1: The staff have skills in building monitors using the VRTX real-time operating system.

T1.1, T1.2: The processor speed is likely to change frequently, even during development. The number of processors may increase in future releases.

P3.1: Provide real-time presentation of the current monitoring state.

P3.2: Several processing priority levels are needed to support multiple processing deadlines.

P7.1: Trade off processor speed, memory size, and other factors to meet the fixed product cost.

Continued

High Performance *(continued)*

Solution

Use multiple processors and a real-time operating system to meet the high performance requirements. Prepare for different processor configurations in the future. Partitioning the system into separate components gives flexibility in allocating them to different processes.

Strategy: *Use multiple processors.*

Use a digital signal processor for signal filtering, use the fastest general-purpose processor available for main processing, and move low-level graphics processing and waveform drawing to a graphics processor.

Strategy: *Use the VRTX real-time operating system.*

The VRTX operating system has a strict priority scheduler, supports message sending and receiving, and has semaphores. These are typical real-time operating system features.

Strategy: *Divide logical processing into multiple components.*

Divide logical processing into software components, called *entities*, to meet timing deadlines.

Strategy: *Separate steady-state real-time processing from event-driven asynchronous processing.*

Separate components with critical real-time performance requirements from those with less stringent requirements.

Strategy: *Create a task for each unique processing deadline.*

Use rate monotonic analysis for assigning software components to tasks based on processing deadlines, and to give higher priority to tasks that run more frequently or have a shorter deadline.

Strategy: *Do not allow entities to make blocking calls.*

Decouple requests from replies into separate messages.

Strategy: *Minimize the copying of data.*

Analyze the impact of data copying and eliminate it when necessary. Consider using a shared memory queue for high-volume data when appropriate.

Strategy: *Don't produce data unless it is needed.*

Write high-volume data (for example, waveforms) to the data repository only if at least one consumer is registered on that type of data.

9.2 Conceptual Architecture View

For Healthy Vision, the conceptual view was not explicitly described; however, scenarios in the design documentation showed how data flows among the major software components.

The scenario in Figure 9.3 uses a UML Collaboration Diagram to show how raw data is acquired from the patient, processed, and displayed on the screen. Data flow between software components is indicated by arrows, labeled with a sequence number and the type of the data. First the waveform data is acquired. This waveform data is displayed directly on the monitor and it is also sent to the Analyze component. The Analyze component produces raw physiological parameter values, which it sends to the AlarmProcessing component. The AlarmProcessing component implements application policy rules such as the ones listed earlier. The alarms are then also displayed on the monitor. Although scenarios do not give the complete picture of the conceptual view, they do show the peer-to-peer communication that is missing in the module view.

The software components in these scenarios are a particular type of component called a *software entity*. In the conceptual view, the entity concept is the result of applying the following two strategies:

1. *Separate monitor functionality into loosely coupled components* (issue Easy Addition of Features)

2. *Divide logical processing into multiple components* (issue High Performance)

A software entity produces data that is used by other entities. Thus, it is possible to describe the conceptual view of the Healthy Vision system using software entities as the lowest level components. Figure 9.4 shows that an entity communicates with other entities through its ports via messages (global data object message [GDOMessage]). Some of the message types for the monitor entities are the raw data coming in from the devices, waveform samples, parameter values, and alarm status. Each message type is produced by only one entity, but many entities can consume it. Entities are decoupled in the sense that producers don't know which entities consume its data and consumers don't know which entity produces the data.

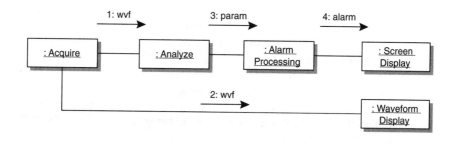

Figure 9.3. Producer/consumer processing scenario

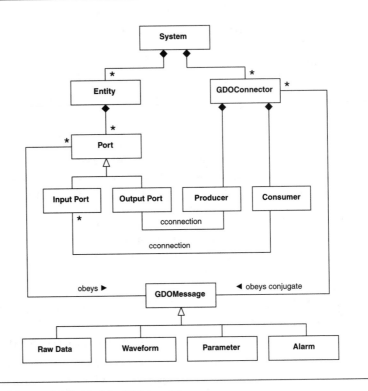

Figure 9.4. Meta-model for Healthy Vision entities

The meta-model in Figure 9.4 is a restricted version of the conceptual view meta-model presented in Figure 4.16. The most important simplification is that Healthy Vision has only one level of decomposition; neither the components (Entities) nor the connectors (GDOConnectors) can be decomposed. A GDOConnector has exactly two roles—a producer and consumer—and these can only be connected to output ports and input ports, respectively. Because a GDOConnector cannot be decomposed, the protocol (GDOMessage) is associated with the connector instead of with its roles. And lastly, because an entity cannot be decomposed, there is no need for bindings between ports.

The conceptual view can also explicitly describe abstract connections between entities by describing the protocol associated with a GDOConnector. It contains information about the characteristics of the data and events flowing between the entities, including their type, direction, size, and rate. The strategy *Use publish/subscribe communication* (issue Easy Addition of Features) applies to this protocol.

The protocol adhered to by entities communicating via the GDOConnector is shown in Figure 9.5. The information exchanged between entities via the GDOConnector is represented as a GDO. Entities first register for data of interest. When published data is writ-

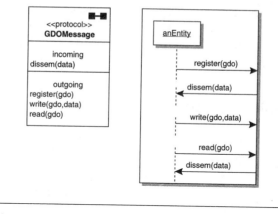

Figure 9.5. GDOMessage protocol

ten, it is disseminated to all entities subscribed to it. An entity can also explicitly read data rather than wait to be notified of an update.

There is a special kind of entity called an *agent*, which acts as an intermediary between other (non-*agent*) entities and device managers. A device manager is a software component that interacts directly with a hardware device, and presents to agents an abstraction of this device. The device managers are the result of applying the strategy *Encapsulate device communication* (issue Changes in Hardware).

Figure 9.6 shows a portion of the conceptual configuration for Healthy Vision. This configuration corresponds to the scenario depicted in Figure 9.3, but here the input and output device managers are also shown. There are three types of GDOConnectors in this configuration: WGDO, PGDO, and AGDO. These connectors handle the communication

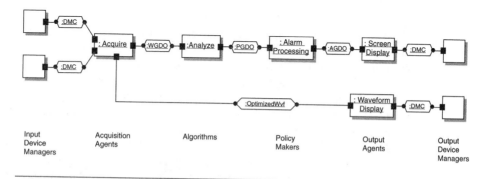

Figure 9.6. Example of a Healthy Vision conceptual configuration

between entities and convey waveform, parameter, and alarm data respectively. Connectors of type DMC handle the communication between the device managers and the agents. There is a special OptimizedWvf connector for the high-speed data transfer used to display the waveforms on the screen in real time.

9.3 Module Architecture View

In the module view, Healthy Vision software is divided into application software and platform software.

9.3.1 Decomposition of the Application Software

The application software of the Healthy Vision system is organized into the following subsystems:

- SignalAcquisition is responsible for acquiring and preprocessing physiological data.
- SignalAnalysis is responsible for deriving the parameter values and detecting physiological conditions as well as alarm limit violations.
- Communication is responsible for network access. Healthy Vision communicates with other bedside units and the central station using common interproduct protocols.
- GraphicalUserInterface is responsible for serving as the link between the user and the underlying functionality of the unit. It is responsible for the visual and audio presentation of information to the user.
- UserApplications is responsible for the high-level logic that implements the user requirements.
- StateControl is responsible for coordinating major state transitions such as start-up, shutdown, standby, and transfer.
- SystemApplications is responsible for battery management, diagnostic management, log management, and system resource utilization management.

The UserApplications and SystemApplications subsystems are further decomposed into device manager modules and entity modules. These are abstract modules that implement the device managers and entities in the conceptual view.

For example, there are entity modules in the module view for functionality such as data acquisition, alarm detection, drawing the home screen, discharging a patient, and network support. Figure 9.7 shows how entity modules are contained in Healthy Vision's subsystems. These are some of the entity modules needed for the conceptual configuration of Figure 9.6.

An EntityModule is decomposed into EntityControl, EntityData, and multiple EntityFunctions—one for each GDO to which it subscribes (Figure 9.8). It has an interface for each of the GDOs it publishes or to which it subscribes. When an entity receives a GDO,

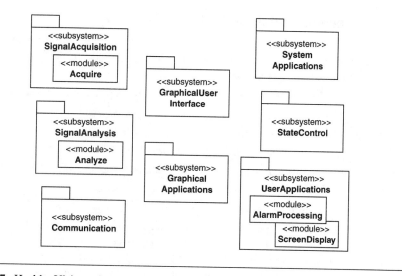

Figure 9.7. Healthy Vision subsystems in the application software

the EntityControl initiates the corresponding EntityFunction for processing the GDO. When publishing a GDO, the EntityFunction returns control to the EntityControl. Entity-Functions share a common EntityData space. Services provided by the platform software handle the publication and subscription requests so that entity modules do not interact directly with each other.

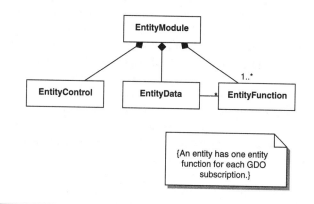

Figure 9.8. Meta-model for Entity module structure

9.3.2 Decomposition of the Platform Software

The platform software provides services for communication between entities, communication with devices, and other general system services. Its design is the result of applying the following four strategies:

1. *Use reentrant repository for data sharing* (issue Easy Addition of Features)
2. *Use a central data manager and repository to exchange information* (issue Easy Addition of Features)
3. *Create a device manager interface* (issue Changes in Hardware)
4. *Encapsulate the operating system and communication mechanisms* (issue Changes in Software Technology)

The platform software contains the following subsystems:

• DataManagement provides an interface for entity modules to publish and subscribe to data. Entity modules share information via GDOs provided by this subsystem. It is responsible for managing the centralized repository in which the GDOs reside and for providing services for data publishing and registration, data distribution, and access to local and remote data.

• DeviceManagement defines a standard for interfacing to product-line devices. The standard is based on POSIX and UNIX to enhance portability. It is responsible for providing a stable, standardized device environment for the rest of the system. It protects the software from the hardware details, allowing applications and other subsystems to be ported to other hardware environments.

• SystemServices provides an interface to the host platform. System services include file handling, IPC, logging interfaces, operating system support, system console interface, system resource protection, and time services.

Entity modules access GDOs through the DataManagement subsystem of the platform software. Instead of the peer-to-peer communication between entities in the conceptual view, the Entity modules communicate via the data manager in the DataManagement subsystem. The decomposition of the data manager is show in Figure 9.9. The data repository is encapsulated in the GDOData module. The GDOControl module provides the data manager functionality and access via an interface that adheres to the GDOMessage protocol defined in Figure 9.5.

The strategy *Do not allow applications to share global memory directly* (issue Quality Assurance) applies here. The strategy *Do not allow entities to make blocking calls* (issue High Performance) also applies here. In-line reads of data are not allowed unless an entity is the owner of the data. When an entity issues a data read or registration request to the data manager, the data request reply comes back to the entity in a separate message. This allows applications to be written without knowing whether data is coming from a local data repository, from a repository on a different processor, or from across the network.

Having this additional infrastructure in the platform software meant that all software engineers were trained and could communicate using a common framework. For example,

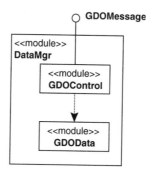

Figure 9.9. Data manager

more than 95 percent of interentity communication uses common data distribution techniques and common event notification techniques implemented by the data manager. Because there is only one way for entities to communicate, it is easy to explain and understand. This additional infrastructure eliminated reentry issues for entity modules because global data is not shared between entities.

The platform software design ensures that moving to a faster processor affects the software only at the lowest level of interface with the host platform. The software design makes it relatively easy to distribute the application software onto multiple processors.

9.3.3 Layering Structure

The layering structure is used to implement the global analysis strategies for providing abstract interfaces and isolating dependencies. This structure, shown in Figure 9.10, is orthogonal to the subsystem decomposition just described. Although all the modules in the platform software are assigned to the Platform layer, modules in the application software are spread over multiple layers.

Within the Applications layer, entity modules are further separated into policy makers and procedural applications, to separate the functionality for product-specific requirements from more generic algorithms that are used across the product line.

The subsystems for application software in Healthy Vision fit into the layering structure in the following way. Entity and agent modules are located in the Applications layer. Device manager modules are located in the DeviceManagers layer.

The SignalAcquisition subsystem is the interface to the hardware devices that monitor the patient. It consists of device manager and agent modules that convert the incoming signals into GDOs. The device manager modules are located in the DeviceManagers layer and the agent modules are located in the Applications layer.

The SignalAnalysis subsystem is in the Applications layer. It contains two kinds of entity modules: procedural applications and a policy maker. The procedural applications

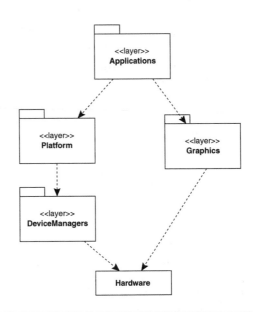

Figure 9.10. Layering structure in Healthy Vision

analyze the acquired signals. They contain generic algorithms used in the product family that were developed independently from and prior to Healthy Vision. An entity wrapper around each algorithm ensures that the resulting code follows the architecture model. The policy maker entity synthesizes the information from the algorithms and reports it to modules in the UserApplications subsystem.

The StateControl subsystem, which is also in the Applications layer, is the chief policy maker. It provides top-level coordination for the operational states of the Healthy Vision system (for example, monitoring, standby, and shutdown).

Networking code in the Communication subsystem was ported from a previous product. The ported code was partitioned into device manager and agent modules to follow the architecture model.

9.3.4 Error Logging

Because error logging is used throughout the system, it is important to minimize the impact of any change to it by creating a separate error logger module and guidelines for its use.

The error logger allows callers to log an entry containing the file name and line number where the error was detected. As many as nine 4-byte integers of information, including an error code, a severity level, the time of the error, and a trace of addresses and arguments of the call can be logged. This gives the context for debugging and fits within the resource constraints of the embedded system, in accordance with the strategy *Create RAM-based error logging* (issue Quality Assurance).

One of the usage guidelines is that services do not produce fatal errors if an input argument is invalid. Instead, the service passes an error back to the caller, and the caller must take appropriate action. An error log can be examined locally via the monitor menu system, over the network at the central station, and by TELNET access to the central station via a modem.

9.4 Execution Architecture View

Healthy Visions's execution view focused on meeting the real-time performance requirements given the constraints of an embedded system. Guidelines for designing tasks call for a task assignment that minimizes operating system context switching and thus overhead, increasing system throughput and reducing processing latency.

Figure 9.11 uses a UML Deployment Diagram to show the processors located in the base unit, and the communication paths between them. In this section we discuss task allocation for the main processor.

The choice of operating system was guided by the strategy *Use the VRTX real-time operating system* (issue High Performance). Figure 9.12 shows some of the platform elements provided by the VRTX real-time operating system. There is one common address space shared by a number of tasks and interrupt service routines. To create an instance of a task, the programmer assigns to it a message queue and a program counter. Entity modules are assigned to tasks, and device managers are assigned to interrupt service routines.

9.4.1 Defining Runtime Entities

The strategy *Create a task for each unique processing deadline* (issue High Performance) was used to assign entity modules to tasks. Entity modules are organized into priority groups during resource budgeting. There is one priority group for each processing deadline found in the timing requirements of the requirements specification. Then each priority group is assigned to a separate task.

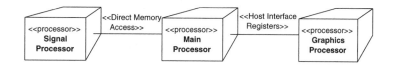

Figure 9.11. Processors for Healthy Vision's base unit

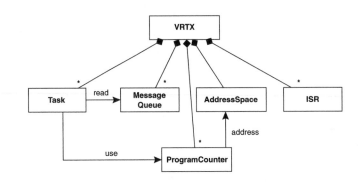

Figure 9.12. VRTX platform elements used in Healthy Vision. ISR = interrupt service routine.

Healthy Vision tasks have the structure shown in Figure 9.13. A priority group is implemented in the module view by a GroupControl module. The GroupControl module contains the control logic software that routes the message to the appropriate entity (EntityModule). Messages contain the GDOs to which an entity has subscribed. The entity module has its own control logic (EntityControl) that selects the appropriate entity function based on the message type. When message processing is complete, the entity module returns control to the GroupControl module.

Because entity modules receive all inputs from the GroupControl module and do not make blocking calls waiting for inputs, they can be moved among processors and tasks. The assignment of an entity module to a task is based strictly on timing deadlines. If a timing deadline changes it is very easy to move an entity module from one task to another. A tool uses a text description of the GroupControl module to generate a new c file for it, it is recompiled, and the software is relinked.

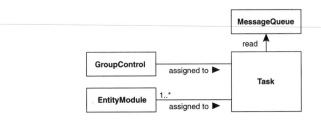

Figure 9.13. Meta-model for Healthy Vision task structure

The concept of priority groups made the definition of the tasks in the execution view straightforward. A task was created for each priority group. For example, the requirements give the maximum delay for displaying waveforms, and audio and alarm information, as seen in Table 9.2. Subtracting the time spent outside of the task (for example, digital signal processing in hardware) gave tasks for each of the deadlines of 20 msec, 1,200 msec, 50 msec, and 500 msec.

In a couple of cases special tasks needed to be added to meet deadlines that arose because of the way the code was implemented. An example of this is the networking code ported from a previous product. Although the logical deadline was 300 msec, the way the ported code was designed meant that the networking activity had to be completed within a few tens of milliseconds. A new task was created to meet this timing deadline.

The end result was 17 unique deadlines giving rise to 17 tasks. The cost of adding tasks was a concern because each task has dedicated stack space and the system has very limited memory. To keep the task stack sizes under control, the general rule for developers was that temporary buffers of 1K or smaller could be put on the stack, but larger buffers should be allocated from the heap.

9.4.2 Communication Paths

Figure 9.6 in the conceptual view shows two types of connectors between entities. The GDO connector is the typical connector between entities, and its communication is as follows. When an entity produces new GDO data, it uses the data manager's write service. The data manager maintains a list of entities registered to receive updates of a particular GDO. In addition to updating the GDO data in the data repository, the data manager calls the IPC service in the SystemServices subsystem. This service maintains the mapping between an entity module and the mail queue of the task in which it resides.

To meet the stringent real-time requirements of acquiring and displaying the waveform data, an additional communication scheme was developed. This is represented in Figure 9.6 as an OptimizedWvf connector. The system must keep up with the hardware acquisition of the incoming data by accepting new data every 10 msec and displaying it within 20 msec. Processing the data has a less stringent deadline. The algorithms for signal analysis expect data every 300 msec. The overhead of writing more than 60 waveform streams to the data repository to meet the 20-msec deadline requires more than 1,200 calls per second, which is prohibitive from a CPU loading standpoint.

The OptimizedWvf connector is implemented as a direct pathway between entities, bypassing the data manager as a mechanism for transferring waveform data. Thus each waveform is written to the data repository once every 300 msec, which saves significant CPU time. To decouple the acquisition entity from the waveform display entity's processing requirements, the waveform display tells the acquisition entity which waveforms it wants.

9.4.3 Conceptual and Module Views Revisited

For components with critical real-time performance requirements, the strategy *Separate steady-state real-time processing from event-driven asynchronous processing* (issue High Performance) was used.

An example of this is the Acquire entity from Figure 9.6. As initially designed, the Acquire entity is responsible for acquiring the data, sending the waveform to the display within 10 msec, and writing it to the GDO data repository within 50 msec so that it can be processed by the Analyze entities. The 10-msec deadline could not be met with a single entity performing both activities.

The Acquire entity was split into two entities to solve this problem. The original Acquire entity is now responsible only for meeting the 10-msec deadline for displaying waveforms and for passing the acquired data to the new entity. The new entity writes the waveforms to the data repository, where it will be read by the Analyze entities.

If the two acquisition entities were to communicate via the data manager, it would defeat the purpose of splitting them apart. Therefore, the entities communicated via a shared memory queue (strategy *Minimize the copying of data*, issue High Performance).

In addition, the strategy *Don't produce data unless it is needed* was employed to enhance performance. The new entity writes waveforms to the data repository only when at least one consumer has registered for that waveform type.

A naming service supported distribution (strategy *Use a naming service*, issue Changes in Hardware). Servers advertise their service by informing the name server. The name server stores this information and broadcasts the availability of that service locally as well as to all of the other products in the system. The name server entry contains a description of the service and routing information.

9.4.4 Execution Configuration

Figure 9.14 shows a representative set of tasks for Healthy Vision's main processor. The interface to the signal processor is through direct memory access. Graphics queues provide the interface to the graphics processor via the host interface registers. Although all of the tasks have a message queue, to simplify the figure not all of these are shown.

As previously mentioned, entity modules that are defined in the module view are assigned to a task based on processing deadlines. Modules with similar processing deadlines are placed in the same task, and the task itself is assigned a deadline. The longest executing function in the entity must take less time than the deadline of the task. Following the principles of RMA, task priorities are based on the task deadline so that tasks with a shorter deadline have a higher priority.

The tasks range from the highest priority 10-msec task to the lowest priority background task. The background task is the result of the strategy *Implement watchdog mechanisms* (issue High Availability), and it uses all spare CPU time to verify that the software image is not corrupt.

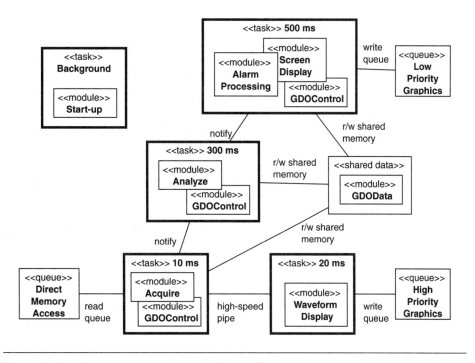

Figure 9.14. Tasks on the main processor in Healthy Vision

The default connection between tasks is via the data manager. The data manager is divided into two modules: one for control and one for the GDO data. The GDOControl module is linked to each of the tasks, and it controls the access to the module containing the shared GDO data and notifies the tasks that have subscribed to the data. An exception to the default connection is a direct message passing between the 10-msec and 20-msec tasks that provides a high-speed pipe for passing waveforms. The other platform software, device management and system services, is placed in libraries and is also linked statically to each of the tasks that require these services.

The entity concept was used only on the main processor, and not on the graphics processor or the signal processor. These specialized processors perform a limited set of activities, and do not need the full services supplied by the platform software or an operating system. The entity concept could have been supported on these processors by making minor modifications to the data management and IPC services.

A key strategy for the execution view is that all tasks are created at start-up; tasks are never dynamically created or deleted. A very different architecture with different rules about blocking would have evolved if each entity, especially user interface menus, dynamically created and deleted its task on demand.

The experienced developers believed that dynamic task allocation was inherently more complex and created additional exception conditions. By creating all tasks permanently at start-up, programming bugs related to forgetting to free resources when a task is deleted were avoided. This also eliminated the need to handle certain exception conditions such as sending a message to an entity in a task that no longer exists.

A similar strategy was employed with respect to dynamic memory allocation: The less dynamic memory allocation the system did, the less susceptible it would be to memory leaks and the more reliable the product would be. Some developers wanted to prohibit all dynamic memory allocation because of a fear of memory leaks, but others were less concerned. The system ended up with some dynamic memory allocation and deletion, but far less than usually exists in C++ object-oriented designs that employ object lifetime models for the creation and destruction of objects.

Healthy Vision is a medical device, not a personal computer. It must guarantee that the resources needed to perform the monitoring functions are available when needed. All design decisions that help to meet this guarantee improve the quality of the product.

9.5 Code Architecture View

The directory structure (that is, code groups) for Healthy Vision's code architecture view is shown in Figure 9.15. It follows the module decomposition to the extent that there are directories for subsystems and entity modules. There are additional directories for version control (VersionControl), documentation (Doc), include files (Inc), libraries (Lib), and testing (Test). An entity module is typically implemented as a group of one or more source code files, each of which contains one or more functions.

The code view should help enforce the design constraints established in the module view, such as preventing entity modules from directly calling another entity module's functions or directly accessing another entity module's data. Therefore global .h files are located at the top of the source code tree. Each entity module has its own directory (Entity-Code) at a lower level of the directory tree. The make system allows an entity module to access only .h files from its Code subdirectories or from an Inc directory at a higher level in the tree. Because entity modules are all at the same level, they cannot access each other's .h files. Each file is stored in the revision control system (RCS). The make system tags each build with a symbolic tag so that any build can easily be reproduced.

9.5.1 Development Environment

The programming language was ANSI C, and developers used a set of coding conventions, most of which were standard. For example, to ensure that names in enumerated lists are unique across the system, the members of each enumerated list (enum) start with the name of the enum itself. If the enum type was COLOR, the color blue might be COLOR_BLUE.

Another convention guiding the partitioning of entity functions into files was that each function had to be in its own file. The benefit of this approach is that file contention is

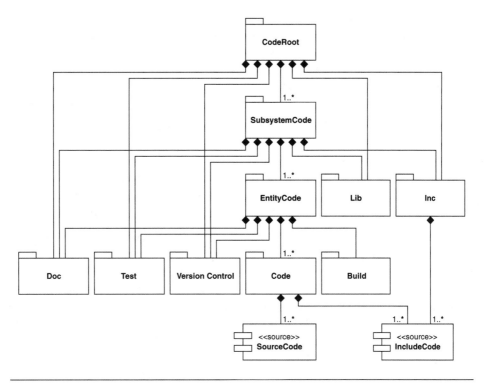

Figure 9.15. Healthy Vision directory structure

minimized when more than one developer is working in the same area. The disadvantage is that a build takes much longer because the cost of opening a file is large compared with reading and compiling its contents. It also increases the size of the executable with debugging information because much of the debug information is duplicated in each file.

In general, one individual was responsible for each device manager and entity module. So over time the development environment gravitated to a model in which each entity or device manager module has a small number of files, which is almost the opposite of the original coding standard.

RCS was not used to merge changes of two developers working in the same file because the automated process could not make the proper decisions about what constituted a proper merge. There are cases when a change applied to a particular version of a file should not be propagated to newer versions of the file. Therefore, an engineer made the merge decisions rather than relying on RCS's automated merge capability.

When software development began, the hardware for the target platform was not yet available. There also wasn't enough space in the development lab for each developer to have a target machine. For these reasons, plus the more friendly and productive workstation development environment, both a workstation and target development environment were supported.

Code was compiled and executed on both a SUN UNIX platform and the target platform. The version of Healthy Vision for the SUN platform runs in a single UNIX process. This made debugging simpler on the workstation. Timing-related problems due to a true multitasking system with interrupt interactions were debugged on the target environment.

9.5.2 Configuration Management and Build Strategies

RCS is the repository for all versions of all files needed across the set of all builds, and it is the mechanism for sharing files. The protocols to network gateways or to other products have major and minor version numbers to ensure compatibility of software releases.

Not all customers have the same release of Healthy Vision software, but the different releases must interoperate. This places an additional requirement on developers because the software must be compatible with other software releases that could be on the network at the same time.

RCS was enhanced to be able to recreate any build. Any time a file is modified and checked back into RCS, the new version is considered to be a new RCS revision of the file. With each build, the files used in the build are symbolically tagged, so that later these same files can be retrieved and the same image rebuilt.

Multiple developers were allowed to change different versions of the same file, then to build different releases at the same time. This is supported by branches in RCS combined with symbolic tagging.

As part of the build process, a tool parses the comment section of each GDO file to determine whether it is located in volatile or persistent (battery-backed) memory. The tool automatically creates code that allocates the GDO to the right area of memory. A GDO can be moved simply by changing the specification in its GDO file and rebuilding the GDO definition section of the configuration.

9.6 Software Architecture Uses

This section summarizes the relation of the software architecture to the software process. As the architecture was being designed, it was evaluated to see how it fulfilled the requirements. Then it was used to plan the development schedule. It provided conventions and implementation strategies that made development more productive. It also helped trace the requirements to the implemented code, which was useful in making sure that all the requirements were covered.

9.6.1 Evaluation

The architecture design was reviewed to identify defects and issues as well as to teach the engineering leaders the architecture. Scenarios were used as the basis for design discussions. They provided a common framework to check that the design would meet the requirements and to verify that the communication among components was understood by all involved in the development.

Scenarios taken from the product architecture described the real-time patient data flow and helped find defects in steady-state processing. Scenarios explained the functional decomposition, showed the main data "highways," showed overall data flow, and showed the relationships between producers and consumers. Figure 9.3 is an example of the steady-state scenario for waveform processing.

The principles of RMA helped in understanding the timing behavior of the system and in determining whether the system would meet its schedule requirements. Separating the module and execution structure in Healthy Vision facilitated this scheduling analysis: It allowed entities to be assigned to tasks based on processing deadlines. Then the priorities of the tasks were set according to RMS, giving tasks with a shorter deadline a higher priority. It was straightforward to apply the RMA techniques for analyzing timing behavior because an RMA model of the system could be extracted from the execution view.

9.6.2 Schedule Planning

The architecture was used to identify and to define subsystem responsibilities, and to define subsystem structure. It was also used to determine which entities needed to be developed, what responsibilities the entity had, and who would develop it. The architecture had little impact on effort estimation in general; it was used primarily for work assignments.

9.6.3 Implementation

The entity and device frameworks in the module view dictated a standard API to all entities and to all devices, which made it easier to manage the module interfaces and to perform change impact analysis. A GDO can only be modified by one owner entity, so there was no possibility of concurrent updates. Reentrancy issues were not a concern at the entity level because entities must be nonblocking. These architectural rules simplified the task of implementation.

Often on the target platform the developers needed a trace of the executing code, when the events being traced occurred within microseconds of each other. Using printf statements was too slow, so a memory-based service in which logging an event takes a few microseconds was designed. Software developers put "antibug" calls in their code at all the points that might be useful in tracing code execution. Each antibug can be turned on or off via a diagnostic console. Additional features were built into the antibugger, such as the ability to stop the logging of antibugs if a particular antibug was logged, or the ability to configure antibugs at compilation time that are turned on by default in the product.

Designing services explicitly for antibugging and giving guidelines for their use meant that developers consistently used this feature. This saved development time, improved testing, and improved service on the product.

9.6.4 Requirements Tracking

As part of quality assurance, every requirement was tested on the finished product; however, tracking requirements to implementation was performed informally. Developers were assigned a user feature based on the Entity modules or other modules they were assigned. They read the requirement sections related to that feature, then designed code to meet the specification. When a requirement involved more than one person's modules, they discussed jointly how the requirement was being fulfilled.

Formally tracking requirements in the software was considered. Because quality assurance procedures would eventually test every feature in the specification, the decision was based on the trade-off of spending more to analyze the design for missing features versus spending more to fix the code because of missing features. The program manager and senior developers decided not to put in the extra analysis effort. In retrospect, although there were cases when requirements were overlooked during the early design phase, these cases represented less than 1 percent of the total requirements. An informal process for checking that every requirement is being addressed, in conjunction with a product validation suite that tests every requirement, was a good mix.

9.7 Summary

9.7.1 Software Architecture Concepts

Because of rigid performance requirements, short development time, and severe hardware constraints, an ad hoc solution would not have worked; the product release date would not have been met. Advanced software architecture concepts were needed, such as the entity model and the flexible entity-to-task assignment. Thus the implementation costs plus the requirement to design a range of products (albeit a small range) drove the use of these concepts:

- **Entities**—Most of the system is composed of loosely coupled entities. Entities do not communicate directly with one another; all communication occurs via connectors. Inside the entity, the control is separated from the processing, and it is standard across all entities. Entities are nonblocking, enabling entities to be moved to different tasks.

- **Connectors**—Healthy Vision's connectors use a data manager and repository to support data sharing among components such as entities. The connector protocol is publish/subscribe, with asynchronous responses to data requests. An optimization was added that aggregates messages to or from the data repository. This lowers the IPC message rate by sending multiple data repository updates to an entity in one message.

- **Tasks**—The assignment of entities to tasks is based on the similarity of their deadlines rather than the similarity of their functionality. Like entity control, task control is standard across all tasks.

- **Mediators**—Interaction between subsystems that use different interaction mechanisms is done through mediators. Mediators provide uniform data access to both producers and consumers, hide the location of the data, and decouple both sides from each other. Agents are an example of mediators, mediating between software entities and device managers that use different protocols and different data formats.

- **Layers**—Standardized APIs are used to isolate dependencies among layers. Healthy Vision uses interface libraries for isolating the dependencies on the hardware, operating system, and device managers.

With these concepts as the basis for the architecture, Healthy Vision was successfully built. These concepts were developed without deliberate use of design patterns or component/connector architecture concepts, which were not generally known at the time of the architecture design. Similar concepts were invented, but it would have been more efficient to have used existing concepts.

9.7.2 Experience

In general the architecture responded well to change, largely because of the layers built into the design. The system runs on three operating systems, communicates on two networks, uses three different graphics libraries, and executes on two different target hardware platforms (one with one main processor and one with two main processors). It was easy to move the product to each of the new environments. Porting to a new operating system only affected the IPC libraries and implementation of the operating system library interfaces. Moving to a different graphics library only required a rewrite of the implementation of the generic graphics library.

The system also responds well to functional change. This is due largely to the strategy of separating application policy rules from the mechanisms that support them. Major new features are constantly added to the system, usually with little or no modification to the rest of the system. Minor requirement changes can usually be handled by changing a single software component. Adding new features or implementing requirement changes has not affected the integrity of other established working features.

One drawback to the current design is in the protocol of the GDO connectors. Rather than routing messages implicitly back to the calling entity, the data management service could have executed an entity-supplied callback function. This would have given the entity designers more flexibility in processing data updates. It would have decoupled the data manager from any knowledge of the entities, and simplified entity control so that no dispatching would be needed.

The same applies to the protocol of the device management connectors. The interface to devices could have allowed agents to specify callback functions rather than routing response messages back to the agent.

To enforce the architecture and reduce development time, the developers were equipped with code templates for tasks and entities. This caused developers to replicate a lot of infrastructure in each entity, rather than inheriting it (as supported by an object-oriented language) or generating it.

Another useful implementation guideline would have been to use a single structure definition for all global data in an entity. Currently, all entity functions in the entity can access this data, and if putting multiple instances of an entity in a single task is desired, separate global data areas need to be manually created. With the entity's global data in a single structure, the entity functions would access the data via a pointer. Of course, the best solution would be to use a programming language that supports the class/instance concept.

If the development of Healthy Vision were starting over today, C++ would be chosen over C for the implementation language. It provides support for making many of these improvements, and the toolsets have matured quite a bit since the original language decision was made. An object-oriented design methodology would be used throughout the entire product.

Separating the control from the procedural applications, which are the generic algorithms used for many products, enabled reuse of existing procedural applications. However, the combination of the entity-centric model, schedule pressure, and 30 people developing the product meant that not as much was put in common libraries as should have been. Developing an object model may have helped with uncovering and enforcing reuse. There should have been a more active effort to create common application libraries that could be shared among entities.

Performance could be addressed separately from functionality because of the clear separation between the module and execution views. Strict guidelines for designing entities limited interactions between them and ensured that they could be independently assigned to tasks. The trade-off inherent in this approach was that it did not allow in-line data repository access, which sometimes added to the size and complexity of the code, and took more time to train the developers.

In certain cases exceptions were made to the design principles for optimization. For example, in a few cases, entities in the same task communicate directly with function calls rather than through the data manager.

Healthy Vision—Lessons Learned

- Don't think that advanced architecture concepts are a luxury you can't afford; you may not be able to afford doing without them.
- The decision whether to adopt a new technology is always hard to make; there's no simple answer (for example, the decision not to use C++).
- Separate the module view from the execution view, especially for high-performance systems. Don't rely merely on optimizations. Exploit the performance increases you can gain by regrouping processes/tasks to use the CPU more efficiently.
- Think about debugging, testing, and service right at the beginning, and build any support you need into the architecture (for example, antibugging).
- Plan for change.

Chapter 10

Central Vision

with Contributions by
Jeffrey Melanson

Central Vision is a central patient-monitoring station. The system's primary function is the display of continuous real-time data for multiple patient bedside monitors. Like Healthy Vision (Chapter 9), Central Vision displays physiological data consisting of discrete, intermittent parameter values (for example, heart and respiration rates), alarm status, and continuous waveform samples (for example, EKG, arterial pressures). Central Vision also provides remote control of the patient bedside monitors and viewing of stored patient information such as physiological events and trends.

The typical hospital configuration is organized around the concept of a "care unit," in which a single Central Vision system is connected to many bedside monitors within a hospital ward (for example, Intensive Care). From a single location, clinicians can monitor, view, and control recordings on any patient's bedside monitor within the unit. Central Vision can also span care units and view devices within a hospitalwide network.

The hardware for Central Vision consists of a single cabinet, high-resolution display, mouse, keyboard, and uninterruptible power supply. A laser printer and second display can be added as options. Figure 10.1 shows the full hardware configuration.

A Central Vision system is a peer within a network of patient bedside monitors and strip chart recorders. These devices support proprietary protocols for real-time monitoring, control, distributed time, and name services.

Central Vision replaces an existing embedded systems product that uses proprietary hardware. It was important for Central Vision to be adaptable and long lived, because it is intended to host future applications in the domain of patient information management.

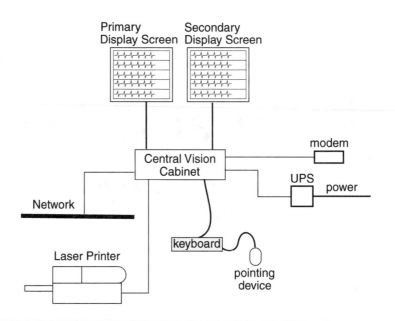

Figure 10.1. Central Vision hardware configuration. UPS = uninterrupted power supply.

To this end, the design followed an "open systems" approach, using off-the-shelf hardware and software. Additionally, an object-oriented design and implementation language (C++) were used. These new technologies added considerable risk to the project. To help mitigate these risks, the architecture needed to be simple, well-defined, and testable.

What follows is a description of the architecture, design, and rationale used to deliver the Central Vision product.

10.1 Global Analysis

Global analysis identifies the key factors that affect the architecture design of Central Vision. Central Vision presents four kinds of application functionality to the user:

1. The Cluster View display lets the user keep track of as many as 8 patients on a single screen, and 16 patients on two screens.

2. Bed View displays any bedside monitor screen.

3. Trends displays all patient information saved by the monitors for the last 24 hours in tabular and graphical formats.

4. Setup provides the user with the ability to configure the central station.

Configuration can be performed at start-up and during operation of the system. Changes that can be made include what view is displayed, audio levels of tones, menu time-outs, the location of a bed in the display, and alarm limit settings. Changing the configuration may involve sending commands (for example, setting alarm limits) to remote bedside monitors.

Central Vision offers two packages to meet different monitoring needs. Central Vision systems are preconfigured with the Basic package. The Enhanced option is enabled via a software licensing mechanism that allows customers to upgrade easily when needed.

The Basic package has the following features: display of numeric values and waveforms of two to eight bedside monitors on a single screen, alarm annunciation, context-sensitive on-line help, configurable views, and remote dial-in for diagnostics. The user has the option to display from two to eight bedsides in the Cluster View and the ability to toggle between a view of the bedsides and a view of the EKG leads.

The Enhanced package includes a full remote view of a bedside main screen, remote control of bedside monitors, a dual display option allowing for the display of 16 bedside monitors, and increased configurability. The user can select as many as 16 bedside monitors on the two screens. More information is displayed for a single bed, and additional applications are available with the Enhanced package.

10.1.1 Analyze Product Factors

In addition to the features already described, Central Vision was designed to meet the product requirements listed in Table 10.1. The features and user interface sections show the product requirements visible to the user. The data for these views come from the remote bedside monitors. Central Vision must handle multiple monitors entering and leaving the network as needed. The data arriving from the bedside monitors and user input are asynchronous and event driven in nature. The system is configurable by the user and is designed to be used by medical personnel without needing advanced skills in computer use.

In the future, Central Vision may need to support wireless monitoring, when there is no remote bedside monitor. In this case the central station must provide services that a bedside monitor currently provides. New types of data may need to be processed and presented as connections are made to other medical information systems.

The performance factors (factor P3) require that the high-volume data streams from bedside monitors be presented to the user in real time. Tuning is required during development and any time the system is modified.

As part of the service factors (factor P6), it is noted that the product must be extensible through a software upgrade path. The system is designed as a product and also as a platform for future applications. Given the strategy of delaying features to meet the schedule, new applications are added regularly during the product's lifetime.

The reliability factors (factor P7) require that the correct information be provided to the user 24 hours a day, 7 days a week.

Product Factor	Flexibility and Changeability	Impact
P1: Features		
P1.1: High concurrency		
The product must monitor many independent bedside monitors.	The number of bedside monitors could increase.	There is a moderate impact on acquisition performance.
P1.2: Very dynamic		
Bedside monitors enter and leave the network as needed.	Networks are growing.	There is a moderate impact on resource allocation. This affects acquisition and the user interface.
P1.3: Asynchronous, event-driven control		
User input and real-time, asynchronous events occur on the network.	The rate is affected by changes in the user interface paradigms and devices on the network.	This affects the user interface and the network.
P1.4: Configurable		
Users can tailor applications and the hardware configuration.	There is a high likelihood that the setup may change.	This affects acquisition and the user interface.
P2: User interface		
P2.1: Ease of use		
The product must accommodate unsophisticated computer users.	The product must adapt to new paradigms and domain standards as needed.	This affects the user interface.

Table 10.1. Product Factors Influencing Central Vision

Product Factor	Flexibility and Changeability	Impact
P3: Performance		
P3.1: Real-time presentation		
High-volume, continuous real-time bedside monitoring data must be presented.	Performance must be tuned during development and retuned whenever the product is modified.	There is a large impact on the components meeting performance requirements, process priorities, and process scheduling.
P6: Service		
P6.1: Extendable		
An open-ended system and a platform for future applications are required.	Networks are growing and medical information systems could be added. New applications are added yearly.	There is a high impact on all components.
P7: Reliability		
P7.1: High reliability		
The system must operate 24 hours a day, 7 days a week.	The requirements are stable.	There is a moderate impact on error handling and recovery.
P7.2: Data integrity		
Correct up-to-date information is provided to the user.	The requirements are stable.	There is a moderate impact on acquisition, process control, and the user interface.

Table 10.1. Product Factors Influencing Central Vision *(continued)*

10.1.2   Analyze Technological Factors

Technological factors are summarized in Table 10.2. A key decision for the Central Vision product was to use off-the-shelf technology. The UNIX operating system and X Windows/ Motif GUI framework running on a standard personal computer was the chosen platform.

Adopting an open systems approach based on a UNIX platform meant choosing a shorter development time at the expense of less programming control. This approach minimized coding by using platform services, third-party libraries, and off-the-shelf applications. The open systems approach was motivated by a desire to take advantage of hardware advances and to minimize development efforts by using third-party applications, tool kits, and standards. Additional benefits included a rapid prototyping capability and rich development/runtime environments.

Although there were many advantages to this technology choice, it was not without pitfalls. The set of potential risks included

- Reliability/integration problems with third-party or host software and hardware
- Inadequate vendor support
- Steep learning curves (for example, X/Motif programming)
- Performance/flexibility trade-offs

These potential risks were identified early to develop strategies for avoiding them or reducing their impact.

Technological Factor	Flexibility and Changeability	Impact
T1: General-purpose hardware		
T1.1: Hardware for processing		
A standard personal computer, memory, and disk are required.	Upgrade the technology based on the application need.	The impact of change is transparent, provided it does not require a change to the operating system.

Table 10.2. Technological Factors Influencing Central Vision

Technological Factor	Flexibility and Changeability	Impact
T2: Domain-specific hardware		
T2.1: Proprietary, networked devices		
Bedside monitors, recorders, and other medical devices are required.	New device types and versions need to be supported.	There is a large impact on acquisition components.
T3: Software technology		
T3.1: Operating system		
A UNIX-based operating system is required.	Flexibility depends on the hardware. There is a market-driven change within two years.	The impact is transparent, provided it conforms to current interface standards.
T3.2: System services		
Interprocess communication mechanisms, process scheduling/control, and device driver support are needed.	Control of process granularity, priorities, and memory usage, and efficient communication mechanisms are needed.	There is a significant impact on system performance characteristics and scalability.
T3.3: Third-party applications and tool kits		
An on-line help application is employed, as well as X Windows and the Motif graphical user interface.	Best results have been realized with tool kits, libraries, and standards. Upgrades are required as technology improves.	The cost/benefit ratio for applications is too high. There are risks in upgrading, such as memory leaks and performance.

Table 10.2. Technological Factors Influencing Central Vision *(continued)*

Technological Factor	Flexibility and Changeability	Impact
T5: Standards		
T5.1: Operating system standards		
A POSIX interface is required for the operating system.	This feature is stable.	There is a large impact on system services.

Table 10.2. Technological Factors Influencing Central Vision *(continued)*

10.1.3 Analyze Organizational Factors

The organizational factors are summarized in Table 10.3. The preference for buying reflects the open systems approach. To meet an aggressive schedule there was some flexibility in delaying nonessential features and in hiring a mentor for needed expertise.

Organizational Factor	Flexibility and Changeability	Impact
O1: Management		
O1.1: Buy versus build		
There is a preference for buying.	Use off-the-shelf technology when possible.	There is a moderate impact on the schedule and integration.
O1.2: Schedule versus functionality		
Nonessential features can be delayed to meet the schedule.	Several features are negotiable.	There is a moderate impact on meeting the schedule.

Table 10.3. Organizational Factors Influencing Central Vision

Organizational Factor	Flexibility and Changeability	Impact
O2: Staff skills		
O2.1: Domain experience		
All developers have extensive domain knowledge.	Staff must remain assigned to the project.	Losing domain expertise would affect the schedule.
O2.2: Object technology/C++		
One person knows object technology and C++. All team members know structured design and C.	It is feasible to hold training.	There is a moderate impact on meeting the schedule.
O2.3: X/Motif		
Team members have some knowledge of X/Motif but no development experience.	It is feasible to hire an expert.	There is a moderate impact on meeting the schedule.
O2.5: Concurrency		
Most team members have little multithreading experience, but most have multiprocessing experience.	Software abstraction may alleviate the lack of skills.	There is a large impact on meeting performance.

Table 10.3. Organizational Factors Influencing Central Vision *(continued)*

Organizational Factor	Flexibility and Changeability	Impact
O4: Schedule		
O4.1: Time-to-market		
The schedule is aggressive.	There is no flexibility.	There is a large impact on all design choices.
O4.2: Delivery of features		
The features are prioritized.	The features are negotiable.	There is a moderate impact on meeting the schedule.
O5: Budget		
O5.1: Head count		
Personnel assignments are fixed.	One contractor can be hired.	There is a moderate impact on meeting the schedule.
O5.2: Budget		
There is a software budget.	There is some flexibility to hire a mentor for missing skills.	There is a moderate impact on meeting the schedule.

Table 10.3. Organizational Factors Influencing Central Vision *(continued)*

The initial team consisted of six in-house developers, all with extensive domain knowledge. The majority of the team was familiar with structured design techniques, C programming, and embedded systems development. One member had object-oriented design, C++, and UNIX systems development experience. The team had some knowledge of X/Motif but no development experience.

To be successful, the team needed to increase its competency in object-oriented design and C++ and X/Motif programming. The team leader accomplished this through extensive training and by adding an experienced consultant to the team to serve as a mentor. The consultant worked with the architect to develop the core functionality for team members either to reuse or to use as an example. Within six months team members produced a working system containing the basic functionality. Within a year they were developing new functionality on their own.

10.1.4 Develop Strategies

The organizational, technological, and product factors presented so far led to the following issues and their accompanying strategies.

Reliability Using Many Off-the-Shelf Components

The choice of a UNIX-based platform is a significant architectural challenge because past experience with central monitoring is with embedded systems. Such systems offer a high degree of programming control at the expense of a longer development time. Open systems, on the other hand, improve development time but offer less programming control; for example, third-party and platform-supplied software components implement different levels of error handling.

Influencing Factors

O2.1, O2.2: The staff is skilled in the monitoring domain and structured design. Skills are needed in object technology.

O4.1: The time-to-market is short and is not flexible.

T3.1, T3.2, T5.1: A software platform based on UNIX and interprocess communication (IPC) is fairly stable.

P7.1, P7.2: Correct information needs to be provided to the user 24 hours a day, 7 days a week.

Solution

Improve developer productivity by using off-the-shelf components, abstractions, and focusing developers within their areas of expertise. Design the system to be robust, and easy to test and prototype. Make it mandatory that all components avoid, handle, recover, and identify problems when they occur.

Strategy: *Create a layered design.*

Focus developers within their areas of expertise in X/Motif, UNIX, and real-time monitoring by using a layered design. This helps insulate applications from vendor and platform specifics, thereby improving developer productivity.

Continued

Reliability Using Many
Off-the-Shelf Components *(continued)*

Strategy: *Provide abstraction for services.*

Provide abstract mechanisms for handling platform services such as input/output, IPC, and access to the execution environment. This benefits platform independence and reliability.

Strategy: *Define an error-handling policy.*

Develop and enforce a consistent approach to error and exception handling, diagnostics, logging, and trace/debugging. Adopt defensive coding techniques.

Issue: Turnkey Operation

Turnkey operation including autostart and restart is needed to accommodate unsophisticated computer users.

Influencing Factors

P1.3: User input is affected by changes in user interface paradigms. Real-time asynchronous events arrive from devices over the network.

P1.4: Users can tailor applications.

P2.1: The system must be easy to use and must accommodate unsophisticated users.

P7.1: Information needs to be provided to the user 24 hours a day, 7 days a week.

Solution

Ensure the system is tunable and the user interface is easy to adjust.

Strategy: *Implement a framework for process monitoring and recovery.*

A data-driven process control mechanism enables processes and groups to be configured easily for autostart and restart policies.

Related Strategies

Parameterize system configuration, Separate the user interface from the application logic (issue, Modifiability).

Modifiability

The system must support multiple, separately controlled physical displays, be highly configurable, and support the incremental development of features.

Influencing Factors

O4.2: Features are prioritized in the schedule and will be delivered in incremental releases.

T2.1: The central station is part of a network of heterogeneous devices. New device types and versions need to be supported.

P1.2: Bedside monitors enter and leave the network as needed; physiological parameters can be added or deleted.

P1.4: Users can tailor applications and the hardware configuration.

P6.1: Central Vision is designed as an open-ended system with a platform for future applications.

Solution

An important decision was to use object-oriented technology. The rationale for this decision was the desire to build a more understandable and manageable software platform, to maximize reuse of the design and code, to be resilient to change, and to provide technical challenge and interest to the team. A well-known design methodology, Object Modeling Technique, and the C++ programming language were the chosen tools.

Strategy: *Use an object-oriented design, not just an object-oriented language.*

Take full advantage of object-oriented concepts (for example, inheritance, polymorphism, encapsulation, composition) and "programming by object lifetime." Don't do a traditional structured design dressed in C++.

Strategy: *Provide for loose coupling and high cohesion.*

Provide for loose coupling and high cohesion of modules and processes. For example, design services so that they do only one thing, and the process to which they are assigned can run alone.

Continued

Modifiability *(continued)*

Strategy: *Minimize dependencies at all levels.*

Minimize dependencies at all levels: between processes, components, and objects. For example, ensure that the system is platform independent. The design should insulate applications from vendor and platform specifics to achieve portability to new platforms. The dependencies to the bedside monitors can be encapsulated in a virtual bedside monitor.

Strategy: *Separate the user interface from the application logic.*

Clearly separate the user interface from the core application logic. Encapsulate display components and behavior.

Strategy: *Parameterize system configuration.*

Separate the information needed to configure the system to provide the flexibility to configure the system according to need. The system configuration can be defined using resource files so that the components responsible for configuring the system don't have to change.

Related Strategies

Create a layered design, Provide abstraction for services (issue, Reliability Using Many Off-the-Shelf Components).

Performance

For the graphical user interface, the performance issue is the real-time display of moving waveforms using a standard, single-threaded X-Server. The architecture design must be able to meet this performance criterion.

Influencing Factors

T3.1, T5.1: Real-time capability of the UNIX operating system (time-slicing process scheduler) is needed.

T3.3: It is expensive to allocate X-Windows resources.

P3.1: Physiological data must be presented in real time. The data streams coming from the bedside monitors are high volume and real time.

Continued

Performance *(continued)*

Solution

Ensure the system is tunable. System performance characteristics may need to be determined empirically.

Strategy: *Adopt a flexible process model.*

It is not clear whether the real-time performance requirements of drawing waveforms can be met using X-Windows. A flexible process model allows for tuning. If performance by tuning is not adequate, the alternative is to use a direct hardware interface.

Strategy: *Separate time-critical activities.*

Time-critical activities can be assigned to separate processes to help ensure the performance requirements are met.

Strategy: *Minimize resource usage.*

Minimizing resource usage can help conserve system resources and enhance start-up and runtime performance.

Strategy: *Allocate resources statically.*

Certain problems are well known from experience. For example, it is expensive to allocate X-Windows resources, and there is the risk of memory leaks. This influenced the decision to allocate resources statically.

10.2 Conceptual Architecture View

The conceptual view of the design began with an object-oriented domain model to identify the significant elements of the system, their functional responsibilities and their relationships. A guiding strategy was to *Minimize dependencies at all levels* (issue Modifiability). This domain model was used to identify four groups of conceptual elements: Virtual Bed, Network, Presentation, and System Control.

The purpose of Central Vision is to gather data and present it to the user. There are a variety of beds and this led to the concept of a *Virtual Bed*. Virtual Bed is responsible for producing a single, abstract view of each bedside monitor on the network. This insulates other parts of the system from the specifics of multiple bedside monitoring devices on the network.

Virtual Bed in turn needs to communicate with remote bedsides over a network. This functionality is encapsulated in *Network*. It is responsible for handling the connections to the remote bedside monitors. It provides for network access, distributed time, and name services, enabling Central Vision to be a peer within the real-time monitoring network.

Although Virtual Bed is responsible for gathering data, *Presentation* is responsible for its presentation as visual and audio information to the user. It presents available services to the user (for example, a list of connected bedside monitors) and publishes local services. This element contains most of the policies for implementing user-level requirements and is expected to be the most volatile element in the system.

System Control is responsible for system start-up, shutdown, cleanup, and monitoring whether other elements are in operation or not. This element has knowledge of all elements in the system and addresses requirements for reliability and turnkey operation.

These groups of conceptual elements were refined to identify conceptual components and their relationships. We focus on the Bed View and Cluster View application functionality for the purposes of this example. The Bed View application functionality is supported by the architecture shown in Figure 10.2.

The Virtual Bed is represented by the BedAcq component, which acquires bedside data over the network and provides an abstract view of each bedside monitor. The Network is represented by the BedNet connector from the BedAcq component to a remote bedside monitor. The Presentation is represented by the BedPresentation component. The connector of type BedData provides dynamic notification of new bedside data. The System Control is represented by the SystemControl component. It has responsibilities for life-cycle management, diagnostics, and failure detection. SystemControl is shown as a single component. It has connections to each of the other components in the system. The BedPresentation component is refined in Figure 10.3.

The BedPresentation component is decomposed into two components: BedModel and BedDisplay. The BedModel component provides the virtual representation of the remote bedside data that contains the patient information, physiological parameters, waveforms, and alarm status. The presentation aspects are captured in the BedDisplay component, which contains the corresponding display aspects of the information contained in Bed-

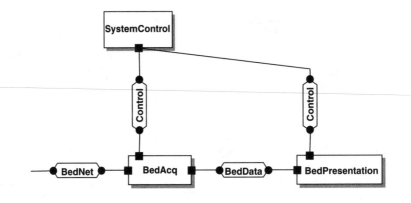

Figure 10.2. Central Vision conceptual architecture supporting Bed View

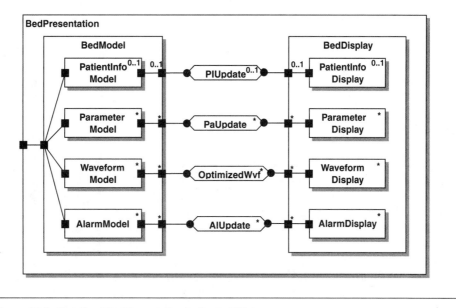

Figure 10.3. Details of BedPresentation in Central Vision

Model. The displays contain all the presentation knowledge and are responsible for handling user input and implementing visual layout and formats. The ports on BedModel and BedDisplay have multiplicities associated with them. Because each model has a direct connection with its corresponding display, the number of ports is dependent on the number of connections. Connectors of type PIUpdate, PaUpdate, and AlUpdate provide the dynamic notification of new bedside data. There is a special OptimizedWvf connector for handling the high-speed data transfer necessary to display the waveforms on the screen in real time.

The Cluster View provides information on as many as 8 patients on a single screen, and 16 patients on two screens. Multiple BedAcq components provide information to the cluster presentation that is displayed on the screen. The architecture supporting the Cluster View application is shown in Figure 10.4.

There is a BedAcq component for each of the remote monitors that are part of Cluster View. Instead of being connected to BedPresentation, BedAcq provides the information for ClusterPresentation. The ClusterPresentation component is decomposed into two components: ClusterModel and ClusterDisplay. These in turn contain BedModels and BedDisplays that present the data for each of the bedsides, as shown previously in Figure 10.3.

The primary and secondary display screens have unique and separately configurable instances. Specifically, a ClusterModel is first instantiated for each display screen. It creates its component BedModel objects for each configured bedside monitor. BedModels access

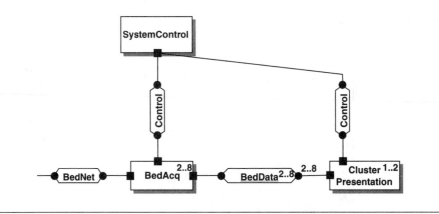

Figure 10.4. Central Vision conceptual architecture supporting Cluster View

the network and determine the state of the bedside monitor. BedModel in turn creates its component objects such as ParameterModel and AlarmModel.

After instantiating a ClusterModel, the application instantiates a ClusterDisplay, binding the two together and initiating real-time monitoring and display. This relationship is similar to the Document View pattern, where the model is acting as the document and the displays are acting as the views.

The scenarios that follow highlight the components in Central Vision's design that participate in asynchronous event processing. Events may be either user input events or asynchronous network events. Asynchronous network events signal the availability of new bedside monitor data on the network.

Scenario 1, featured in Figure 10.5, is an example of what happens when Central Vision responds to a network event and disseminates data to registered clients via dynamic update notification. In this example, a bedside monitor produces a new parameter value and writes it to the network, triggering a network event at Central Vision that new data is available. This network event triggers BedModel to read the associated bedside network connection via BedAcq. When the data is returned, the BedModel component routes it to the appropriate subcomponent, in this case, ParameterModel. ParameterModel in turn notifies registered ParameterDisplay components that the data has changed. The ParameterDisplay components read the new parameter value and update the display.

Scenario 2, featured in Figure 10.6, shows what happens when responding to a user input event that is a control request for a remote bedside. In this example, a Central Vision user hits the Alarm Silence button for a bedside being displayed, triggering a user input event at Central Vision. AlarmDisplay is triggered directly by the application, which causes an alarm silence message to be sent to the AlarmDisplay model, and in turn to BedModel. BedModel sends the message to the bedside network connection via BedAcq.

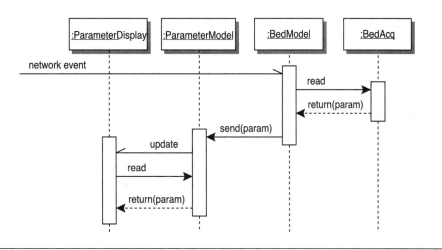

Figure 10.5. Scenario 1: Heart rate parameter change

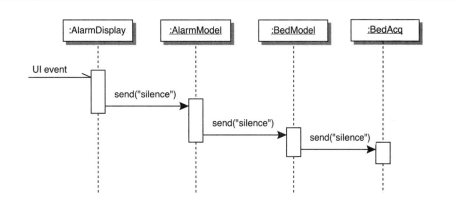

Figure 10.6. Scenario 2: Remote control of a bedside monitor alarm. UI = user input.

10.3 Module Architecture View

The module architecture view focuses on addressing the issue Reliability Using Off-the-Shelf Components. One starting point for identifying modules was the software platform. The point of interaction between the applications and the software platform identified the need for abstractions for GUI and system services in the module architecture. The other starting point was the conceptual components that identified the initial modules. Working top-down from these initial modules, and bottom-up from the software platform, a growing number of modules were identified and organized into layers to fulfill the strategy *Create a layered design*, and to manage the dependencies.

10.3.1   Decomposition and Layering

The Presentation, Virtual Bed, and Network groups of conceptual elements formed the initial layers in the module view, namely Applications, BedService and SystemServices respectively (Figure 10.7). The main conceptual components and connectors were then associated with the layers. In addition to BedNet being assigned to system services, the BedData connector was assigned to this layer because modules were needed to implement the communication protocols.

Figure 10.8 shows the final assignment of modules to layers. What follows are the steps that led to this picture. The initial modules were identified from the conceptual elements shown in Figure 10.7. System Control is decomposed into three modules shown in the Applications layer: Startup, Shutdown, and Watchdog. Start-up spawns all other processes, Shutdown provides for the orderly shutdown and release of system resources, and Watchdog monitors processes, detects failures, and implements recovery policies.

There are modules for the application functionality. There is a direct correspondence of the conceptual elements for display and model components to the modules that implement them (for example, ClusterDisplay, ClusterModel, BedDisplay, BedModel). The

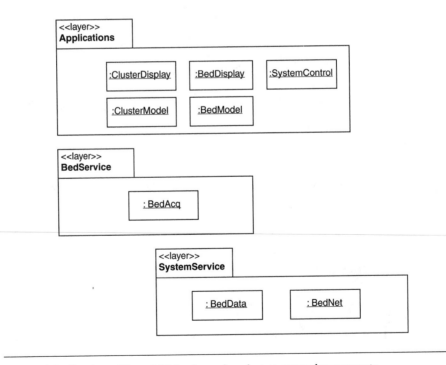

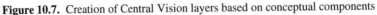

Figure 10.7. Creation of Central Vision layers based on conceptual components

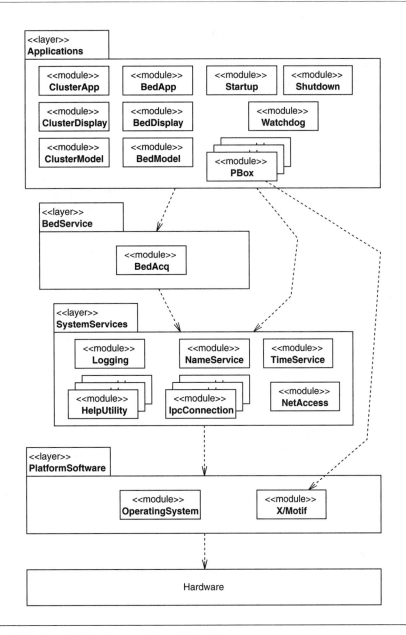

Figure 10.8. Central Vision layers with module assignments

same holds true of BedAcq in the BedService layer. BedNet is decomposed into modules for NetAcess, NameService, and TimeService in the SystemServices layer. The BedData connector is implemented by modules in system services for supporting IPC and for the protocol between components (for example, IpcConnection, Client, Server).

Additional modules are needed in the Applications layer. The application functionality acts as clients and is represented as the modules ClusterApp and BedApp. These modules contain the client functionality and coordinate the interaction of the displays and models defined in the conceptual scenarios (Figure 10.5 and Figure 10.6). All of the modules in this layer access the user interface via GUI service modules following the strategy *Provide abstraction for services* (issue, Reliability Using Many Off-the-Shelf Components). GUI services have two purposes: to insulate applications from X/Motif and to provide abstractions that map closely to user display requirements. An example is a patient's parameter display region, commonly referred to as a *PBox*. The PBox module contains and manages all display components of a PBox. Modules of this kind fulfill the strategy to *Minimize dependencies at all levels* (issue, Modifiability) and provide reusable units. Additional modules of this kind are shown behind PBox in Figure 10.8.

Moving to the BedService layer, its purpose is to acquire, translate, and communicate bedside data and control requests. The BedAcq module acquires real-time data from bedsides on the network. There is one instance of the BedAcq module for each remote bedside.

Following the strategy *Provide abstraction for services* (issue, Reliability Using Many Off-the-Shelf Components), the SystemServices layer contains abstract interfaces to platform services. As with the GUI services, the system services have two purposes: to insulate other modules from the host platform (operating system, devices, file system, and so forth) and to provide an abstraction to system services (for example, diagnostics and logging support). System services provide benefits such as type safety, robustness, standard error handling, and portability.

System services include interfaces to proprietary and purchased third-party libraries. Examples include IpcConnection, Timer, SharedMemory, ProcessLock, FileLock, SignalHandler, ChildExec, ShellExec, and utilities. Other services include a time service to synchronize platform time with the network, a name service to provide a list of network services, and network messaging standards to enable product-independent access to bedside data and control. The logging service is motivated by the strategy *Define an error-handling policy* (issue, Reliability Using Many Off-the-Shelf Components). It provides persistent storage for diagnostic events.

The PlatformSoftware layer contains two elements: X-Windows/Motif provides the framework for building user interfaces, and OperatingSystem provides a set of standard POSIX/UNIX services such as file and device input/output, IPC, timers, and process control.

10.3.2 Decomposition

With these layers and modules identified, the focus then turned to an object-oriented decomposition, looking for important classes, relationships, and patterns. The strategies

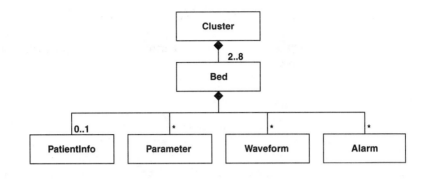

Figure 10.9. Structure used for ClusterModel and ClusterDisplay

Use an object-oriented design and *Separate the user interface from the application logic* (issue, Modifiability) guided refinement of the Document View pattern, which was identified in the conceptual architecture as the pattern of interaction between the applications and the user interface.

Both displays and models have a similar structure for capturing the multibed grouping. How this structure is captured in object-oriented design is shown in Figure 10.9. A Cluster is a hierarchical structure that contains from two to eight beds. A Bed contains the patient information, physiological parameter values, waveforms, and alarm status.

The Cluster structure allows the dynamics of central monitoring to be modeled. For example, the removal of a bedside monitor parameter triggers the destruction of the associated display and model objects. Likewise, if a Bed object is disconnected from the network, its associated instances and all their contained objects are cleanly removed.

The interface between displays and models is responsible for providing the following three services:

- A common mechanism for displays to register for data of interest from the models. Once bound, displays are notified when new data is acquired.

- A common mechanism for disseminating data via dynamic update notification to all registered clients. This conforms to the scenario presented in Figure 10.5.

- Communication of bedside remote control requests. This conforms to the scenario presented in Figure 10.6.

10.4 Execution Architecture View

Central Vision's execution architecture focused on performance, reliability, turnkey operation, and adaptability requirements. These goals had to be satisfied given the constraints of the host platform and the chosen off-the-shelf components. For example, achievement of near-real-time display performance using a "nonpreemptable" kernel, and a standard, single-threaded X-Server implementation was required. These constraints and the strategy *Adopt a flexible process model* (issue, Performance) led to a simple, client/server model for Central Vision processes.

10.4.1 Defining Runtime Entities

The conceptual view identified the initial process groupings of the execution view by associating each high-level conceptual component with a set of execution elements (Figure 10.10).

The Presentation, Bed Acquisition, and System Control aspects of the conceptual view were mapped to their own processes. Once these initial processes were in place, they were refined by examining the relevant issue cards and strategies and mapping modules and dependencies in the module view to processes and communication mechanisms in the execution view. Figure 10.11 shows the final set of processes that implement the core central monitoring station functionality. The Cluster View application is shown. Other applications, such as Bed View, are created as needed and are similarly connected to a subset of the servers based on needed functionality. What follows are the steps that led to this configuration.

Each of the applications becomes its own GUI application client process (for example, ClusterGUI). The GUI processes are implemented as X-Clients. The client creates and manipulates windows on the screen using the GUI services to insulate the application from the display hardware. The GUI services handle incoming events and send display requests based on standard X/Motif interfaces. A single X-Server process handles the input coming from the keyboard and pointer devices and the output to the physical displays.

The first concern for a central patient-monitoring station is the display of real-time bedside monitor data with minimal delay: The actual requirement was less than or equal to 2 seconds from the time of production. The initial GUI process grouping for Cluster View displayed low-frequency, intermittent data such as parameters, messages, and local time, and it displayed high-frequency data such as real-time waveforms and alarms. To meet the performance requirements, the strategy *Separate time-critical activities* (issue, Performance) was followed, and functionality for displaying high-frequency data was put into

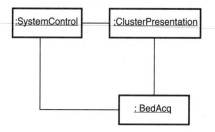

Figure 10.10. Overview of the Central Vision execution architecture view

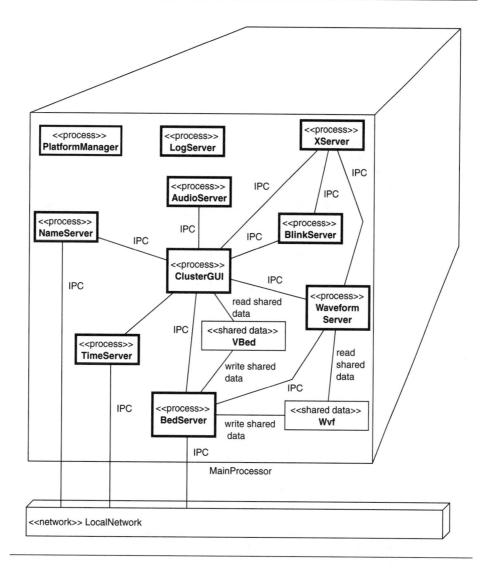

Figure 10.11. Execution view of processes and connection to the network. IPC = interprocess communication.

separate application services that could each be assigned to its own server process. The modules for displaying the real-time waveforms for bedside monitors were grouped into the WaveformDraw module, and it was assigned to the WaveformServer process. Similarly, modules for handling alarms were grouped into the VisualAlarm and AudioAlarm modules. VisualAlarm provides synchronized blinking of alarm regions, and AudioAlarm interfaces with the audio device to implement the audio alarm policy. They are assigned to the BlinkServer and AudioServer processes respectively.

Additional concerns beyond performance were maintainability and extendability. These were addressed by considering the strategies *Provide for loose coupling and high cohesion* and *Minimize dependencies at all levels* (issue, Modifiability) when defining the processes. For example, services such as waveform drawing only do one thing. The bed acquisition, name, time, and logging services are also assigned to their own server processes. The only dependency of a server is on the logger. Therefore, they can run in stand-alone mode with the logger and don't need to know details about the client.

Central Vision's system monitoring and recovery model was designed to enhance reliability, ensure presentation integrity (in other words, minimize the possibility of a "stale" presentation), and provide turnkey operation. This model, guided by the strategy *Implement a framework for monitoring and recovery,* consists of a top-level controller—PlatformManager—which is assigned the System Control modules Startup, Shutdown, and Watchdog. PlatformManager manages individual processes.

The details of the assignment of modules to processes are summarized in Table 10.4. The modules in the system service layer that do not become their own processes are referred to as OperatingSystemServices in the table. GUIServices refers to the collection of modules, such as PBox, that provide access to the user interface.

Process Name	Modules
PlatformManager	Startup, Shutdown, Watchdog, OperatingSystem Services
ClusterGUI	ClusterApp, ClusterDisplay, ClusterModel, GUIServices, OperatingSystemServices
BedGUI	BedApp, BedDisplay, BedModel, GUIServices, Operating-SystemServices
WaveformServer	WaveformDraw, GUIServices, OperatingSystem Services
BlinkServer	VisualAlarm, GUIServices, OperatingSystem Services

Table 10.4. Process Mapping and Priorities

Process Name	Modules
AudioServer	AudioAlarm, GUIServices, OperatingSystemServices
BedServer	BedAcq, NetAccess, OperatingSystemServices
TimeServer	TimeService, NetAccess, OperatingSystemServices
NameServer	NameService, NetAccess, OperatingSystemServices
LogServer	Logging, OperatingSystemServices

Table 10.4. Process Mapping and Priorities *(continued)*

10.4.2 Defining Communication Paths

Central Vision consists of many collaborating processes. This characteristic inspired the development of a common IPC framework to facilitate reuse and consistency. The diagram for the module view of the IPC framework is shown in Figure 10.12.

Server and client processes are related by a communication channel supporting a specific IPC protocol. The Server module represents the general characteristics of all servers (for example, BedServer, WaveformServer). The Client module represents the general characteristics of all clients (for example, ClusterGUI). Behavioral aspects of each IPC protocol are provided by specialized instances of IpcCmdServer and IpcCmdClient and may include synchronous or asynchronous communication.

The IPC protocol is realized in the execution architecture with sockets and shared memory. Sockets are used for communication between the GUI clients and its services. Shared memory is used for transmitting the high-volume data provided by the bed server and is one way to implement the strategy *Minimize resource usage* (issue, Performance).

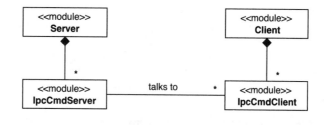

Figure 10.12. IPC framework

10.4.3   Defining the Execution Configuration

There is only one instance of each of the clients and servers in the system; therefore, there is no need to show a picture different than the one in Figure 10.11 for the configuration of runtime entities and entity instances.

Central Vision supports simultaneous monitoring of many patient bedside monitors, and this is shown with multiple BedAcq components in the conceptual view. Concurrency is supported in the execution view by a single-server process model using nonblocked input/output mechanisms. For example, a single BedServer process manages many internal instances of BedAcq modules. Input and output can be triggered via "data ready" events (for example, via the X-event loop) or can utilize a timer-based approach, as is typically needed for the acquisition of time-sequenced, continuous data streams.

The alternative of using blocked input and output in the context of multithreaded processes was not chosen due to unavailability of thread-safe libraries and a perceived increase in complexity. Multiple threads were also not necessary to handle the data sent to the BedServer because the data was transferred over one socket.

At start-up, the PlatformManager process is started by bootstrap mechanisms. All other Central Vision processes are created and monitored by PlatformManager. The ClusterGUI process is the first client application to be created, and a Cluster View is displayed in full size on the screen. Other client applications are created as requested by the user. Creating another application when the Cluster View application is running causes its display to shift right on the screen. Returning to the Cluster View application causes the other running application to be destroyed.

Processes are organized into process groups. Associated with the process-group type are attributes such as disposition on failure (abort, restart, ignore). A process type specifies attributes such as priority and watchdog time-outs. The values of these attributes for a particular system are recorded in configuration description files in the code architecture view.

The PlatformManager process reads a configuration description file that lists the particular process groups for the system and their attributes. Each process group has an associated configuration description file that lists the processes contained in that group, the pathname of their associated executable, and their attributes. This data-driven approach, from the strategy *Parameterize system configuration* (issue Modifiability), allows the particular system configuration to be specified independently of the PlatformManager.

The notion of a process group provides a convenient framework for controlling the lifetime of licensed applications. An application that consists of one or more collaborating processes is mapped to a process group. PlatformManager can, dynamically, start, restart on failure, and shut down individual process groups.

A special consideration is how to monitor third-party applications or platform services such as the X-Server. This is accomplished by creating a dependency with a Central Vision process. For example, the central GUI process is dependent on a functioning X-Server. If the X-Server fails, then the central GUI exits prematurely and this event is detected by the process group, triggering a restart.

This watchdog scheme can also be extended to include the monitoring of global resources for a process group or the entire platform. For example, a small server that monitors memory usage could trigger a restart of its associated process group if a predetermined limit is reached.

The Central Vision process model has proved to be very flexible and is easily extended by adding new servers and GUI applications. To preserve this architectural feature, a set of design guidelines for creating processes was identified. All Central Vision processes utilize the LogServer for capturing runtime errors and diagnostics. All Central Vision server processes support zero or more clients; are autonomous, with the exception of depending on the LogServer connection; and implement a "lazy" connection strategy (for example, WaveformServer will not attempt to connect to BedServer until needed).

10.4.4 Resource Allocation

Central Vision resources of concern included CPU, memory, disk, and the X-Windows display server. The standard X-Server implements a single-threaded, FIFO request queue for all clients and could be monopolized by a misbehaving client.

The first resource considered was the CPU consumption and whether it could support the performance goals. The most time-consuming activity is the acquisition and display of waveforms. Displaying waveforms involves the highest data transfers and CPU consumption. The WaveformServer process is triggered to run every 20 msec to draw smooth waveforms. All other processes were considered secondary to this function and were required to run at intervals between 50 and 100 msec to meet the user response times specified in the requirements.

This led to a two-tiered process priority scheme. A process is either set explicitly to a high priority or it runs at the default system low priority for interactive tasks. Following this scheme, the WaveformServer, AudioServer, and BedServer processes are set to a high priority, whereas the remainder run at the default system low priority.

An architecture that follows the strategies *Minimize dependencies at all levels*, *Minimize resource usage*, and *Allocate resources statically* supported the system in meeting extendability and performance requirements. The following five guidelines were identified to minimize resource utilization:

- Maximize code and data sharing. Utilize shared, dynamically linked libraries to minimize the memory footprint of all executables. Use shared memory for high-volume IPC channels.

- Minimize paging of critical, high-volume memory regions by locking them in memory.

- Utilize a circular buffer scheme for continuous file storage (for example, storage of LogServer events).

- Follow a single-server process model in which a single process serves many clients to minimize the number of executable processes and associated context switches.

- Utilize static allocation of X-Windows resources to minimize X-Server traffic and overhead.

These guidelines helped conserve system resources, enhanced start-up and runtime performance, and enabled future scalability. For example, shared memory supports a one-to-many relationship of writer to readers, allowing new readers to be added with little impact on overall performance.

10.5 Code Architecture View

10.5.1 Central Design Tasks

The concept of a process was seen as a reasonable approach to organizing the source code into the code groups seen in Figure 10.13. This is in keeping with the strategy *Reflect module architecture hierarchies*, because most modules do not get mapped to more than one process. Code groups are directories in the Central Vision code architecture. Each major directory contained all of the modules for a process. This could be for front-end GUI applications or back-end server processes. Additionally, the layers for common services from the module architecture were mapped to directories for shared libraries.

All leaf nodes in the directory tree contain implementation and interface files (.C and .h), binaries (.o), and executables. The libraries contain shared services from system services, network, and functionality. Shared functionality was created when two or more processes needed it.

Directories were organized according to the principle, "look above but not across." Code shouldn't look at other code in sibling directories; otherwise it would introduce unwanted dependencies. This enforces the design constraints and usage dependencies established in the module view of the architecture. It simplifies the include paths and linking. It simplifies building because developers can go to a directory and compile from the node down. They look up the directory hierarchy for shared libraries.

The testing approach contributed additional components that were organized in the source component directory structure. Testing is done at the GUI, module, and process levels. The test methods are part of the modules and classes they test. The test instructions, test harnesses, and test suites become components and are kept in the same directory as the module or server they test. There is a client test program that connects to back-end server processes, makes a request, and validates the results. The makefile has a test option to build the test components. This is documented in the makefile with options for testing without a bedside monitor, with a simulated monitor, or with a hookup to an actual monitor.

As applications were introduced, new directories were added for these GUI front ends. Applic was the first application for Central Vision.

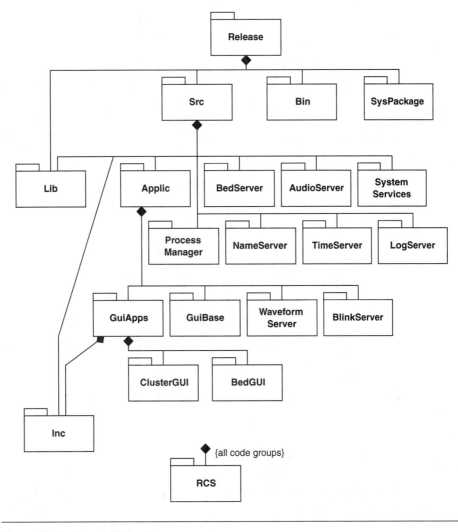

Figure 10.13. Central Vision directory structure

10.5.2 Build Procedure and Configuration Management

The build process was automated with the make utility, which supports conditional processing for building and packaging different software releases from the same source tree. Install directories contained in the Release directory—Bin, Lib, and SysPackage—are used to pull in the appropriate files and package them together into an archive.

RCS was used for source code configuration management. All directories under Src have an RCS directory. RCS provides a feature that is used to tag the source code with the release version.

Development activities were coordinated through the build process:

* Developers make a change to a local copy of the code in their workspace.

* Developers build the process containing the change locally and link against a public tree containing the rest of the system. This public tree is a library in the install directories. If multiple developers are developing code that depends on each other they must coordinate the build process. Typically they share a public tree that has been put in a private workspace.

* Developers test their private version.

* Developers check the revised version in a working directory and send e-mail so no one will touch the system.

* Developers then build and test the whole tree.

* If the testing is successful, they install and release the change.

There are two versions of libraries: static and shared. Shared libraries were utilized to minimize the total memory usage of the system. There is an option for developers to link statically as a convenience because this allows a single process to be moved or tested on any machine regardless of which libraries are installed.

Code is shared through the shared libraries, GuiBase, and SystemServices. GuiBase contains the common GUI code within a particular product. GuiBase is built shared because there are a number of GUI clients under the product that link against it. System-Services contains the common system services. The GuiBase library depends on System-Services.

10.6 Software Architecture Uses

The software architecture facilitated initial project planning, highlighted many of the risks introduced by new technologies, and provided a road map for keeping the integrity and goals of the system on track during its evolution. It was a tool for capturing project knowledge and communicating this knowledge within the team.

The conceptual view helped to organize the team according to knowledge of real-time systems, the UNIX operating system, and GUIs. The conceptual view was used to identify points of interaction among the team members by identifying important interfaces. It also helped to identify points of interaction with other groups in the organization. For example, the Presentation element requires collaboration with clinical specialists; Virtual Bed requires collaboration and integration with bedside monitor groups.

The module view facilitated an iterative, depth-first development approach that allowed the system to evolve incrementally and enabled rapid validation of design. The design team identified the key architectural components and cast them into the object model. They served as "templates," giving members of the development team enough guidance to do detailed design and coding. This allowed them to focus on the functionality of the application domain while providing the necessary architecture infrastructure (for example, communication mechanisms and protocols) that developers could reuse in their detailed designs.

Making the decisions regarding the high-level architectural design, detailed design, and implementation was an iterative process. During system design it was sometimes necessary to go into detailed design in certain areas that were less understood to validate the design. The implementation was built in phases. Getting a working framework in place quickly and building a small vertical slice of functionality helped validate the requirements and build confidence that the design approach was viable. It also provided important feedback to the designers early in the design process.

10.7 Summary

10.7.1 Software Architecture Concepts

The Central Vision architecture design identified key concepts, relationships, guidelines, and strategies that contributed to the successful delivery of the Central Vision product. Developing an architecture should be an organized and planned activity. Partitioning the task into different views, each addressing separate concerns, was beneficial and provided a framework for applying the object-oriented methodology. Following an incremental and iterative approach was a productive strategy in which insights developed in one view were fed into other views.

The Presentation, Virtual Bed, and Network conceptual groupings from the conceptual view identified the initial layers in the module view. Conceptual components were refined to the point where they could be mapped to modules in the module view. The module view helped to identify static structure, layers, and categories of classes needed to construct the system.

The conceptual view was also used to develop a simple execution view. The Presentation, Bed Acquisition, and System Control aspects of the conceptual view were mapped to their own processes. Once this process clustering was in place, the processes were refined. The execution view was further refined by mapping modules and dependencies in the module view to the processes and communication mechanisms in the execution view.

The execution view provided the starting point for the code view, which is organized around the concepts of processes. Each major directory represented all of the modules for a process. The layers for common services from the module view were mapped to directories for shared libraries.

A number of recurring patterns began to surface during the development of the Central Vision architecture. Recognizing these patterns and providing implementations facilitated reuse and consistency because all developers followed the same approach. Frameworks supporting common tasks such as the design and implementation of IPC protocols were developed.

10.7.2 Experience

Central Vision has been in the field for two years. The basic architecture has proved to be very extendable. The architecture also received more visibility than anticipated—the design concepts and some code from system services were used by a number of external development efforts in the medical domain.

New applications have been added that required changes to Cluster View and the way windows are managed. Previously, Cluster View had exclusive control of a window. Now, with the addition of new applications, Cluster View has to share the window. To handle this, a top-level window manager was introduced to coordinate the clients accessing windows. An additional interface and protocol was required for Cluster View to respond to the window manager's request for it to resize itself or to shift over so that other applications could have access to part of the window. This affected primarily the Presentation aspects.

The core services were unaffected because they were designed to be independent of clients. The process model made adding new applications and configurations straightforward, because this could be specified in the resource description files. Another change was adding dependencies at start-up. Because the ability to configure the system at start-up was already addressed, this meant no change to the architecture. The only change necessary was the one made to the system configuration description file.

New products have been built on the Central Vision platform that required adding functionality for bedside monitoring on top of the Central Vision platform. The existing system services could be used intact. In addition, the platform had to be changed to allow processes to share more and different kinds of data. This required the introduction of a broker to allow processes to subscribe for and to publish any kind of information.

As new products were identified, separate product directory structures were added under the Src directory in the code view. Even among products, 90 percent of the source was in common. They shared utilities and back-end server processes. It was also observed that the products shared front-end GUI code. So a new GUIsys directory was created to share generic GUI services common among products.

Ensuring reliability using many off-the-shelf components was a challenge. The off-the-shelf components were not always fully documented, and any problems were inherited in the system. For example, memory leaks with X/Motif was an issue in meeting the reliability requirements. This risk was mitigated by statically allocating memory at system start-up and reusing the memory during system operation. Tools such as heap debuggers and process information reporting identified memory leaks.

The architecture enabled the goal of turnkey operation to be met. The process-monitoring and recovery model ensured the system was operating properly and provided a way to easily configure the system for autostart and restart. The modifiability goal was achieved and did not affect the performance requirements for the first release. User interface and system configuration were driven by resource files.

Meeting performance requirements using the Central Vision platform for some new products turned out to be a challenge. It was necessary to adjust process priorities and the order in which they were created at start-up. Using resource files provided the flexibility to make these adjustments. Shared libraries were introduced. This affected the code view in terms of the build tools needed to generate different types of libraries. Because the operating system provides an abstraction for accessing libraries, the interface remained the same.

Central Vision—Lessons Learned

- Developing an architecture should be an organized and planned activity.
- The architecture is distinct from detailed design.
- The discovery and application of common patterns is a powerful design technique.
- An iterative, depth-first development approach helps to validate designs quickly and provides working frameworks that developers can flesh out.
- Use existing architecture and software technologies (for example, existing frameworks, tool kits, applications, and development of local domain- and platform-specific class libraries) to minimize the amount of new design and implementation.
- Strive for simplicity. It is better to have a small set of descriptions that are accurate than a large pile of stale or inaccurate information.

Chapter 11

Comm Vision

with Contributions by
Cornelis H. Hoogendoorn and
Heinz Kossmann

Telecommunication networks have been evolving from dedicated service-specific networks (for example, telephony, data transfer, TV transfer) to networks that provide an integrated set of services. This evolution has been facilitated by recent advances in networks based on asynchronous transfer mode (ATM). Such networks support a variety of communication requirements such as low and constant bandwidth for telephony to high and varying bandwidth for data transfer, to high and bursty bandwidth for video conferences—all using the same equipment.

Comm Vision is a product line of highly reliable switching nodes for ATM networks. A switching node establishes and controls connections between arbitrary pairs of input and output lines. The system can also interoperate with a variety of existing communication networks.

A Comm Vision system has a long lifetime of 20 years or more. During its lifetime, new software upgrades are regularly integrated without interruption in service. Over the lifetime of the switch, a customer's requirements may change due to the changes in traffic patterns: traffic type (for example, voice versus video) and traffic volume (for example, number of subscribers). A customer has the option to add or to upgrade processors and channel capacity over the lifetime of the product.

Different customers also have considerably different requirements, and as a result, Comm Vision products are not predefined. Comm Vision software architecture meets the evolving and differing requirements of customers using a set of reusable components called service provision units (SPUs), which can be packaged and deployed in many different ways.

The Comm Vision architecture has been used for two different applications or products: Broadband Switch and Signalling System Network Control (SSNC). Internet applications will comprise the next product.

The overall system architecture of Comm Vision is shown in Figure 11.1. The ATM switching network provides the hardware for interconnections between all the processors on the system as well as communication channels to other network nodes. The access units support connections to subscriber terminators (such as telephones) and other networks. The access units consist of specialized peripheral control processors such as line interface cards (LICs) and ATM multiplexers. The control cluster of main processors supports the main functionality of Comm Vision.

The system architecture is scalable and may include as many main and peripheral control processors as required. A low-end system could have a single main processor whereas a high-end system could have as many as 50 main processors spread over several ATM multiplexers.

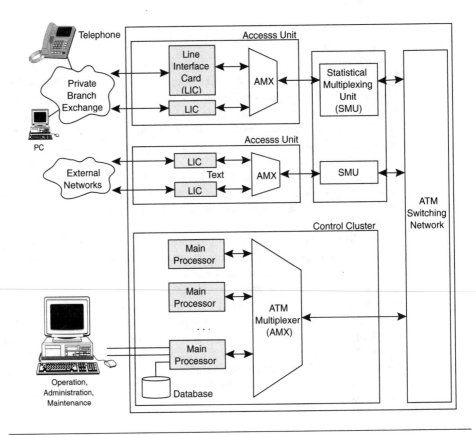

Figure 11.1. Comm Vision system architecture. ATM = asynchronous transfer mode.

Comm Vision software runs on the main and peripheral control processors. It supports various applications, including Call Processing and Operation, Administration, and Maintenance (OA&M). Call Processing supports services for establishing and managing logical and physical connections. OA&M provides an interface for the operator to install new subscribers, receive alarms, and reconfigure the network. It is also used to control the loading of all software on the switch.

In this chapter, we focus mainly on the aspects of software architecture related to the call-processing subsystem.

11.1 Global Analysis

11.1.1 Analyze Product Factors

The key product factors for Comm Vision are summarized in Table 11.1.

Product Factor	Flexibility and Changeability	Impact
P1: Features		
P1.1: Long lifetime		
A switch may remain in operation for a period of 20 years or more.	This requirement is not likely to change.	This places stringent requirements on software maintainability.
P1.2: Customized and flexible functionality		
Comm Vision software must be tailored to support considerably different requirements of customers.	The software may be upgraded to support new hardware, connection to new types of networks, and new applications.	The need for reusable components is greatly increased.
P1.3: Interoperability with standard services		
Comm Vision software interoperates with many standard communication services to connect to a variety of networks.	New standard services may be added over the lifetime of a switch.	This determines the externally visible services and their extensions.

Table 11.1. Product Factors Influencing Comm Vision

Product Factor	Flexibility and Changeability	Impact
P3: Performance		
P3.1: High performance		
Comm Vision supports hundreds of thousands of fixed or virtual connections per hour and five to several hundred gigabits per second in bandwidth.	Customers will demand higher and higher performance.	There is a tension between high performance and greater flexibility throughout the system.
P3.2: Flexible and scalable performance		
Comm Vision supports changing performance requirements through load balancing, reallocation of software on processors, and addition of hardware.	This requirement is quite stable.	This requires software components to be able to be relocated and amenable to load balancing.
P4: Dependability		
P4.1: High availability		
The switch is expected to be available 24 hours a day, 7 days a week with a downtime of less than 1 minute per year. At least 90 percent of the system failures should not require human intervention.	The availability requirement may become more stringent in the future.	Redundant hardware must be used in part to meet this requirement. Software must be designed to be fault tolerant.

Table 11.1. Product Factors Influencing Comm Vision *(continued)*

Product Factor	Flexibility and Changeability	Impact
P4.2: Fault recovery		
Comm Vision is required to detect all hardware and software failures and to recover with minimum overhead. The system may revert to an earlier version of the software if necessary.	This requirement is stable. Decisions related to the manner and the level of recovery are left to the software designers.	This has a global impact on the architecture and mechanisms for fault detection and recovery. All components must deal with faults in their clients and servers.
P6: Service		
P6.1: Maintainability		
Comm Vision can accept hardware and software changes with minimal impact. It offers separate evolution paths for software and hardware.	This requirement is quite stable.	Hardware must be encapsulated and software must be designed to be modifiable.
P6.2: On-line software upgrade		
In light of high availability requirements, all software upgrades are required to be made on-line.	There is no flexibility.	Communication between two software components must use protocols to facilitate upgrade of either component.

Table 11.1. Product Factors Influencing Comm Vision *(continued)*

Historically, communication switches have had a long life. Only the modes of maintenance and upgrades have changed. This factor affects all other factors of Comm Vision.

For example, the development environment used to develop the software for a switch must be preserved for future use. New software may be added and must interoperate with old software versions.

The software architecture must anticipate and accommodate the most common types of changes, which include changes in requirements over the lifetime of a switch to provide support for as yet unknown communication services.

Comm Vision offers scalable high performance measured by the number of connections and bandwidth without introducing any bottlenecks. Such flexibility and scalability in performance cannot be achieved without a flexible distribution of software. Performance requirements for the switch must be translated into performance requirements for individual components and must be managed explicitly.

The switch is expected to be available 24 hours a day, 7 days a week with a downtime of less than 1 minute per year. This goal is only partly achieved with redundant and microsynchronous hardware. To achieve the required level of availability, all software must be designed to detect faults and to recover from them with minimum time and overhead.

Comm Vision offers changes to hardware and software without interruption in service and with minimal impact to the customer. Thus, software components must be designed to be upgraded and to work with different versions of other software. In particular, all software components must be able to be upgraded while the system is in operation.

11.1.2 Analyze Technological Factors

The key technological factors for Comm Vision are summarized in Table 11.2.

Technological Factor	Flexibility and Changeability	Impact
T1: General-purpose hardware		
T1.1: Processor type		
The switch hardware includes a number of main processors.	Processor types will change with advances in technology.	The impact is reduced through encapsulation.
T1.2: Processing number		
The number of processors may vary from 1 to 50.	The number of processors varies during the lifetime of a switch.	This has a large impact on the execution architecture view.

Table 11.2. Technological Factors Influencing Comm Vision

Technological Factor	Flexibility and Changeability	Impact
T2: Domain-specific hardware		
T2.1: ATM switching network and multiplexers		
The switching network manages connections. Multiplexers allow processors to multiplex to the switching network.	Both kinds of hardware are likely to change.	This has a large impact on performance.
T2.2: Line interface cards (LICs)		
LICs connect the switch to various communication networks.	LICs will change over time with technology and with requirements to connect to new types of networks.	Comm Vision software must interoperate with other communication networks through standard services.
T3: Software technology		
T3.1: Programming languages		
Software is written in CHILL for main processors and C for LICs.	The choice of programming languages is not likely to change.	This has a large impact on the design of software components and their services.
T3.2: Operating system		
The proprietary operating system, VOCOS, supports various CHILL concepts.	For main processors, VOCOS will continue to be used. It may be modified over time.	This has a large impact on the design of the execution architecture view.
T3.3: Interprocess communication (IPC) mechanisms		
IPC mechanisms include remote procedure calls, message passing, and shared data.	The IPC mechanisms supported by VOCOS are not likely to change drastically.	This enables loose coupling between components and flexible allocation to processors.

Table 11.2. Technological Factors Influencing Comm Vision *(continued)*

Processor technology is expected to change several times over the lifetime of the system. To minimize the impact of changes in processor technologies, all processor-dependent software, including the operating system, must be encapsulated. The number of processors is expected to increase over the lifetime of a switch to meet increases in performance. This implies that the software must be designed so that it can be flexibly distributed over the changing number and kind of processing platforms.

The ATM switching network, multiplexers, and LICs are the main domain-specific hardware used in Comm Vision. The switching network establishes and manages interconnections and channels between two points on a communication network. Its size and nature, which affect the bandwidth and performance of the switch, are expected to change over the lifetime of the system. Multiplexers allow several processors to multiplex to the switching network. LICs are used to connect to a variety of communication networks. The types of LICs supported will change over the lifetime of a switch. The C programming language is used for software resident on LICs.

The CCITT[1] High Level Language, or CHILL, is used as a programming language for software resident on main processors. CHILL was developed for telecommunication software in the late 1970s, and it incorporates many constructs of high-level languages available at the time. It supports concurrent execution through constructs such as CHILL process, which is a unit of concurrent execution; region, which provides mutually exclusive access to shared data; and message buffers, signals, and events, which provide mechanisms for communication and synchronization.

A CHILL module is the unit of compilation that may define constants, data, procedures and the process type. CHILL supports a separation compilation model in which CHILL modules and their specifications are compiled into a hierarchical library.

The proprietary operating system, called VOCOS, supports a variety of CHILL software concepts. It also supports C, and facilitates the interoperation of software written in C and CHILL. It is expected that VOCOS will be ported to new processor types as they are incorporated in the switch. The impact of changes in the operating system are minimized by using its services only through published interfaces. The operating system offers several different mechanisms for IPC, including RPC and message passing. The selection of an IPC mechanism has a significant impact on the communication overhead and, therefore, the performance of the overall system. Guidelines are used to facilitate the uniform selection of IPC mechanisms.

11.1.3 Analyze Organizational Factors

The key organizational factors for Comm Vision are summarized in Table 11.3.

---

1. CCITT: The International Telegraph and Telephone Consultative Committee.

Organizational Factor	Flexibility and Changeability	Impact
O2: Staff skills		
O2.1: Communication software		
The staff is highly skilled, having built several generations of telecommunication software.	The staff stays abreast of advances in communication technologies.	Techniques and strategies used in new development are influenced.
O3: Process and development environment		
O3.1: Software production environment		
A comprehensive production environment supports various phases of development, including requirements, development, and testing.	The production environment is modified or extended when required.	This makes architecture concepts explicit in code.
O3.2: Software development process		
A flexible development and configuration management process also addresses the management of architectural issues such as performance budgeting.	The process is adapted to suit the needs of various development teams.	This makes development more systematic and predictable.
O3.3: Distributed development		
Large development teams, organized around functional areas and projects, are located on several continents.	The development is likely to be even more distributed in the future.	This has a large impact on the production environment and the development process.

Table 11.3. Organizational Factors for Comm Vision

The organization has built several generations of telecommunication software and, therefore, the staff is highly skilled in this area. They took advantage of experience (for example, use of static task and memory allocation) gained in development of previous products, and look forward to tackling state-of-the-art technologies in the area of telecommunications.

The organization has successfully used a sophisticated production environment that supports development from concept to implementation and release of software. At the time of its development, a suitable, integrated set of tools for CHILL was not available on the market. However, its ownership gives the organization a lot of flexibility in being able to enhance functionality of production tools, including checking of conventions and architectural guidelines. It provides a direct route to correction of errors in and extensions to the basic software and production tools, thus improving the organization's ability to introduce technology faster. It also reduces the maintenance problems related to integrating tools from multiple vendors.

The flexible production environment has had a large impact on the development process. With time, production tools are enhanced or added to track adherence to the process. The process has enabled the organization to track and manage changes and to streamline production. It also facilitates the distributed development of Comm Vision software across several continents.

11.1.4   Develop Strategies

The issues arising from the factors presented in the previous sections, and the strategies designed to address these issues, are summarized below.

Size and Complexity of the System

The size of communication systems varies from 10 to 20 million lines of code. The number of components and their interconnections of such large systems result in an architecture that is also large and complex. There is a need to reuse old as well as new code to improve productivity and reliability.

Influencing Factors

O3.3: In a large software project, many teams of people must cooperate, often in geographically distributed locations.

T3.3: The VOCOS operating system supports loosely coupled interprocess communication through remote procedure calls and message passing.

P1.1, P1.2: Proliferation of customer variants must be controlled by representing each system as a set of standard components. In a long-lived product, upgrades to the system must be packaged coherently for sale to customers.

Continued

Size and Complexity of the System *(continued)*

Solution

The size and complexity of the architecture is addressed by a two-level architecture that is defined at the level of the system and at the level of service provision units (SPUs).

Strategy: *Use services and service provision units.*

Separate the Comm Vision functionality into clearly defined services. A service (for example, printing) is a well-defined set of operations that may be implemented by any number of components (for example, printers). Decompose the system into standard components, called SPUs, that offer one or more of the defined services. This will reduce the number of variations in functionality by packaging related services into SPUs. SPUs provide the designer with large and complex building blocks. When possible or desirable, encapsulate the old code as SPUs. This will facilitate its reuse and integration.

Strategy: *Use system-level and SPU-level architectures.*

Decompose the architecture design problem into two levels: system level and SPU level. This will reduce the number of components and interconnections at the system level, thus making the system-level architecture design manageable. The system-level architecture will address only the SPUs and service provided by them. Regard SPUs as systems in their own right with particular architectural needs, and delegate the responsibility for their architecture design to respective development teams.

Strategy: *Use loosely coupled communication between SPUs.*

To make SPUs more readily reusable, maintainable, and able to be upgraded, use only remote procedure calls or message passing to communicate among them.

Related Strategies

Introduce generic services (issue, Customized, Flexible, and Maintainable Functionality).

Customized, Flexible, and Maintainable Functionality

The system must be designed to accept changes in hardware and software easily and with minimal impact. It must be possible to customize the system according to a customer's requirements. It must be possible to add new features or enhancements to the existing system.

Influencing Factors

T1, T2: The system must accommodate changes in both general-purpose and domain-specific hardware.

P1.3: The software must interoperate with universal and standard services. New standard services may be added over the lifetime of the system.

P6.2: It must be possible to make changes to the software while the system is on-line.

Solution

Separate concerns to isolate the effect of changes to parts of the system. Developers of Comm Vision have traditionally used a layered architecture to develop previous generations of systems. Layers, called *shells*, were defined as a means for separation and encapsulation. The solution calls for a uniform and a rigorously followed shell model.

Strategy: *Separate and isolate concerns.*

Isolate concerns in such a way as to contain most likely changes without replacing the whole system. For example, separate the global functions (for example, call processing and signaling) from the hardware, so that they can evolve independently. Also separate application-specific functions from generic and basic functions.

Strategy: *Use the shell model uniformly and rigorously.*

Achieve the separation and isolation of concerns using clearly defined layers, called *shells*. Keep the definition of these shells uniform over all products in the Comm Vision product line to promote reusability across products and projects. Enforce the limitations of intershell usage and communication rigorously.

Strategy: *Introduce generic services.*

When possible, make services generic so that applications and features can be added and combined without changing lower layers or the rest of the software.

Related Strategies

Use services and service provision units (issue, Size and Complexity of the System).

Flexible and Scalable Performance

Differences in performance requirements are considerable, requiring a very flexible system. As processing platforms are added to the switch, the software must be able to take advantage of additional processing power. Flexibility is needed to interconnect additional processors, to allocate processor power to switching demands, and to balance the load among them. Flexibility is also needed to allocate tasks flexibly and to dedicate tasks to individual processors. However, this flexibility must be achieved with minimal development effort.

Influencing Factors

P3.1: Scalability is necessitated by high performance requirements.

P3.2: Requirements for flexible and scalable performance are important and stringent.

T1, T2: The hardware architecture is scalable through the addition of various processors.

Solution

Use the principles of distributed processing environments when applications are designed as a collection of interacting components that are independent of the processing platform to which they are assigned.

Strategy: *Use capsules to package and allocate SPUs to processors.*

Introduce a new architectural element, called a *capsule*, to package logically separate functionality of SPUs into an executable. Capsules are then allocated or dedicated to different processors to achieve the desired performance. This allows vertical distribution when different SPUs are allocated to different processing platforms, and horizontal distribution when SPUs are replicated to deal with subsets of physical resources. Capsules also improve performance of communication among its SPUs through optimization of remote procedure calls.

Strategy: *Use services of SPUs independent from their location.*

Introduce a service-addressing mechanism to use the services of SPUs in a manner that is transparent to their location. When allocation of capsules to processors changes for the purpose of load balancing, clients of its SPUs will not be affected. This will also facilitate on-line software upgrades because new service requests from clients will be transparently directed to newer versions of SPUs.

Continued

Flexible and Scalable Performance *(continued)*

Strategy: *Use performance-modeling techniques.*

Use performance-modeling techniques to predict performance based on capsule allocation long before code may be available for the SPUs. This requires making predictions about performance characteristics and resource needs of SPUs.

Related Strategies

Separate and isolate concerns (issue, Customized, Flexible, and Maintainable Functionality), *Use loosely coupled communication between SPUs* (issue, Size and Complexity of the System).

Fault Recovery

The software is required to detect all hardware and software failures and to recover from them with minimum overhead.

Influencing Factors

P3.1, P4.2: Fault recovery should not interfere with high performance.

P4.1: The recovery time and overhead must be minimized to avoid interfering with the high availability requirement.

Solution

Employ common recovery guidelines and components.

Strategy: *Use a stratified recovery mechanism.*

Make the system more reliable by containing the effects of software failures to small, recoverable units and take corrective measures such as restart with or without reinitialization. Start with a single process in an SPU, and then escalate the level of recovery from recovery suites within a SPU, to SPU, capsule, processing platform, and the entire system. Use well-defined measures such as error counts to raise the recovery level.

Strategy: *Make all software responsible for its own fault detection and recovery.*

All software must be developed using defensive programming techniques. It should detect and isolate effects of common faults such as plausibility and type compatibility of parameters, and access violations. It must report such occurrences to a centralized fault reporting system.

Development Based on Architecture Principles

The development environment must facilitate application of architecture principles and strategies. It is also essential to verify that architecture principles are not violated during development.

Influencing Factors

O3.1: The software production environment is the appropriate mechanism to introduce checks.

O3.2: The software development environment produces architecture documents to facilitate the application of architecture principles and checks for errors in the results of their application.

T3.1: The main programming languages are CHILL and C.

Solution

Extend the production environment.

Strategy: *Introduce architecture concepts into CHILL.*

The production tools are extended to support concepts such as services, SPUs, and capsules. For example, the concept of a group module is introduced to describe SPUs and to map them to CHILL constructs.

Strategy: *Introduce architecture guidelines.*

Introduce a set of well-defined and understandable guidelines that facilitate the application of architecture principles. The system design authority team is responsible for defining and enforcing architecture principles.

11.2 Conceptual Architecture View

The conceptual architecture of the Comm Vision system is informally documented in design documents and papers for the purpose of improved understanding. It is not described at a sufficiently detailed level to be able to generate code.

For example, as illustrated in Figure 11.2, a pipeline of SPUs is constructed when a subscriber places a call to subscriber B. For the sake of simplicity, connectors representing these protocols have not been shown. The signaling SPUs interface to the telephones at the subscriber sites. The call control SPUs manage the logical and physical connections between the two subscribers.

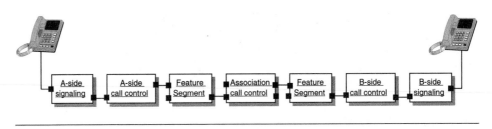

Figure 11.2. Call-processing pipeline

The core of the call-processing pipeline consists of two smaller pipeline segments called *feature segments*. These segments are composed of SPUs that support features visible to the two subscribers; for example, call waiting and call forwarding. These feature segments are constructed dynamically and may contain an arbitrary number of SPUs that can be linked together to form customized processing chains, with each chain representing a call.

Each feature SPU provides the same set of ports to permit them to be linked to the chain of a particular call as required. An event (in other words, a message) for a certain call (for example a hookflash) is passed through the chain for each linked SPU to address using that unit's internal state information. Essentially, each SPU takes a local view when it decides to act on a message; for example, requesting a tone to be connected or deciding to pass it on to the next SPU in the chain.

Such architectural diagrams were produced for a normal call and later for calls with additional features. Later, the functionality was decomposed to the point of individual services. The Specification and Description Language standardized by the International Telecommunication Union is used to describe the behavior of SPUs and interactions among them.

Although these diagrams are described in terms of design-level procedures and events, interfaces and interactions at the conceptual architecture level are described in terms of more abstract operations and events.

11.3 Module Architecture View

11.3.1 Decomposition

The module architecture view of Comm Vision software is decomposed (Figure 11.3) into functional areas, functional groups, and SPUs. Comm Vision is divided into platform and application software, each of which consists of a number of functional areas. A functional area is a unit used for project and line management. It is a set of one or more functionally related components that can be conveniently developed together. A functional area may be

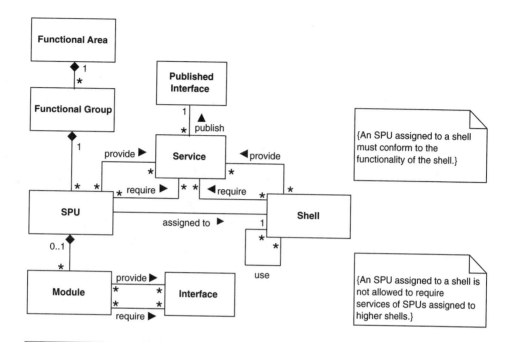

Figure 11.3. Meta-model for Comm Vision module architecture view. SPU = service provision unit.

further decomposed into functional groups. Functional groups provide an optional sub-structure for a large functional area. Figure 11.4 shows the decomposition of the functional area Logical Call Processing, which handles individual calls independent of the physical topology of the switch.

A functional group is decomposed into SPUs, which are the fundamental units of functional partitioning in Comm Vision software. For example, the functional group Usage Metering in Figure 11.4 is decomposed into two different SPUs to provide metering services for permanent and switched virtual connections respectively.

SPUs provide the designer with larger, more abstract functional building blocks. Each SPU provides a set of common and well-publicized services to the rest of the system. In doing so, it may make use of services provided by other SPUs. Thus it is visible externally only by way of its services.

Each SPU provides a certain functionality and an associated set of services to its environment. In most cases the services are organized around the need for common data or the

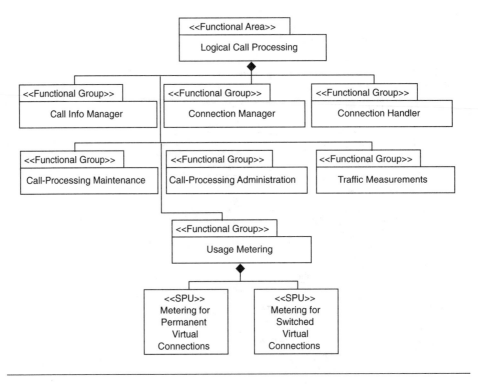

Figure 11.4. Decomposition of software related to call processing

administration of common resources. The realization of these services therefore requires a certain minimum SPU size.

SPUs are the smallest units that can be relocated. SPUs should be as small as possible to ensure that the units of relocation do not become too large.

11.3.2 SPU Interfaces and Inter-SPU Dependencies

A service is a related set of functionality made available by a server to its clients. Services are accessed by way of their interface, which specifies the functionality they offer. To make a service visible outside an SPU, its interface must be published, and it is known as a *published interface*. A published interface specifies the synchronous and asynchronous operations of the service, and the types of parameters and messages to these operations. It is possible for different services to offer the same set of operations but to implement quite different functionality.

SPUs use only RPCs and messages to communicate with other SPUs. Within an SPU, however, local procedure calls and shared memory interfaces may be used. As a consequence, intra-SPU communication will be faster than the communication between different SPUs.

For the purpose of tracking and architecture control, information about SPUs providing the published interface as well as SPUs using the interface is entered in a database, from which various reports are generated. For example, a report may describe all the SPUs with which a particular SPU communicates, or all SPUs that provide a particular service.

11.3.3 Layering Structure or Shell Model

The shell model structures Comm Vision software into large layers, called *shells*, to help manage its complexity. The shell model follows the following three principles:

1. Separation of basic functions from application-specific functions

2. Separation of logical and physical concerns (for example, hardware independence)

3. Separation of database and application-specific logic

These considerations led to the design of generic shells that are used throughout the Comm Vision product line. The shell model shown in Figure 11.5 contains seven generic shells. Shell 1 represents the hardware of the switch. Shell 2 contains the core software that provides the core functionality of the hardware. Shell 3 provides the operating system and supervisory software. Shell 4 provides basic functionality, including the DBMS and administrative functions. Shell 5 provides maintenance functions. Shell 6 provides protocol and resource-handling functions. Lastly, shell 7 provides switching functionality. Each instance of the Comm Vision system employs an adaptation of this generic shell model.

The decomposition structure and the shell model are related by assigning all SPUs to shells. The assignment to the shell constrains the SPU to conform with the functionality of the shell and to initiate communication with only those SPUs that are assigned to the same or to a lower level shell.

Such restrictions make shells independent of higher shells, and help management plan and monitor the software development process. Starting with shell 1, each shell is produced and tested together with lower shells in a stepwise fashion. Carefully designed implementation techniques are used to make the shells independent of higher shells, and to manage exceptions for invoking use of services from higher shells without sacrificing the advantage of stepwise production.

Documentation of the SPU-to-shell assignment is done in tables, thus allowing a check for completeness and violation of interfacing rules of the shell model. Tabular representation also allows the assignment information to be reproduced in appropriate reports.

```
<<Shell>>
┌──────────────────────────────────────┐
│              Shell  7                 │
│          Switching Software          │
└──────────────────────────────────────┘
<<Shell>>
┌──────────────────────────────────────┐
│              Shell  6                 │
│      Protocol and Resource Handling   │
└──────────────────────────────────────┘
<<Shell>>
┌──────────────────────────────────────┐
│              Shell  5                 │
│             Maintenance              │
└──────────────────────────────────────┘
<<Shell>>
┌──────────────────────────────────────┐
│              Shell  4                 │
│             I/O and DBMS             │
└──────────────────────────────────────┘
<<Shell>>
┌──────────────────────────────────────┐
│              Shell 3                  │
│           Kernel Software            │
└──────────────────────────────────────┘
<<Shell>>
┌──────────────────────────────────────┐
│              Shell 2                  │
│            Core Software             │
└──────────────────────────────────────┘
<<Shell>>
┌──────────────────────────────────────┐
│              Shell 1                  │
│             Hardware                 │
└──────────────────────────────────────┘
```

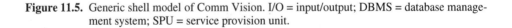

{An SPU assigned to a shell is only allowed to use services of SPUs assigned to lower shells.}

Figure 11.5. Generic shell model of Comm Vision. I/O = input/output; DBMS = database management system; SPU = service provision unit.

11.4 Execution Architecture View

The execution architecture view is distinguished from the module architecture view in recognition and anticipation of potential changes to the RTE. As evidenced in the global analysis described in Section 11.1, a Comm Vision system evolves with time both in terms of new functions and in terms of performance and capacity. Section 11.3 described how addition of new functions is facilitated through the use of the shell model. Growth in Comm

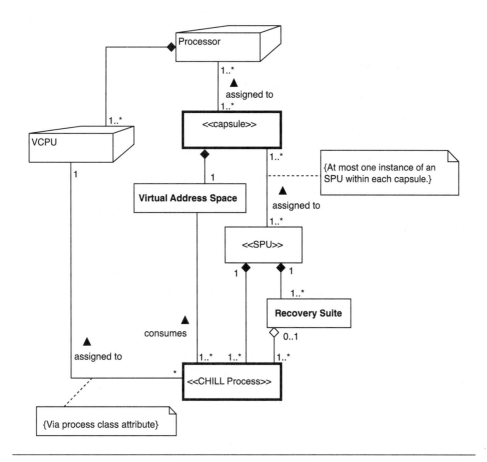

Figure 11.6. Model for system-level execution architecture view. VCPU = virtual central processing unit; SPU = service provision unit.

Vision performance is achieved through addition of faster, additional processors and switching network capacity.

The execution architecture of Comm Vision is designed at two different levels: the SPU level and the system level (Figure 11.6). SPU-level execution architecture is localized to particular SPUs and is the responsibility of the SPU design team. Information about resource requirements of all SPUs is propagated to determine the resource requirements of the system-level execution architecture.

11.4.1 Defining Executables and Configurations

In Comm Vision, an executable is defined in terms of *capsules*. Capsules are used to separate functionality flexibly from its runtime packaging without sacrificing performance. A capsule comprises a set of SPUs that are allocated a common, protected virtual address space (Figure 11.6). A capsule is defined completely by its list of SPUs. Capsules provide data protection by protecting against addressing errors in other capsules.

Assigning SPUs to capsules is independent from assigning SPUs to shells. Capsules normally reside within one shell; however, a small number of capsules may span shells for performance reasons.

The capsule is also a unit of optimization; it enables communication between its SPUs to be optimized. Additionally, at build time, RPCs that stay within the same capsule are automatically optimized to ordinary procedure calls. Thus, context switching between SPUs within a capsule is more efficient than context switching between SPUs in different capsules.

The capsule is also a unit of enhancement and build-time migration within Comm Vision. A capsule may be replaced at runtime when enhancements to its SPUs are available. A capsule may be replicated and allocated to different or the same processing platforms. In Comm Vision, system-level configurations are described by assigning capsules and their replications to processing platforms.

SPUs are autonomous units with their own sets of CHILL processes, shared data regions, and process configurations. An SPU, as a collection of processes, also has runtime characteristics, which are described and designed in terms of its execution structure. In this sense, every SPU can be regarded as a moderate-size system in its own right.

Configurations of SPUs are designed in terms of CHILL processes and regions. They are not described here.

11.4.2 Communication

Comm Vision software is structured as a collection of SPUs interacting as clients and servers, and can be distributed over several processors. Because SPUs can be replicated, more than one SPU can provide a particular service. For communication with a server, the client does not need to know its location or even its identity. The client should, as much as possible, request a service without specifying a server to get benefits like load balancing, fault tolerance, and upgrade. Therefore a service-addressing mechanism is needed to set up communication between client SPUs and server SPUs. This service-addressing mechanism is similar but more sophisticated than the name service mechanism provided by many distributed system platforms.

The communication between client and server SPUs is split into two phases. First, a client SPU requests the service-addressing mechanisms to select a server SPU for a particular service interface. This selection is based on selection criteria, which may include a local processor (least dynamic cost), specification of a well-defined service partition, load balancing, recovery states (fault tolerance), a specific server using an explicit processor number, a capsule number, or an SPU identifier. The service-addressing mechanism selects a suitable server and returns a communication path to the client. The client then uses the communication path to use the service provided by the selected server SPU.

Service addressing is also used during enhancement when a capsule is replaced by an upgraded version. The service manager is able to direct the messages to SPUs in the new capsule instead of those in the old one.

11.4.3 Recovery Suites and Recovery-Tolerant Communication

In general, CHILL processes have to be designed so that each process is capable of being recovered independently of any other. There are cases when this is not feasible. Single-process recovery may impose dynamic overheads and may increase design complexity. For example, if shared data used by several processes is corrupted, it might be necessary to recover together all processes that access the shared data. For this reason, the concept of a recovery suite is introduced.

A recovery suite is any set of CHILL processes within one SPU that may need to be recovered together from a fault without disturbing the operation of other software within the SPU or elsewhere. These processes must detect common conditions such as lost, out-of-sequence, or duplicated messages; loss of communication; partially executed messages; waiting messages; and so forth—and recover from them.

11.4.4 Resource Allocation

On each processing platform the operating system kernel has to support a wide variety of different, real-time requirements. Some tasks such as call-processing requests are urgent and must be performed as quickly as possible. They are given a high priority. Others are less urgent and are given a lower priority. However, they have to be completed some-time—possibly within a certain time. A few processes that ensure system integrity must always be able to run.

The operating system must ensure that even under high-load conditions less important tasks still get a fair chance of meeting their objectives. This is achieved via a refinement of priority-based scheduling through the means of virtual CPUs (VCPUs). Associated with each VCPU are processor-specific load models that specify the time budget for various execution modes (for example, start-up, normal operation, and overload operation) of the system. A set of processes assigned to a VCPU is guaranteed a certain percentage of the CPU time budget. Within the time allocated to each VCPU, priority-based scheduling is used.

Process priority and process class properties of an SPU process are statically assigned and are used to indicate real-time requirements. The dynamic priority of a process is determined based on these two properties, as described later. Resources such as stack size and maximum number of instances can also be controlled for each process. Systemwide limits for resources are defined and must be observed by SPU designers. For example, the maximum number of process instances is 20 by default.

Resource needs of an SPU are based on the resource needs of its processes. Resource needs of a capsule are determined from the cumulative resource needs of its SPUs. The resource needs of capsules are used to get an estimate of resources needed for each processor.

11.5 Code Architecture View

The code architecture view makes explicit design decisions about code components, their interconnections, and their organization. It facilitates the development, construction, integration, and testing of a system and its versions. For Comm Vision, we focus narrowly on how architectural components are mapped to code components, how development productivity is improved through the use of hierarchical compilation libraries, and we describe configuration management for geographically distributed development teams.

11.5.1 Source Components

The organization of source components follows the decomposition in the module decomposition down to the level of SPUs, where different development teams take over and make their own decisions about the organization. In this section we only discuss how elements of the module and execution architecture views are mapped to elements of the CHILL language.

The CHILL language has been extended to support the architectural elements discussed in the previous sections. These extensions are of two kinds: compiler directives and new modules. CHILL group modules have been introduced to support elements such as shells, capsules, and SPUs. An InterfaceSpecification module has been introduced to support published interfaces. Compiler directives have been added to address concepts such as recovery suites.

The interface between CHILL and C software is specified in terms of CHILL interface specification modules, which are then translated into C header files by a production tool. Interfaces within C software are specified using C header files.

Tables are used to describe VCPUs, mapping of process classes to VCPUs, and available processing platforms.

11.5.2 Intermediate Components

The CHILL compiler and accompanying production tools produce a large number of intermediate components. We mainly focus on the hierarchical library concept developed to facilitate separate, independent development of SPUs by their respective teams.

The CHILL compiler supports the separate compilation model in which specification and implementation of a module can be separately compiled in a library. CHILL hierarchical libraries are used to organize the intermediate components generated by the compiler. For example, each SPU team can compile their source components independently in their own CHILL library.

Stability of interfaces is an important issue contributing to productivity of development teams. This problem is aggravated by the number of SPU internal interfaces. To reduce the production time, the concept of a global hierarchical library (Figure 11.7) was

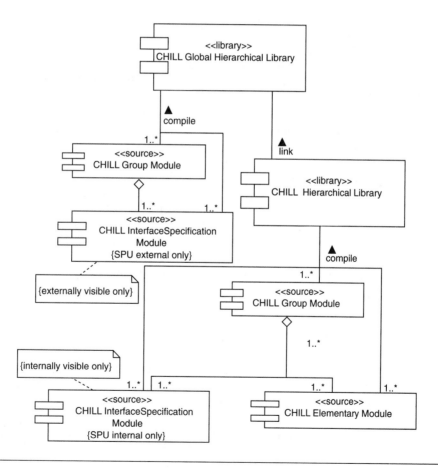

Figure 11.7. Global hierarchical library and separate compilation. SPU = service provision unit.

introduced to separate systemwide interfaces from SPU internal interfaces. With the help of the global hierarchical library, a production cycle is divided into three steps:

1. All the SPU group modules and their interface specification modules related to external published interfaces are compiled in a global hierarchical library. This library is made error free and stable first.

2. All the SPU development teams then use this global hierarchical library while stabilizing independently their SPU internal interfaces in parallel, and developing implementation components, both of which are compiled in their own hierarchical library.

3. Production of a complete hierarchical library, compilation of all modules, and generation of runtime components is carried out in the third and last step.

During the last two steps, the global hierarchical library is not changed, thus reducing the number of recompilations and improving the development productivity.

11.5.3 Configuration Management

The development of Comm Vision is geographically distributed over several continents. Configuration management plays a critical coordination role in the development process. In addition, there are special requirements introduced due to the need to support customer or project-specific enhancements and versions, and the need to reproduce any specific system version.

First, all architecturally visible components, code components, as well as documents are subject to configuration control. This includes the entire set of development tools. When a system version is produced, a version of the associated set of production tools is also produced to be able to reproduce that system version in the future.

A hierarchical configuration management process is used to support geographical distribution of development. Each development team uses their own local configuration management system. This eliminates the bottleneck of a centralized system and gives flexibility to the respective team. The controlled objects of all local configuration systems are integrated through a centralized configuration management system. Furthermore, the common development process ensures the compatibility of the local configuration management systems.

11.6 Software Architecture Uses

Comm Vision uses tables extensively to capture all architecture information. Given the large number of SPUs, published interfaces, and interconnections between them, tables were necessary to capture complete information about all interfaces. Tables are used in situations when complete lists regarding certain special questions with a suitable sorting are needed; for example, an overview of used published interfaces or alphabetical list with SPU names.

The tables are also the basis for analysis tasks (for example, for estimating the storage trend). For example, message catalogs are generated on the basis of the tables to support the system test after implementation.

Diagrams are not used to capture all architecture information because diagrams are often insufficiently detailed and cannot show all interfaces. Furthermore, creation and maintenance of tables is easier than creation and maintenance of diagrams.

Diagrams are preferred in situations in which the interdependence of components has to be clarified and when an overview of a system is required. In some cases, diagrams are derived from generated reports.

11.6.1 Simulation and Code Generation

The information at the level of conceptual architecture is described in SDL to describe the behavior of SPUs and their processes using process diagrams, which are a variation of finite-state machines. Collaboration diagrams and message sequence charts are used to describe the communication interaction among SPUs and their processes.

The precise syntax and finite-state semantics of SDL make it possible to simulate configurations of SPUs and to catch design errors early. Code generators transform the control flow of the process diagrams to the control structure of the target programming languages (CHILL, C, Assembler).

11.6.2 Higher Productivity of Software Production

Software production becomes much faster with SPUs. Instead of checking all the interfaces of the entire system, the global interfaces between SPUs can be checked first, and then as a second step the SPU internal interfaces can be checked in parallel for every SPU. The ratio of global to SPU internal interfaces is approximately 20 percent.

Code generation tools improve consistency between SDL models and code as well as support interworking of software written in C and CHILL.

11.6.3 Stepwise Production Testing of Shells

The shell model provides a structuring of the software into several large layers, called *shells*, which are made independent of higher shells through constraining the usage of higher shells and specialized implementation techniques. Development schedules are divided into steps. Starting with Shell 1, each step delivers a shell along with lower-level shells, which are then tested together.

11.6.4 Architecture Control Process

A system design authority is responsible for producing the architecture documents. All inter-SPU interfaces identified in these documents are under the control of this authority, which is involved in assessing the system-level impact of any proposed changes and determining the resource requirements for SPUs, capsules, and processors.

11.7   Summary

11.7.1   Software Architecture Concepts

Important architectural concepts introduced in Comm Vision include the following:

- **Services and SPUs**—Comm Vision products are composed of SPUs that are packaged to meet a customer's requirements. Services provide a standard interface for common functionality. SPUs provide well-defined services to their clients. Communication between SPUs is loosely coupled so that SPUs can be migrated or upgraded without affecting their clients.

- **Capsules**—Capsules package Comm Vision functionality at a granularity that is coarser than SPUs without sacrificing performance. Capsules also provide data protection and optimize communication between its SPUs. It is through capsules that SPUs are replicated and allocated to particular processing platforms to meet evolving performance requirements. It is at the level of capsules that Comm Vision software is upgraded to meet evolving functional requirements.

- **Shell model**—The shell model structures the Comm Vision software into larger layers to manage its complexity. A set of seven generic shells are defined for all Comm Vision products. SPUs are assigned to one of the shells, where they are expected to conform to the functionality of the shell, and are constrained to use the services of SPUs assigned to lower-level shells only. These conventions make it possible to develop and test shells in a stepwise manner starting with Shell 1.

- **VCPUs**—VCPUs support a variation of priority-based scheduling. Through carefully controlled CPU budgets for VCPUs and assignment of processes to VCPUs, Comm Vision ensures that processes with critical real-time requirements are always run while less urgent processes still run and complete their tasks.

- **Stratified fault recovery**—Through distribution of the responsibility for fault recovery, and use of fault-tolerant communication protocols, Comm Vision is able to limit the effects of software failure to a process, and then incrementally expand this limit to recover suites of processes, SPUs, capsules, individual CPUs, and the entire system.

With the use of these architectural concepts, Comm Vision has managed to address difficult requirements of high, scalable performance; flexible functionality; and high availability and fault recovery. They provide a smooth evolutionary path from the formerly proprietary system to an open, flexible system that enables integration of software in cooperation with partners, and exploits new hardware technologies.

11.7.2   Experience

The Comm Vision architecture has been used for two different applications or products: Broadband Switch as described in Figure 11.1, and the SSNC. Internet applications will comprise the next product. The architecture has proved itself by remaining stable at the top level of published interfaces. With relatively minor disturbances, the architecture at the level of functional areas and functional groups has remained more or less stable. Although there have been no major changes, new architectural concepts have been added and current concepts have been extended or refined. New SPUs and protocols were also added.

There has been a positive impact of the shell model, which is used extensively in production planning, and which facilitates functionality enhancements and hardware changes. It would not have been possible to handle such a large system without a separation of concerns. New protocols have been easy to add and most changes have been confined to the higher shells.

Many architectural concepts are described using a combination of formal and informal notations. This can lead to varying and sometimes inconsistent interpretations. When development is geographically distributed, one cannot easily ask the author for an explanation. Only tool support for architecture can reduce the differences and enforce consistent semantics.

Comm Vision—Lessons Learned

- The design environment and the architecture are evolving entities, and one must keep refining them.

- One must keep a very strong focus on performance and identify places to optimize performance without sacrificing architecture principles. As design and implementation mature, take advantage of optimization opportunities that arise locally. Use a rich toolset to model capacity and performance, and to predict performance long before availability of code or hardware.

- One must resist the temptation to take shortcuts. There is a tension between the cleanest possible decomposition, flexibility, and objectives related to performance and memory size.

- Documentation and tracking of the architecture is important. Make documentation of components and SPUs a part of the development process. Start tracking components and interfaces early to stay on course—this is hard work!

PART IV

Software Architecture in Your Future

In this book we've described our approach to designing software architecture. This approach is based on defining four separate, loosely coupled architecture views, using global analysis to drive the design decisions for each view, and global evaluation to assess them. The design approach gives you guidance in

- Tracing influencing factors and requirements through the architecture
- Sequencing the design activities
- Making design trade-offs
- Supporting system-specific qualities like performance or reliability
- Supporting general qualities like buildability, portability, testability, and reusability
- Ensuring that no aspects of the architecture are overlooked
- Producing useful documentation of the architecture

For global analysis, we provided a format for capturing the key information and a sequence of activities for gathering that information. This is a considerable advance over most current practices, and we expect this to be the focus of much additional research. The activities will be further refined in the future, and we will see them integrated into the software process along with global evaluation and architecture design reviews.

The software process is also being influenced by what is often called *architecture-centered development*, in which the software architecture design is used to organize development activities. This architecture-centric approach helps in making the implementation conform to the architecture design.

Having a common notation for describing the architecture makes the architect's job easier. The use of UML for describing the architecture will continue to increase, and we expect that UML will have more explicit support for architecture in the future. It is already being influenced by today's architectures description languages, and these will continue to be used and useful to cover domains, to meet analysis needs, and to express concepts that a single language can't.

In the future we expect more and more systems to have an explicit conceptual view, with more levels of decomposition. This becomes more feasible because architects will be able to reuse existing component and connector types—for example, by using an architectural style.

Having an explicit conceptual view also opens up the possibility for more systems to use code generators or application builders in the way that Safety Vision does. For standard architectural styles, these could be off-the-shelf tools. A custom solution like Safety Vision's must make economic sense, which depends on the domain characteristics, market conditions, and company strategy.

In organizations there is an increasing recognition of software architectures as valuable company assets. Along with this comes the recognition that product-line architectures can be a worthwhile investment.

The future will also bring more architecture-level reuse through the conscious use of architecture technologies such as architectural styles and product-line architectures, and the availability of more reference architectures as domains mature.

The importance of software architecture will only increase in the future. More sophisticated tools, techniques, and technologies will improve the architect's productivity, but designing software architecture will always be a challenge. The availability of more off-the-shelf components for composing a system may improve overall productivity, but the architect must select the appropriate components and figure out how to make them work together. Balancing design trade-offs will be even more difficult in this case.

We close this book with a chapter that describes the role of the software architect. The software architect is the key technical consultant to the project manager and a coach for the development team. An architect is a decision maker, a coordinator, and sometimes an "implementor." But most importantly, an architect is a visionary and an advocate for software architecture.

Chapter 12

The Role of the Software Architect

We've spent the rest of the book describing the technical aspects of designing software architecture. In this final chapter, we put this into the context of the organizational structure. These technical aspects are essential to being a good architect, but they alone aren't enough to succeed as a software architect.

An architect interacts with many other people in the organization: managers, system architects, software developers, and sometimes other software architects, marketing personnel, or customers. To be a successful architect you must understand what these people expect from you, and vice versa. You must coordinate with them, listen to them, and communicate your vision of the architecture to them.

The software architect has a responsibility beyond the product currently being designed. A good architect will look to the future and be an advocate for the organization's investment in software architecture.

12.1 Creating a Vision

To be a successful architect, you must be a visionary. This means you must know in advance what the system will look like when it is done, what it will accomplish, and how it fits in with the rest of the company's technology and business objectives.

In this role, an architect who knows something about the application domain and targeted product market is more valuable. One who doesn't have this background should put some effort into learning the business, market characteristics, and capabilities of the company's and competitors' products. An architect without this knowledge must find other sources for it, because it is essential to designing a good software architecture.

As an architect, you must understand the global requirements and constraints of the product. You'll use them to come up with a global view of the system. Initially you may just have a feeling for what the components will be, but to make your vision concrete invariably requires a leap of faith. You'll sketch some preliminary ideas, consider the implications of the design, get feedback, and refine the ideas or try again. This is an iterative process.

Often a project that uses new, advanced technologies is targeted to new markets, or has a fast time-to-market. If the architect and project manager don't truly believe the vision can be achieved, they'd be better off looking for another project rather than risking involvement in a project that can't succeed.

To feed their creativity, architects need to stay in touch with innovations in the field. You must stay up-to-date with the company's technology as well as what's new in the marketplace. Users of the product are another important source of inspiration. To get the user's perspective, you should talk to specialists in applications, technical marketing, and customers. However, there's no substitute for visiting the user site to get first-hand knowledge of how the system is actually used in practice, what problems users are encountering, and how they would like to see the product improved.

Once the initial architecture design is sketched, often on a single sheet of paper, the architect needs to communicate the vision effectively as coach, coordinator, decision maker, and implementor. You will work with the project manager to coach the team during high-level design and throughout product development.

As an architect, you need to coordinate and to control the key interfaces of the architecture design because you know the key components and how they fit together to form a system. The system architect selects and configures the hardware of the system, but you provide requirements and inputs about how the software fits into the overall product, and later verify that the agreed system interfaces can be met.

With a sketch of the architecture you can start to think about how commercial components or existing software can be used to implement pieces of the system. Realizing your vision may require introducing new technology or making changes to the organization. Often you will be the trailblazer in learning new technologies and introducing them to the rest of the team. Whenever you discover defects or holes in your vision, you'll have to make mid-course corrections (even as the product is being developed) and communicate any changes to the development team.

12.2 The Architect as a Key Technical Consultant

The software architect is the key technical consultant to the project manager, and is involved with making many of the major technical decisions for the project. The architect has a close working relationship with the project manager. They aren't peers in the organizational hierarchy because the project manager still has ultimate responsibility for the project. However, the project manager must have an architect with trusted abilities, and must give the architect the technical authority needed to succeed.

Some projects have the same person as project manager and software architect. By combining these roles there is a risk of the architect's duties being neglected because the project manager's must be met, or vice versa. But for smaller projects, the roles may be combined successfully, or the duties of the architect may be shared between project manager and technical lead.

For larger projects, when control of interfaces is essential, one individual acting as architect may not be enough. Here there may be a group of architects forming a system design review board, with formal authority for maintaining the integrity of the architecture.

Table 12.1 shows some of the complementary activities of the project manager and the software architect. The project manager is responsible for the organization of the project and manages the resources, budgets, and schedules. The architect's part is coaching the team in the design and implementation tasks associated with the architecture. The architect is the one who knows the technical details of how things fit together and how they are dependent on each other, and should use this information to advise the project manager of work assignments and needed resources.

For many projects, the development team organization mirrors the structure of the software to be developed. Thus the architect's inputs to the project manager concerning

Topic	Project Manager	Software Architect
Software development	Organize project; manage resources, budgets, schedules	Organize team around design; manage dependencies
Requirements	Negotiate with marketing	Review and negotiate requirements
Personnel issues	Handle hiring, performance appraisals, salary; motivate employees	Interview candidates; provide input on technical capabilities of staff; motivate development team
Technology	Introduce new technology per architect's recommendations	Recommend technology, training, tools
Quality	Ensure quality of product	Track quality of design
Metrics	Measure productivity, size, quality	Ensure design goals are met

Table 12.1. Activities of Project Managers and Software Architects

selection of team leaders, size of the subsystem development teams, skills required, and so forth, are extremely valuable. In many cases, the members of the high-level design team go on to lead the subsystem and major component developments. The architect's input on their design skills and potential people management skills will likely be requested by the project manager and other managers.

The project manager negotiates with marketing and is responsible for taking the product's requirements and translating them into requirements specifications. The architect doesn't define the requirements, but does need to critique them and to determine whether they are technically feasible. As the architecture design proceeds, the architect may need to negotiate changes in the requirements, either because they are impossible to fulfill or can be fulfilled only at the expense of more important issues.

The project manager handles personnel issues such as hiring, firing, performance appraisals, salary, and bonuses. The architect is needed to interview candidates and give input on the technical capabilities of the staff. Both are responsible for keeping the staff motivated and working as a team throughout the development.

When the relationship is working right, the project manager supports the architect's recommendations on technology, and assists by scheduling training for the staff, purchasing computer-aided software engineering tools, or hiring a consultant to make it happen.

Although the project manager ensures the quality of the product, the architect tracks the quality of the design. The architect needs to keep track of whether the detailed designs and dependencies in the code conform to the architecture design, but need not go down to the level of ensuring that the code conforms to the detailed designs. That is better handled by peer reviews.

The project manager is responsible for measuring the productivity of the project team. The architect is concerned with ensuring that the architecture meets its design goals. One way to do this is to define and enforce guidelines (for example, coding standards, component templates) for the team.

12.3   The Architect Makes Decisions

The high-level design team typically consists of the software architect plus team leaders of the subsystems or experts in technology or domain specialty areas. As the software architect you are the leader of the design team and the one who, ultimately, has to make the early design decisions. There are conflicting demands that need to be balanced and you help the team make these trade-offs.

As the architect, you need some knowledge of the domain in which you are working but you don't necessarily have to be an expert. Because the architect bridges the gap between the domain and software engineering, you must have enough domain knowledge to analyze design trade-offs, but you won't need as much as it requires to implement the design. If you don't have enough domain experience yourself, you can often rely on specialists in the application domain.

You won't always have all the information you need or the complete consensus of your team, but you must make decisions in a timely manner to meet your deadlines. It is up to you to know when it is time to end discussions and simply make a decision.

You must make the key global decisions early and identify the risks involved. There is an art to making the other decisions "just in time." This means delaying decisions as long as possible but no longer. The advantage to delaying decisions is that the design remains flexible and can more easily accommodate changes to requirements or other factors. But remember, making a decision that you later change is often better than making no decision at all and holding up the development.

Take a look at the scheduling dependencies to figure out the appropriate time to make various decisions. By working forward from your resources and backward from your goals, you can order your decisions to satisfy a number of constraints. You must factor in marketing priorities for releasing product features, the project schedule, and the impact of new technology. Choices in technology affect other choices. For example, the choice of the software platform could affect the choice of commercial tools or the training needed for the team. These all get factored into the component release plan, which determines the strategy for developing the system.

You, as the architect, are responsible for global decisions. You don't have the time or the resources to be a micromanager. You should delegate some decisions to experts in specialty areas, and you should leave the appropriate design and implementation decisions in the hands of your team, coaching when necessary.

12.4 The Architect Coaches

The software architect acts as a coach for the software development team. Once marketing has established the concept for a new product and established the product requirements, the architect works with the project manager to put a design team in place. Software development typically starts with a small number of people to define the high-level architecture design. Resist the temptation to involve too many people at the beginning. At this phase of the project, smaller is definitely better.

Additional staff are added as low-level design and implementation tasks are introduced. The architecture design is a good starting point to assign components to particular team leaders or individuals, depending on the size of your project. The architect works with the project manager to assign team members a piece of the work. We recommend that you identify components of the architecture to prototype early in the development, both to minimize project risks and to help train new team members on the architecture and technologies used.

However, it is not enough just to complete the software architecture design. As the architect, your job begins with the design of the architecture; it doesn't end there. You need to make sure everyone understands the design and to convince people it can indeed be implemented. To do this you should establish a dialog with each of the team members, teaching them the important aspects of the design and listening to their feedback. It is very important to get their buy-in, and you must balance the give-and-take needed in your role as coach with your more dictatorial role as decision maker.

Team members need to understand the software architecture design well enough to do a detailed design of their subsystem. One way to get them started is to have them design the decomposition of their subsystem and its interfaces to the rest of the system. Having them estimate the time and complexity of the implementation will provide important feedback to the project manager for the schedule. This exercise can also increase the team members' feelings of ownership in the architecture design and development schedules.

Part of being a good coach is knowing when to let go. As architect, you need to provide the overall structure of the design but at the same time give team members the responsibility and challenge of designing their own piece of the system. So, your duties end when you get down to the appropriate level of design. What is appropriate is highly subjective, depending on the novelty of the design, the risks involved, and the skills of the team. Sometimes you may allow team members to make small mistakes in their detailed designs, provided that they learn from these mistakes and the overall project goals are not jeopardized.

As the system evolves, you need to stay involved to maintain the architectural integrity of the system. Your duties change as the product moves into the maintenance phase, which should require less involvement on your part. Sometimes, though, a major effort is needed to restructure an architecture that has drifted from its original design and is no longer maintainable. Or, an existing system may be updated to a new product version, and the architecture needs to be restructured to accommodate new product goals. Most software products today are incrementally enhanced with new version releases. In many cases, the original vision of the architecture cannot accommodate the long-term evolution of the product because of unexpected changes in technology or product requirements.

12.5 The Architect Coordinates

The software architect coordinates the activities of the team members around the design elements of the architecture. Software architecture is a unifying theme for the engineering and management compromises that must be made to complete a product development: It provides the central element around which many aspects of a project revolve. A project manager may view the architecture as a vehicle for decomposing a complex effort into more manageable tasks. Technical marketing may use the architecture to support new features over the life span of a product. Software engineers may be concerned with performance, reusability, and evolution. The choice, development, and refinement of the software architecture is thus critical to the success of software development.

As the keeper of the architecture, you coordinate with the activities of these people that influence and are influenced by the architecture. As the design unfolds, you establish and control the key interfaces.

The architect should also keep track of the software process, and make sure important milestones like the architecture design review are met. Design reviews serve the dual purpose of ensuring the consistency and quality of the architecture, and ensuring that the participants understand the design.

The architect needs to work with the project manager to establish team leader responsibilities for different aspects of the design. You should also facilitate how team leaders relate to each other. They need to coordinate to ensure the subsystems under their responsibility fit into the architecture.

It is your responsibility to maintain the integrity of the design and to ensure that the architecture is followed. If there are special cases when it cannot be followed, the rationale must be documented.

12.6 The Architect Implements

In addition to analysis and high-level design, the software architect has a role to play in implementing the system. Software engineers progressing along a career path to software architecture need to keep their programming skills current, and track technology trends and standards (for example, IEEE, ANSI, OMG, OSF).

There isn't always a sharp cutoff between software architecture and detailed design. Sometimes an architect finds it necessary to go into more detail for parts of the system that are high risk because the design implications are unknown. Looking at the low-level details can help validate the initial design concepts. An architect may implement a vertical slice of the system to minimize implementation risk. Prototyping can help in understanding a design trade-off, predicting the performance of the system as designed, or educating the team on how to begin implementation.

Keep in mind that what the architect implements may also be used to instruct team members. If you are using an object-oriented approach, for instance, the architect may be designing the initial base classes and coding the initial implementations for others to learn from this example.

12.7 The Architect Advocates

Perhaps the most important role of the software architect is as an advocate for software architecture. Software architecture is a critical asset of your organization, and an architect should help the company recognize the value of this asset.

You should keep track of the existing software architectures in your company so they can be mined for new architectures or perhaps combined into a product-line architecture. You should also look for opportunities in which the investment in a product-line architecture makes economic sense. Product managers are naturally more focused on an individual project, but an architect should look beyond the boundaries of the product for reuse opportunities.

The architect must assess and advocate software architecture technologies, including new ones as they appear. You should keep track of research results and the experiences of other organizations to help you assess these technologies. These outside results and experiences give you evidence to help convince management to support new efforts in your organization.

The software architect should also work to incorporate software architecture into the development process, making the software architecture design activities and resulting artifacts part of the standard operating procedure of the organization. This could mean producing a high-level architecture design document and holding an architecture design review for organizations that follow a more formal, methodological approach. Or it could mean producing a series of prototypes that serve as a baseline for the structure and interfaces of the design. In all cases, the architect must advocate architecture design reviews and set the standards for architecture documentation.

If your organization has a software engineering process improvement group or champion, you should make sure your role is correctly defined. Projects that run into trouble usually have neither a well-defined architecture nor a well-defined development process for implementing it.

Even though a project often has an official software architect, this may not be a formal position of authority. You must work with the project manager in this case to ensure that your role is understood and valued. Otherwise, when the project starts coming under pressure, your role can be reduced to responding to one crisis after another, with no time to do the job of architect. Without a watchful architect, the architecture is often undermined with short-term expediencies that are harmful in the long run. The architecture begins to drift from its intended design and becomes more difficult to manage. The vision of the system being implemented begins to disappear.

12.8 Software Architecture as a Career

If you are just starting out in the software field and your goal is to become a software architect, you first need to set your sights on becoming an expert in software engineering. Above all else, experience is what matters in becoming a successful software architect. As you progress along this career path you need to develop your technical, leadership, communication, and people skills.

You may start off as an individual contributor, making your way from software engineer to senior software engineer and then taking on the responsibilities of a team leader. You must accept increasing responsibility and more challenging tasks. Ideally, you will have the opportunity to serve in an apprenticeship with an experienced architect.

The challenges for the software architect are great. Table 12.2 summarizes the many aspects of this job. An architect needs to have a vision of the product to be developed, the courage to strive to achieve that vision, and the conviction and communication skills to influence the entire development team to believe that the vision can be achieved.

The architect creates a vision.	Keeps up with innovations and technologies of the company and the marketplace; understands the global requirements and constraints of the product; creates a vision (global view) of the system; communicates the vision effectively; provides requirements and inputs to the system architect
The architect is the key technical consultant.	Organizes the development team around the design; manages dependencies; reviews and negotiates requirements; interviews candidates and provides input regarding the technical capabilities of staff; motivates the team; recommends technology, training, and tools; tracks the quality of the design; ensures that the architecture meets its design goals
The architect makes decisions.	Leads the design team; makes early design decisions (the key global ones); knows when to end discussions and make a decision; identifies risks
The architect coaches.	Establishes a dialog with each team member; teaches them the design; ensures that they understand the design; gets their buy-in; listens to their feedback; knows when to yield to design changes; knows when to let others take over the detailed design
The architect coordinates.	Coordinates the activities of those whose tasks influence the architecture; coordinates the activities of those whose tasks are influenced by the architecture; maintains the integrity of the design; ensures that the architecture is followed
The architect implements.	Considers the design implications of introducing a new technology; may look at low-level details to validate initial concepts; may prototype to explore and to evaluate design decisions; may implement a vertical slice to minimize implementation risk; may implement components as an implementation model for developers

Table 12.2. The Role of the Software Architect

The architect advocates.	Advocates investment in software architecture; works to incorporate software architecture into the software process; continues to assess and advocate new software architecture technologies

Table 12.2. The Role of the Software Architect *(continued)*

Glossary

acquisition performance—Measured by the size and number of images, and acquisition response time measured in terms of end-to-end deadlines.

acquisition procedure—The sequence of steps from positioning the probe to processing images that are part of an image acquisition. The system has a set of built-in acquisition procedures that can be customized by setting parameters before or during the acquisition.

AMX (for Comm Vision)—ATM multiplexing.

ANSI—American National Standards Institute. Creates standards for the computer industry.

API—Application programming interface.

application—Software designed to fulfill the customer's product requirements.

architectural style, architectural pattern—Define element types and how they interact.

architecture description language—Provides a way of specifying the elements used in the architecture, generally both as types and instances. It also provides support for interconnecting element instances to form a configuration.

ASN (for Comm Vision)—ATM switching network.

asynchronous—Not occurring at regular or predetermined intervals.

ATM—Asynchronous transfer mode.

binding—The binding relation is used when a conceptual component or connector is decomposed, either to bind an inner port to a port of the enclosing component or to bind an inner role with a role of the enclosing connector.

build procedure—The procedure for building the intermediate and deployment components; a final design task in the code architecture view.

CALLP (for Comm Vision)—Call processing.

capsule (for Comm Vision)—The fundamental unit of resource protection. It defines a protected virtual address space comprising a collection of SPUs. The capsule is also a unit of optimization. RPCs that stay entirely within the same capsule are optimized to ordinary procedure calls.

CASE—Computer-aided software engineering.

CCITT—The International Telegraph and Telephone Consultative Committee.

central design task—The process of defining the elements of an architecture view and the relationships among them and (if appropriate for that view) defining how these elements are configured. Strategies developed during global analysis are used to guide design decisions and to improve the ability of the system to respond to change.

CHILL—CCITT High-Level Language.

client/server—A pattern of interaction in which each component is either a client or a server. Clients rely on servers to provide services. On the server side, the requests are accepted, and on the client side the requests are sent and the corresponding replies are received.

code architecture view—The code architecture view is a view of the software architecture. For this view, the architect determines how runtime entities from the execution view are mapped to deployment components (for example, executables), how modules from the module view are mapped to source components, and how the deployment components are produced from the source components.

COM (for Comm Vision)—Communication manager.

communication path—One of the basic elements in the execution view. The communication paths identify the expected and/or allowable communication between runtime entities, including the mechanisms and resources used for the communication. Defining communication paths is a central design task in the execution view.

component—The conceptual components or code architecture elements (for example, source component, deployment component). Note that UML defines a component as a modular, reusable unit of implementation. This corresponds to components in the code architecture view (for example, source, binary, executable).

conceptual component—Conceptual components are independently executing peers within a component-connector model. A critical goal of this model is to keep the control aspects of the components simple, concentrating functional behavior in the components and control aspects in the connectors. A component interacts with its surroundings through ports. Defining conceptual components is a central design task in the conceptual view.

conceptual configuration—The relations among components and connectors. A conceptual configuration that contains component and connector types constrains how instances of these types can be interconnected. A conceptual configuration that contains instances defines which instances exist in the product and how they interconnect. Defining conceptual configuration is a central design task in the conceptual view.

conceptual connector—Connectors mediate the interactions among the conceptual components. A connector's roles define the behavior of the participants in the interaction. Defining conceptual connectors is a central design task in the conceptual view.

conceptual view—The conceptual view is a view of the software architecture. In this view, the functionality of the system is mapped to architecture elements called *conceptual components*, with coordination and data exchange handled by elements called *connectors*.

configuration management—Design decisions related to management of versions and releases of code components; a final design task in the code architecture view.

connection—Components and connectors are interconnected through their ports and roles. Connections are possible only when the associated protocols are compatible, and only when the elements are nested within the same component or connector.

connector—*See* conceptual connector.

CORBA—Common Object Request Broker Architecture.

COTS—Commercial off-the-shelf.

data driven—A strategy to separate data and control concerns to enable easy configuration (for example, putting information in a resource file).

DBMS—Database management system.

DCOM—Distributed Component Object Model.

decomposition—The decomposition of a system captures the way the system is logically decomposed into subsystems and modules.

deployment component—Deployment components are required for the system to start up, to operate, to be used, and to be shut down. The deployment code components include executables, shared or dynamic libraries, the system configuration files, and resources such as storage for data and shared memory. Defining deployment components is a central design task in the code view.

design pattern—A recurring design problem with its generic solution. Design patterns are a technology that may be relevant to architecture or may be relevant only to detailed design. When a design pattern describes the interactions of architecture elements, it is considered to be part of the software architecture. When it describes the structure and interactions within architecture elements, it is part of the detailed design.

DLL—Dynamic link library.

DMA—Direct memory access.

Document View—The Document View pattern separates the application (the document) from the way it is presented on the screen and the way the user interface reacts to user input (the view).

domain—An area of knowledge characterized by a set of concepts understood by practitioners of that area; often used as *application domain* to denote the area an application addresses.

domain-specific software architecture—Defines element types, allowed interactions, and how the domain functionality is mapped to the architecture elements. Similar to reference architecture.

DPRAM—Dual ported random access memory.

DSP—Digital signal processor.

EEPROM—Electrically erasable programmable read-only memory.

EKG—Electrocardiogram. The curve traced from the electric potentials associated with the electric currents that traverse the heart; used to diagnose heart disease.

EM (for Comm Vision)—Elementary module.

embedded system—A specialized computer system that is part of a larger system or machine. Typically an embedded system is housed on a single microprocessor board with the program stored in ROM.

engineering system (for Safety Vision)—The Safety Vision engineering system defines its product-line architecture and provides an engineering toolset that is used to create individual I&C systems, or projects, for each plant.

enhancement (for Comm Vision)—Replacing a unit of software on one or more processing platforms with a new version of the software that may differ from the old one by some corrected errors or by extended functionality. For Comm Vision, the units of enhancement are *capsules*.

event—An action or occurrence detected by a program. Events can be user actions or system occurrences.

event driven—Programs that are designed to respond to events.

execution configuration—Describes the system's runtime topology by characterizing the instances of the runtime entities and how they are interconnected. Defining the execution configuration is a central design task of the execution view.

execution view—The execution view is a view of the software architecture. It describes how modules are mapped to the elements provided by the runtime platform, and how these are mapped to the hardware architecture. The execution view defines the system's runtime entities and their attributes, such as memory usage and hardware assignment.

FB (for Safety Vision)—Function block.

FD (for Safety Vision)—Functional diagram.

FDG (for Safety Vision)—Functional diagram group.

Feature (for Comm Vision)—A unit visible to the customer; for example, multiparty conference service.

FEPROM—Flash erasable programmable read-only memory.

FIFO—First in, first out.

final design task—Architecture-level decisions are made in the central design tasks; the design decisions in the final design tasks are more localized.

framework—Frameworks specify structure and the flow of control and/or data. The specification is in the form of a partial implementation—an implementation of the infrastructure.

Functional area (for Comm Vision)—A unit enabling project and line management. It is a set of one or more functionally related SPUs that can be developed together conveniently; for example, logical call processing.

GDO (for Healthy Vision)—Global data object.

global analysis—The analysis of organizational, technological, and product factors that globally influence the architecture design of a system. The result of the analysis is a set of global strategies that can be used to guide the architecture design and improve its changeability with respect to the factors identified. The first task for each of the four views.

global evaluation—The process of continual evaluation of design decisions to see that the results of the global analysis are being followed. During the central design tasks, interactions among decisions must be evaluated periodically.

GUI—Graphical user interface.

hardware architecture—The organization of hardware components for a system (components and their topology or interconnections).

hardware platform—The kinds of hardware components used in the system.

HOT (for Safety Vision)—Hardware organization tool.

I&C (for Safety Vision)—Instrumentation and control.

image acquisition—Acquisition of raw signal data and their conversion into two- and three-dimensional images.

interface—The services of a module are defined by the interfaces it provides. A module may also need the services of another module to perform its function. These services are defined by the interfaces it requires. This is an approximate but not exact fit with UML semantics.

interface design—The description of the interfaces for each of the modules and layers. This involves the detailed design of interfaces required or provided by modules or layers based on their use-dependencies. This is a final design task in the module architecture view.

intermediate component—Intermediate components are specific to the implementation language and the development tools. For C++, each .CPP file gives rise to an .obj file. The .obj components are related to their respective source components through the "is compiled from" dependency relation. Defining intermediate components is a central design task in the code view.

IPC—Interprocess communication.

ISM (for Comm Vision)—InterfaceSpecification module.

issue (architecture design issue)—Issues arise from the need to accommodate the driving factors that influence the architecture design.

issue card—Format for describing an architecture design issue. Information that is captured includes the issue, influencing factors, solution, and strategies.

layers—Layers organize the modules into a partially ordered hierarchy. A module is assigned to a layer, which then constrains its dependencies on other modules. Defining layers is a central design task in the module view.

LCD—Liquid crystal display.

LIC (for Comm Vision)—Line interface card.

LOC—Lines of code.

meta-model—Describes how the elements of a view are related to each other. This is in contrast to a normal UML model, which we reserve for describing the architecture elements of a particular system. There's nothing in the notation that distinguishes a model from a meta-model, but the term *meta-model* tells you that you've stepped up a level of abstraction.

module—A module encapsulates data and operations to provide a service. These services are defined by the interfaces it provides. A module may also need the services of another module to perform its function; these services are defined by the interfaces it requires. Defining modules is a central design task in the module view.

module view—The module view is a view of the software architecture. In this view, the components and connectors from the conceptual view are mapped to subsystems and modules. Here the architect addresses how the conceptual solution can be realized with today's software platforms and technologies.

MP (for Comm Vision)—Main processor.

OA&M (for Comm Vision)—Operative administration and maintenance.

OMG—Object management group.

open systems—A system that uses off-the-shelf hardware and software and industry standards when possible.

organizational factors—Organizational factors arise from the business organization. Organizational factors constrain the design choices while the product is being designed and built. They are external to the product and exert a one-time, indirect influence on it.

They include aspects of the project such as the schedule and budget, and the skills and interests of the people involved.

physiological parameters (for Central Vision and Healthy Vision)—Heart rate, temperature, and so forth.

platform element—The elements available in a hardware or software platform. In the execution view, a runtime entity is mapped to an element of the software platform (for example, operating system tasks, processes, threads, address spaces).

port—The interaction points for the conceptual component. Ports define both incoming and outgoing messages (operations), so the components can truly be peers. Each port has an associated protocol that mandates how the incoming and outgoing operations are ordered.

POSIX—Portable operating system interface for UNIX; a set of IEEE and ISO standards that define an interface between programs and operating systems.

probe hardware—The hardware used to detect and process signals.

probe network—The network that connects components of the probe hardware and general-purpose hardware.

processing platform (for Comm Vision)—A physical processor in the distributed Comm Vision system.

product factors—Used to describe the product's requirements for functionality, the features seen by the user, and nonfunctional properties such as performance. As the market changes, the product factors may also change, sometimes drastically. The product factors may also change during development when schedule versus features trade-offs are made.

product line—A family of similar products marketed by a company.

product-line architecture—Defines element types, how they interact, and how the product functionality is mapped to them. It may also go further, by defining some of the instances of the architecture elements. This term generally applies to a set of products within an organization or company.

project specification (for Safety Vision)—A project specification is decomposed into a software and a hardware specification phase. The software specification is a domain-specific formal specification that defines the signal processing used to implement the functional units defined in the system requirements specification. The hardware specification defines the hardware structure of the target system, with all of its hardware components. To specify the software/hardware assignment, each functional diagram created in the software specification is assigned to one processor board.

protocol—A protocol describes how conceptual components and connectors coordinate and synchronize their interactions and communicate with each other. A protocol is defined as a set of incoming message types, outgoing message types, and the valid message exchange sequences.

PSS (for Comm Vision)—Physical Switching subsystem.

Published interface (for Comm Vision)—SPU designers have to know what services are available within the system, and must publish the services that their SPUs provide. This is achieved using a published interface. For each service provided by an SPU, there is a published interface that acts as a specification of the service.

RAM—Random access memory.

Rate monotonic analysis—A collection of quantitative methods and algorithms that allows engineers to specify, understand, analyze, and predict the timing behavior of real-time software systems.

RCS—Revision control system.

real-time—A real-time system is required to perform its function within the specified time constraints.

recovery suite (for Comm Vision)—A unit of recovery. A recovery suite is a collection of process types within a single CPU that may need to be recovered together. They can be recovered as an individual entity without disturbing the operation of other software.

redundancy (for Safety Vision)—An I&C system, or project, is a distributed, redundant computer system. Typically it consists of four independent, redundant data-processing paths, called *redundancies*. Each redundancy is physically isolated in a separate room. It contains four computers, each serving a different processing role and communicating via networks.

reference architecture—Defines elements types, allowed interactions, and how the domain functionality is mapped to the architecture elements. Similar to domain-specific software architecture.

resource allocation—The runtime instances and budgets defined in the execution configuration are allocated to particular hardware devices and are assigned specific values to the budgeted attributes (for example, by setting process priorities). This is a final design task of the execution architecture view.

resource budgeting—Assigning resource budgets to the conceptual components and connectors in the conceptual configuration. These budgets are refined later during resource allocation in the execution view. The initial budgets help identify potential resource problems. Resources include devices, memory, and compute time from the operating system. This is a final design task of the conceptual architecture view.

RMA—Rate monotonic analysis.

RMS—Rate monotonic scheduling.

role—Similar to conceptual components having ports, connectors have roles as the point of interaction with other architecture elements. The roles, like ports, obey an associated protocol.

ROM—Read-only memory.

ROOM—Real-time object-oriented modeling.

RPC—Remote procedure call.

RS (for Comm Vision)—Recovery suite.

RTE (for Safety Vision)—Runtime environment.

runtime entity—One of the basic elements in the execution view. The modules from the module view are assigned to runtime entities. A runtime entity is allocated to one of the platform elements defined for the software platform. There may also be runtime entities such as daemons or other server processes that have no direct correspondence to modules but are needed to support the other runtime entities. Defining runtime entities is a central task in the execution view.

runtime platform—The hardware and software platform on which a system (product) runs.

safety instrumentation and control system (for Safety Vision)—A safety I&C system supports parts of operational I&C (such as closed-loop control of the reactor coolant temperature or pressure), but it mainly supports safety-related and safety-critical I&C systems. Examples of these are reactor limitation systems and reactor protection systems. These I&C systems interface with sensors and actuators in the plant, and interact with monitoring and control systems in the control room.

separation of concerns—A separation of design concerns and artifacts according to certain criteria to achieve certain goals. For example, one may separate or decompose modules according to processing, communication, control, data, and user interface aspects of the software design to achieve modifiability and performance goals.

service provision units (for Comm Vision)—A fundamental design unit. An SPU provides a set of services to the rest of the software or to the subscriber. Because SPUs can be updated, interfaces of SPUs have to be defined in terms of IPC.

shell model (for Comm Vision)—Provides a layered structuring solution that enables large-scale testing with stepwise extended application program systems and a stepwise increasing functionality.

SMU (for Comm Vision)—Statistical multiplexing unit.

software platform—The infrastructure software between the product and the hardware platform, which traditionally has been the operating system. Today it certainly includes the operating system, but there may also be networking software, other middleware layers on top of the operating system, or something like a database management system, which is considered to be part of the software platform. Often products within a company share a common custom software platform, particularly when they are part of a product line.

source component—Source components are language-specific interfaces and language-specific modules or components that produce them. For languages such as C and C++, language-specific modules and interfaces are files named *.h, *.H, *.c, and *.CPP. For languages such as Ada, these components are package specification and package implementation. Defining source components is a central design task in the code view.

SPU (for Comm Vision)—Service provision unit.

SSNC (for Comm Vision)—Signalling System Network Control.

strategy—Strategies provide guidance for making architectural design decisions. Strategies address the global concerns but provide guidance for implementing them locally.

system/subsystem—A collection of subsystems or modules grouped by functionality. A subsystem usually corresponds to a higher level conceptual component (one that is decomposed into other components and connectors). This is an approximate but not exact fit with UML semantics.

system architect—One who selects and configures the hardware of a system.

system architecture—Software architecture and the hardware environment. The system architecture shows the physical relationships among software and hardware components in the system.

technological factors—The external technology solutions that are embedded or embodied in the product. These factors are primarily hardware and software technologies and standards. Typical categories of technological factors include general-purpose and domain-specific hardware, software technologies such as the operating system and user interface, architecture technologies such as patterns and frameworks, and standards such as image data formats.

Unified Modeling Language (UML)—A general-purpose modeling language that describes the static structure and dynamic behavior of a system. It is not a design method or a development process.

use—Modules can only interact with each other through interfaces. The "use" relation between modules defines a relation derived from the "requires" and "provides" relations. One module uses another when it requires the interface provided by the other.

VCPU (for Comm Vision)—Virtual CPU.

view (of software architecture)—The idea of separating the software architecture into different views is not unique. However, there isn't a general agreement about which views are the most useful. Fortunately, the reason behind multiple views is always the same: Separating different aspects into separate views helps people manage complexity. The four views presented are the conceptual view, the module view, the execution view, and the code architecture view.

Virtual CPU (for Comm Vision)—A unit of CPU time budgeting. A VCPU is any set of processes to which is assigned a common CPU time budget.

Four Views
Quick Reference

Global Analysis

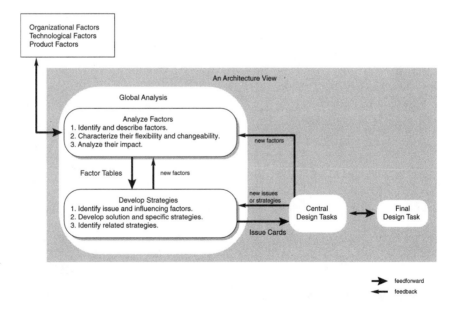

Design Activities

Conceptual Architecture View

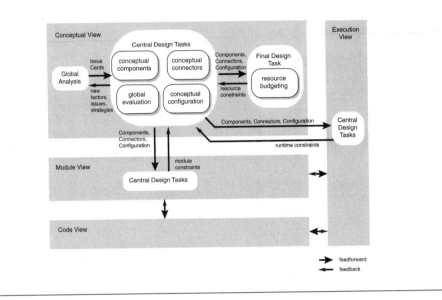

Design Activities

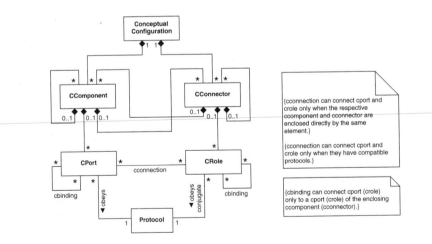

Meta-Model

Element	UML Element	New Stereotype	Notation	Attributes	Associated Behavior
CComponent	Active class	<<ccomponent>>		Resource budget	Component behavior
CPort	Class	<<cport>>	■	—	—
CConnector	Active class	<<cconnector>>		Resource budget	Connector behavior
CRole	Class	<<crole>>	●	—	—
Protocol	Class	<<protocol>>		—	Legal sequence of interactions

Relation	UML Element	Notation	Description
composition	Composition	Nesting (or ↑)	A component or connector can be decomposed into a configuration of interconnected components and connectors.
cbinding	Association	———————	A port can be bound to a port of the enclosing component. A role can be bound to a role of the enclosing connector.
cconnection	Association	———————	A component's port can be connected to a connector's role when both are directly enclosed by the same element.
obeys	Association	obeys	A port or role obeys a protocol.
obeys conjugate	Association	obeys conjugate	A port or role obeys the conjugate of a protocol.

Artifact	Representation
Conceptual configuration	UML Class Diagram (for example, Figure 4.7)
Port or role protocol	ROOM protocol declaration (uses UML Sequence or Statechart Diagrams; for example, Figure 4.9)
Component or connector behavior	Natural language description or UML Statechart Diagram (for example, Figures 4.11 and 4.13)
Interactions among components	UML Sequence Diagram (for example, Figure 4.15)
ROOM = real-time object-oriented modeling; UML = Unified Modeling Language.	

Module Architecture View

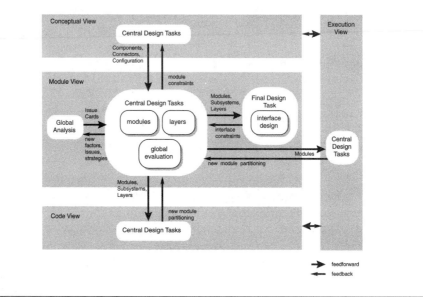

Design Activities

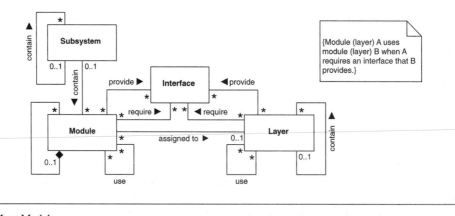

Meta-Model

Element	UML Element	New Stereotype	Notation
Module	Class	<<module>>	\<<module>\>
Interface	Interface	—	O or \<<interface>\>
Subsystem	Subsystem	—	\<<subsystem>\>
Layer	Package	<<layer>>	\<<layer>\>

Relation	UML Element	Notation	Description
contain	Association	Nesting	A subsystem can contain a subsystem or a module. A layer can contain a layer.
composition	Composition	Nesting (or ◆—)	A module can be decomposed into one or more modules.
use (also called use-dependency)	Usage	- - - - ->	Module (layer) A uses module (layer) B when A requires an interface that B provides.
require	Usage	- - - - ->	A module or layer can require an interface.
provide	Realization	—— (with O) - - ▷ (with ▭)	A module or layer can provide an interface.
implement	—	Table row	A module can implement a conceptual element.
	Trace	_ <<trace>> \>	
assigned to	Association	Nesting	A module can be assigned to a layer.

Artifact	Representation
Conceptual-module correspondence	Table
Subsystem and module decomposition	UML Class Diagram (for example, Figure 5.6)
Module use-dependencies	UML Class Diagram (for example, Figure 5.8)
Layer use-dependencies, modules assigned to layers	UML Class Diagram (for example, Figure 5.9)
Summary of module relations	Table

Execution Architecture View

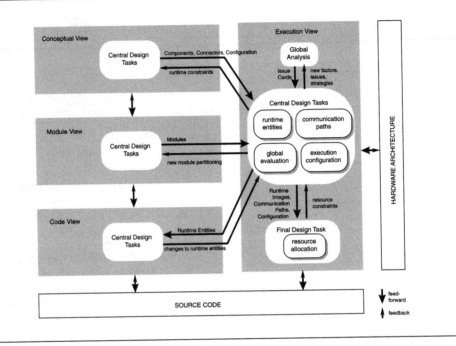

Design Activities

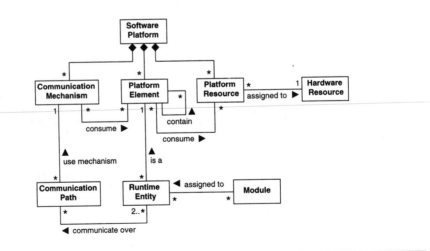

Meta-Model

Element	UML Element	New Stereotype	Notation	Attributes	Associated Behavior
Runtime entity	Process	—	`<< ... >>`	Host type, replication, resource allocation	—
	Thread	—			
	Class or active class	<<shared data>>, <<task>>, etc.			
Communication path	Association	—	———	—	Communication protocol

Relation	UML Element	Notation	Description
use mechanism	Association name	Name of communication mechanism; for example, IPC, RPC	A communication path uses a communication mechanism.
communicate over	—	⬚— (connection of class and association)	A runtime entity (or the module assigned to it) communicates over a communication path.
assigned to	Composition	Nesting (or ↑)	A module is assigned to zero or more runtime entities.

Artifact	Representation
Execution configuration	UML Class Diagram (for example, Figure 6.13)
Execution configuration mapped to hardware devices	UML Deployment Diagram (for example, Figure 6.16)
Dynamic behavior of configuration, or transition between configurations	UML Sequence Diagram (for example, Figures 6.11 and 6.14)
Description of runtime entities (including host type, replication, and assigned modules)	Table or UML Class Diagram
Description of runtime instances (including resource allocation)	Table
Communication protocol	Natural language description or UML Sequence Diagram or Statechart Diagram

Code Architecture View

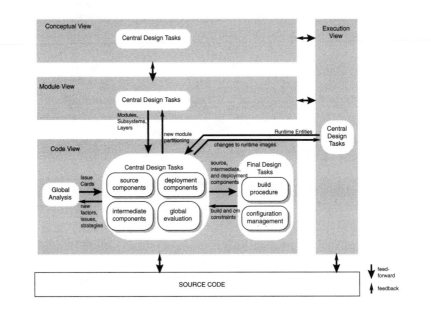

Design Activities

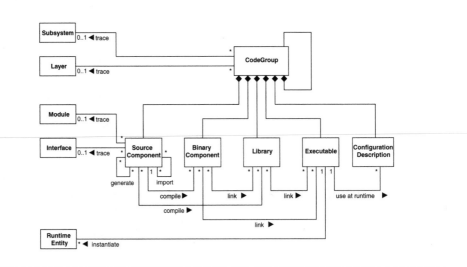

Meta-Model

Element	UML Element	New Stereotype		Notation
Source component	Component	<<source>>		Examples of source components are .H and .CPP files for C++.
Binary component	Component	<<binary>>		These are intermediate components.
Library	Library	—		Static or program libraries are intermediate components. Dynamic libraries are deployment components.
Executable	Executable	—		These are deployment components.
Configuration description	Component	<<configuration description>>		Describes execution configurations as well as resources.
Code group	Package	—		

Relation	UML Element	Notation	Description
generate	Dependency	- - generate - ->	Source components can generate other source components.
import	Import	- - import - ->	Source components can import other source components.
compile	Dependency	- - compile - ->	Source components are compiled to binary components or libraries.
link	Dependency	- - link - ->	Binary components link statically to form libraries or executables. Dynamic or shared libraries link dynamically with and are loaded into executables.
use at runtime	Usage	use at runtime - - - ->	An executable uses configuration descriptions at runtime.

Relation	UML Element	Notation	Description
trace	Trace	———————	A code group may trace to a subsystem or layer. A source component may trace to a module or interface.
instantiate	Instantiate	Table row	At runtime, an executable instantiates a runtime entity (as a runtime instance).

Artifact	Representation
Module view, source component correspondence	Trace dependency, tables
Runtime entity, executable correspondence	Instantiation dependency, tables
Description of components in code architecture view, their organization, and their dependencies	UML Component Diagrams or tables (for example, Figures 7.5 and 7.10)
Description of build procedures	Tool-specific representations (for example, makefiles)
Description of release schedules for modules and corresponding component versions	Tables
Configuration management views for developers	Tool-specific representation

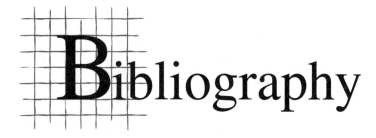

Bibliography

Abowd, G., L. Bass, P. Clements, R. Kazman, L. Northrop, and A. Zaremski. *Recommended Best Industrial Practice for Software Architecture Evaluation*. Technical report CMU/SEI-96-TR-025. Pittsburgh, PA: Software Engineering Institute, Carnegie Mellon University, 1996.

Agha, G., P. Wegner, and A. Yonezawa, eds. *Research Directions in Concurrent Object-Oriented Programming*. Cambridge, MA: MIT Press, 1993.

Allen, R.J., and D. Garlan. "A Formal Basis for Architectural Connection." *ACM Transactions on Software Engineering and Methodology* 1997; 6(3): 213–249.

Allen, R., and D. Garlan. "Beyond Definition/Use: Architectural Interconnection." In: Wing, J. M., ed. *Proceedings of the Workshop on Interface Definition Languages*. New York: ACM Press, 1994: 35–45.

Allen, R., and D. Garlan. "A Formal Approach to Software Architectures." In: van Leeuwen, J., ed. *Algorithms, Software, Architecture*, Information Processing 92, vol. 1. North Holland: Elsevier Science Publishers BV, 1992: 134–141.

Arango, G., and R. Prieto-Diaz. "Domain Analysis Concepts and Research Directions." In: Prieto-Diaz, R., and G. Arango, ed. *Domain Analysis and Software Systems Modeling*. Los Alamitos, CA: IEEE Computer Society Press Tutorial, 1991: 9–26.

Barbacci, M. R., C. B. Weinstock, and J. M. Wing. "Programming at the Processor-Memory-Switch Level." In: *Proceedings of the 10th International Conference on Software Engineering*. Washington DC: IEEE Computer Society Press, 1988: 19–28.

Bass, L., P. Clements, and R. Kazman. *Software Architecture in Practice*. Reading, MA: Addison Wesley Longman, 1998.

Beach, B. W. "Connecting Software Components with Declarative Glue." In: *Proceedings of the Fourteenth International Conference on Software Engineering*. New York: ACM Press, 1992: 120–137.

Beck, K. "Think Like an Object." *UNIX Review*, 1991; 9(10): 39–43.

Binns, P., and S. Vestal. "Architecture Specifications for Complex Real-Time Dependable Systems." In: *Proceedings of the First IEEE International Conference on Engineering of Complex Computer Systems*. Los Alamitos, CA: IEEE Computer Society Press, 1995: 357–360.

Boasson, M., ed. "Special Issue on Software Architecture." *IEEE Software* 1995; 12(6): 13–60.

Boehm, B., and H. In. "Identifying Quality-Requirement Conflicts." *IEEE Software* 1996; 13(2): 25–35.

Booch, G., J. Rumbaugh, and I. Jacobson. *The Unified Modeling Language User Guide*, Reading, MA: Addison-Wesley, 1999.

Brown, A., D. Carney, and P. Clements. "A Case Study in Assessing the Maintainability of a Large, Software-Intensive System." In: Melhart, B., and J. Rozenblit, eds. *Proceedings of the International Symposium of Software Engineering of Computer-Based Systems*. New York: IEEE Computer Society, 1995: 240-347.

Buschmann, F. "Building Software with Patterns." Fourth European Conference on Pattern Languages of Programming and Computing; Writers Workshop C: Patterns of Process and Learning, 1999. URL: *http://www.argo.be/europlop/writers.htm*.

Buschmann, F., R. Meunier, H. Rohnert, P. Sommerlad, and M. Stal. *Pattern-Oriented Software Architecture: A System of Patterns*. Chichester, UK: John Wiley & Sons, 1996.

Chatterjee, S., K. Bradley, J. Madriz, J. Colquist, and J. Strosnider. "SEW: A Toolset for Design and Analysis of Distributed Real-Time Systems." In: *Proceedings of the 3rd IEEE Real-Time Technology and Applications Symposium (RTAS97)*. Los Alamitos, CA: IEEE Computer Society Press, 1997: 72–77.

Chatterjee, S., and J. Strosnider. "Distributed Pipeline Scheduling: A Framework for Distributed, Heterogeneous Real-Time System Design." *Computer Journal* 1995; 38(4): 271–285.

Clements, P. "A Survey of Architecture Description Languages." In: *Proceedings of the Eighth International Workshop on Software Specification and Design*. Los Alamitos, CA: Computer Society Press 1996: 16–25.

Clements, P. C. "Understanding Architectural Influences and Decisions in Large System Projects." In: Garlan, D., ed. *Proceedings of the First International Workshop on Architectures for Software Systems*. Technical report CMU-CS-95-151. Pittsburgh, PA: Carnegie Mellon University, 1995.

Cohen, E. S., D. A. Soni, R. Gluecker, W. M. Hasling, R. W. Schwanker, and M. E. Wagner. "Version Management in Gypsy." In: Henderson, P., ed. *Proceedings of the ACM SIGSOFT/SIGPLAN Software Engineering Symposium on Practical Software Development Environments*. New York: ACM Press, 1988: 201–215.

Coplien, J. O. "A Generative Development-Process Pattern Language." In: Coplien, J., and D. C. Schmidt, eds. *Pattern Languages of Program Design*. Reading, MA: Addison-Wesley, 1995: 183–237.

Davis, A. M. *201 Principles of Software Development*. New York: McGraw Hill, 1995.

Davis, A. M. *Software Requirements: Objects, Functions, States*. Englewood Cliffs, NJ: Prentice-Hall, 1993.

Delisle, N., and D. Garlan. "A Formal Specification of an Oscilloscope." *IEEE Software*, 1990; 7(5): 29–36.

DeRemer, F., and H. Kron. "Programming-in-the-Large versus Programming-in-the-Small." *IEEE Transactions on Software Engineering*. 1976; SE-2(2): 80–86.

D'Ippolito, R., and K. Lee. "Modeling Software Systems by Domains." *AAAI-92 Workshop on Automating Software Design* 1992: 35–40.

Donohoe, P., ed. *Software Architecture: TC2 First Working IFIP Conference on Software Architecture (WICSA1)*. San Antonio: Kluwer Academic Publishers, 1999.

Dorofee, A. J., J. A. Walker, C. J. Alberts, R. P. Higuera, R. L. Murphy, and R. C. Williams. *Continuous Risk Management Guidebook*. Pittsburgh, PA: Carnegie Mellon University, 1996.

Drongowski, P. J. "Software Architectures in Real-Time Systems." In: *Proceedings of the First Workshop on Real-Time Applications*. Los Alamitos, CA: IEEE Computer Society Press, 1993: 198–203.

Ellis, W. J., R. F. Hilliard II, P. T. Poon, D. Rayford, T. F. Saunders, B. Sherlund, and R. L. Wade. "Toward a Recommended Practice for Architectural Description." In: *Proceedings of the Second IEEE International Conference on Engineering of Complex Computer Systems*. Los Alamitos, CA: IEEE Computer Society Press, 1996: 408–413.

Eriksson, H., and M. Penker. *UML Toolkit*. New York: John Wiley and Sons, 1998.

Feather, M. S., and A. van Lamsweerde. "Proceedings of the Seventh International Workshop on Software Specification and Design." *Software Engineering Notes* 1994; 19(3): 18–22.

Feiler, P. *Configuration Management Models in Commercial Environments*. Technical report CMU/SEI-91-TR-7. Pittsburgh, PA: Carnegie Mellon University, 1991.

Feldman, S. I. "Make—A Program for Maintaining Computer Programs." *Software— Practice and Experience*, 1979; 9: 255–265.

Fowler, M., and K. Scott. *UML Distilled: Applying the Standard Object Modelling Language*. Reading, MA: Addison-Wesley, 1997.

Gacek, C., A. Abd-Allah, B. Clark, and B. Boehm. "On the Definition of Software System Architecture." In: Garlan, D., ed. *Proceedings of the First International Workshop on Architectures for Software Systems*. Technical report CMU-CS-95-151. Pittsburgh, PA: Carnegie Mellon University, 1995: 85–95.

Gamma, E., R. Helm, R. Johnson, and J. Vlissides. *Design Patterns*. Reading, MA: Addison-Wesley, 1995.

Garlan, D., ed. *Proceedings of the First International Workshop on Architectures for Software Systems*. Technical report CMU-CS-95-151. Pittsburgh, PA: Carnegie Mellon University, 1995.

Garlan, D., R. T. Monroe, and D. Wile. "ACME: An Architecture Description Interchange Language." In: Johnson, J. H., ed. *Proceedings of CASCON '97*. Toronto: NRC 1997: 169–183.

Garlan, D., and D. E. Perry, eds. "Special Issue on Software Architecture." *IEEE Transactions on Software Engineering* 1995; 21(4): 269–386.

Garlan, D., and M. Shaw. "An Introduction to Software Architecture." In: Ambriola, V., and G. Tortora, eds. Vol. 1. *Advances in Software Engineering and Knowledge Engineering*. Singapore: World Scientific Publishing Company, 1993: 1–39.

Harel, D. "Statecharts: A Visual Formalism for Complex Systems." *Science of Computer Programming*, 1987; 8: 231–274.

Hatley, D. J., and I. A. Pirbhai. *Strategies for Real-Time System Specification*. New York: Dorset House Publishing, 1988.

Hofmeister, C., R. L. Nord, and D. Soni. "Describing Software Architecture with UML." In: Donohoe, P., ed. *Proceedings of the TC2 First Working IFIP Conference on Software Architecture (WICSA1)*. Boston: Kluwer Academic Publishers, 1999: 145–159.

Hofmeister, C., R. L. Nord, and D. Soni. "Architectural Descriptions of Software Systems." In: Garlan, D., ed. *Proceedings of the First International Workshop on Architectures for Software Systems*. Technical report CMU-CS-95-151. Pittsburgh, PA. Carnegie Mellon University, 1995: 127–137.

IEEE Architecture Working Group. *IEEE Recommended Practice for Architectural Description*. 1999. URL: *http://www.pithecanthropus.com/~awg/*.

International Organization for Standardization. *Information Technology, International Standard: Software Product Evaluation, Quality Characteristics and Guidelines for Their Use*. Geneva: ISO/IEC, 1991.

Jackson, M. *Software Requirements & Specifications*. Reading, MA: Addison-Wesley, 1995.

Jacobson, I., M. Christerson, P. Jonsson, and G. Overgaard. *Object-Oriented Software Engineering: A Use Case Driven Approach*. Reading, MA: Addison-Wesley, 1992.

Katz, R. H. *Information Management for Engineering Design*. Berlin; New York: Springer-Verlag, 1985.

Kazman, R., G. Abowd, L. Bass, and P. Clements. "Scenario-Based Analysis of Software Architecture." *IEEE Software*, 1996; 13(6): 47–56.

Kazman, R., M. Barbacci, M. Klein, S. J. Carriere, and S. G. Woods. "Experience with Performing Architecture Tradeoff Analysis." In: *Proceedings of the 21st International Conference on Software Engineering*. New York: ACM Press, 1999: 54–63.

Kiczales, G., J. des Rivieres, and D. G. Bobrow. *The Art of the Metaobject Protocol*. Cambridge, MA: MIT Press, 1991.

Klein, M. H., T. Ralya, B. Pollack, R. Obenza, and M. G. Harbour. *A Practitioner's Handbook for Real-Time Analysis: Guide to Rate Monotonic Analysis for Real-Time Systems*. Boston: Kluwer Academic Publishers, 1993.

Kramer, J. "Configuration Programming—A Framework for the Development of Distributable Systems." In: *Proceedings of the IEEE International Conference on Computer Systems and Software Engineering*. Los Alamitos, CA: IEEE Computer Society Press, 1990: 374–384.

Krutchen, P. "The 4+1 View Model of Architecture." *IEEE Software* 1995; 12(6): 42–50.

Lakos, J. *Large-Scale C++ Software Design*. Reading, MA: Addison-Wesley, 1996.

Lange, R., R. W. Schwanke. "Software Architecture Analysis: A Case Study." In: Feiler, P. H., ed. *Proceedings of the Third International Workshop on Software Configuration Management*. New York: ACM Press, 1991: 19–28.

Luckam, D. C., L. M. Augustin, J. J. Kenney, J. Veera, D. Bryan, and W. Mann. "Specification and Analysis of System Architecture Using Rapide." *IEEE Transactions on Software Engineering* 1995; 21(4): 336–355.

Magee, J., N. Dulay, and J. Kramer. "Regis: A Constructive Development Environment for Distributed Programs." *Distributed Systems Engineering Journal* 1994; 1(5): 304–312.

Magee, J., A. Tseng, and J. Kramer. "Composing Distributed Objects in CORBA." In: *Proceedings of the Third International Symposium on Autonomous Decentralized Systems (ISADS 97)*. Los Alamitos, CA: IEEE Computer Society Press, 1997: 257–263.

Medvidovic, N., and D. Rosenblum. "Assessing the Suitability of a Standard Design Method." In: Donohoe, P., ed. *Proceedings of the TC2 First Working IFIP Conference on Software Architecture (WICSA1)*, Boston: Kluwer Academic Publishers, 1999: 161–182.

Medvidovic, N., and R. N. Taylor. "A Framework for Classifying and Comparing Architecture Description Languages." In: Jazayeri, M., and H. Schauer, eds. *Proceedings of ESEC/FSE'97*. Berlin: Springer, 1997: 60–76.

Meszaros, G., and J. Doble. *A Pattern Language for Pattern Writing*, 1997. URL: *http://www.hillside.net/patterns/Writing/pattern_index.html*.

Mettala, E., and M. H. Graham. *The Domain-Specific Software Architecture Program.* Technical report CMU/SEI-92-SR-9. Pittsburgh, PA: Carnegie Mellon University, Software Engineering Institute, 1992.

Morris, C. R., and C. H. Ferguson. "How Architecture Wins Technology Wars." *Harvard Business Review* 1993; 71(2): 86–96.

Narayanaswamy, K., and W. Scacchi. "Maintaining Configurations of Evolving Software Systems." *IEEE Transactions on Software Engineering* 1987; SE-13(3): 324–334.

Nord, R. L., and B. C. Cheng. "Using RMA for Evaluating Design Decisions." In: *Proceedings of the Second IEEE Workshop on Real-Time Applications.* Los Alamitos, CA: Computer Society Press, 1994: 76–80.

Object Management Group. *UML Revision Task Force.* 1999. URL: *http://uml.shl.com/.*

Object Management Group. *What Is OMG-UML and Why Is It Important?* 1988. URL: *http://www.omg.org/news/pr97/umlprimer.html.*

Orfali, R., D. Harkey, and J. Edwards. *The Essential Client/Server Survival Guide.* 2nd ed. New York: Wiley Computer Publishing, 1996.

Parnas, D. L. "Software Aging." In: *Proceedings of the 16th International Conference on Software Engineering.* Los Alamitos, CA: IEEE Computer Society Press, 1994: 279–287.

Parnas, D. L. "Designing Software for Ease of Extension and Contraction." *IEEE Transactions of Software Engineering* 1979; SE-5(2): 128–137.

Parnas, D. L. "On the Criteria to be Used in Decomposing Systems into Modules." *Communications of the ACM* 1972; 15: 1053–1058.

Parnas, D. L., P. C. Clements, and D. M. Weiss. "The Modular Structure of Complex Systems." *IEEE Transactions on Software Engineering* 1985; SE-11(3): 259–266.

Parnas D. L., and D. M. Weiss. "Active Design Reviews: Principles and Practices." *Journal of Systems Software* 1987; 7(4): 259–265.

Paulish, D., R. L. Nord, and D. Soni. "Experience with Architecture-Centered Software Project Planning." In: Vidal, L., et al., eds. *Proceedings of the Second International Software Architecture Workshop (ISAW-2).* New York: ACM Press, 1996: 126–129.

Perry, D., and J. Magee, eds. *Proceedings of the 3rd International Software Architecture Workshop.* New York: ACM Press, 1998.

Perry, D. E., and A. L. Wolf. "Foundations for the Study of Software Architecture." *ACM SIGSOFT Software Engineering Notes* 1992; 17(4): 40–52.

Prieto-Diaz, R., and J. M. Neighbors. "Module Interconnection Languages." *The Journal of Systems and Software* 1986; 6(4): 307–334.

Purtilo, J. M. "The Polylith Software Bus." *ACM Transactions on Programming Languages and Systems* 1994; 16(1): 151–174.

Rechtin, E. "The Art of Systems Architecting." *IEEE Spectrum* 1992; 29(10): 66–69.

Rechtin, E., and M. Maier. *The Art of Systems Architecting*. Boca Raton, FL: CRC Press, 1997.

Royce, W. "TRW's Ada Process Model for Incremental Development of Large Software Systems." In: *Proceedings of the 12th International Conference on Software Engineering*. Los Alamitos, CA: IEEE Computer Society Press, 1990: 2–11.

Rumbaugh, J., I. Jacobson, and G. Booch. *The Unified Modeling Language Reference Manual*. Reading, MA: Addison-Wesley, 1999.

Schaeffer, J., D. Szafron, G. Lobe, and I. Parson. *The Enterprise Model for Developing Distributed Application*s. Alberta, Canada: Department of Computing, University of Alberta, 1993.

Schmidt, D. C., and T. Suda. "Transport System Architecture Services for High-Performance Communication Systems." *Journal of Selected Areas of Communications* 1993; 11(4): 489–506.

Schwanke, R. W., E. S. Cohen, R. Gluecker, W. M. Hasling, D. A. Soni, and M. E. Wagner. "Configuration Management in BiiN TM SMS." In: *Proceedings of the 11th International Conference on Software Engineering*. Washington, DC: IEEE Computer Society Press, 1989: 383–393.

Selic, B., G. Gullekson, J. McGee, and I. Engelberg. "ROOM: An Object-Oriented Methodology for Developing Real-Time Systems." In: *Proceedings of the CASE'92 Fifth International Workshop on Computer-Aided Software Engineering*. Los Alamitos, CA: IEEE Computer Society Press, 1992: 230–240.

Selic, B., G. Gullekson, and P. T. Ward. *Real-Time Object-Oriented Modeling*. New York: John Wiley & Sons, 1994.

Selic, B., and J. Rumbaugh. *Using UML for Modeling Complex Real-Time Systems*. Kanata, Canada: ObjecTime Limited; Cupertino, CA: Rational Software Corporation, 1998. URL: *http://www.objectime.com/otl/technical/content*.

Shaw, M. "Procedure Calls Are the Assembly Language of Software Interconnection: Connectors Deserve First-Class Status." In: Lamb, D. A., ed. *Studies of Software Design*. Proceedings of a 1993 workshop, lecture notes in computer science no. 1078. Berlin: Springer-Verlag, 1996: 17–32.

Shaw, M. "Some Patterns for Software Architecture." In: Vlissides, J., J. Coplien, and N. Kerth, eds. *Pattern Languages of Program Design, 2*. Reading, MA: Addison-Wesley, 1996: 255–269.

Shaw, M. "Larger Scale Systems Require Higher Level Abstractions." In: *Proceedings of the Fifth International Workshop on Software Specification and Design*. Los Alamitos, CA: IEEE Computer Society Press, 1989: 143–146.

Shaw, M., and P. Clements. "A Field Guide to Boxology: Preliminary Classification of Architectural Styles for Software Systems." In: *Proceedings of the 1st International*

Computer Software and Applications Conference (COMPSAC97). Los Alamitos, CA: IEEE Computer Society Press, 1997: 6–13.

Shaw, M., R. DeLine, D. Klein, T. Ross, D. Young, and G. Zelesnik. "Abstractions for Software Architecture and Tools to Support Them." *IEEE Transactions on Software Engineering* 1995; 21(4): 314–335.

Shaw, M., R. DeLine, and G. Zelesnik. "Abstractions and Implementations for Architectural Connections." In: *Proceedings of the Third International Conference on Configurable Distributed Systems*. Los Alamitos, CA: IEEE Computer Society Press, 1996: 2–10.

Shaw, M., and D. Garlan. *Software Architecture: Perspectives on an Emerging Discipline*. Upper Saddle River, NJ: Prentice Hall, 1996.

Siewiorek, D. P., C. G. Bell, and A. Newell. *Computer Structures: Principles and Examples*. New York: McGraw-Hill, 1982.

Simon, D. *An Embedded Software Primer*. Reading, MA: Addison-Wesley, 1999.

Software Engineering Institute. *Software Architecture* 1999. URL: *http://www.sei.cmu.edu/ architecture/sw_architecture.html*.

Soni, D., R. L. Nord, and C. Hofmeister. "Software Architecture in Industrial Applications." In: Jeffrey, R., and D. Notkin, eds. *Proceedings of the 17th International Conference on Software Engineering*. New York: ACM Press 1995: 196–207.

Soni, D., R. L. Nord, and L. Hsu. "An Empirical Approach to Software Architectures." In: *Proceedings of the Seventh International Workshop on Software Specification and Design*. Los Alamitos, CA: IEEE Computer Society Press, 1993: 47–51.

Soni, D., R. L. Nord, L. Hsu, and P. Drongowski. "Many Faces of Software Architectures." In: Lamb, D. A., ed. *Studies of Software Design*. ICSE '93 Workshop. Berlin: Springer-Verlag. 1996: 6–16.

Stewart, D. B., R. A. Volpe, and P. K. Khosla. "Integration of Software Modules for Reconfigurable Sensor-Based Control Systems." In: *IROS '92: Proceedings of the 1992 IEEE/RSJ International Conference on Intelligent Robots and Systems: Sensor-Based Robotics and Opportunities for Industrial Applications*, Vol. 1. New York: IEEE Computer Society Press, 1992: 325–332.

Taylor, R. N., W. Tracz, and L. Coglianese. *Software Development Using Domain-Specific Software Architectures*. CDRL A011—A Curriculum Module in the SEI Style, ADAGE-UCI-94-01C. Irvine, CA: University of California at Irvine, 1994.

Tichy, W. "Software Development Control Based on Module Interconnection." In: *Proceedings of the Third International Conference on Software Engineering*. New York: IEEE Computer Society Press, 1979: 29–41.

Tracz, W. "LILEANNA: A Parameterized Programming Language." In: Prieto-Diaz, R., and W. B. Frakes, eds. *Proceedings of the Second International Workshop on Software Reuse*. Los Alamitos, CA: IEEE Computer Society Press, 1993: 66–78.

Tracz, W. "An Environment to Support Domain-Specific Software Architectures." In: Deaton, E., ed. *Proceedings of the ACM Symposium on Applied Computing—SAC '94*. New York: ACM Press, 1994: 597–598.

Weiser, M. "Source Code." *IEEE Computer* 1987; 20(11): 66–73.

Williams, L. G., and C. Smith. "Performance Evaluation of Software Architectures." In: *Proceedings of the First International Workshop on Software and Performance (WOSP 98)*. New York: ACM Press, 1998: 164–177.

Wolf, A., ed. *Proceedings of the Second International Software Architecture Workshop (ISAW-2)*. New York: ACM Press, 1996.

Wolf, A. *Language and Tool Support for Precise Interface Control*. Technical report COINS-TR-85-23. Amherst, MA: University of Massachusetts, 1985.

Yokote, Y. "The Apertos Reflective Operating System: The Concept and its Implementation." In: *Proceedings of the Seventh Annual Conference on Object-Oriented Programming Systems, Languages, and Applications (OOPSLA '92)*. New York: ACM Press, 1992: 414–434.

Index